HENRY CLAY

HENRY CLAY

AMERICA'S GREATEST STATESMAN

HARLOW GILES UNGER

DA CAPO PRESS
A Member of the Perseus Books Group

Designed by Trish Wilkinson
Set in 11.5 point Adobe Garamond Pro

Library of Congress Cataloging-in-Publication Data

Unger, Harlow G., 1931–
    Henry Clay, America's greatest statesman / Harlow Giles Unger.
        pages   cm
    Includes bibliographical references and index.
    ISBN 978-0-306-82391-6 (hardcover) — ISBN 978-0-306-82392-3 (e-book)
1. Clay, Henry, 1777–1852. 2. Legislators—United States—Biography.
3. United States. Congress—Biography. 4. United States—Politics and government—1815–1861. I. Title.
E340.C6U57 2915
328.73'092—dc23
[B]   2015010250

First Da Capo Press edition 2015

Published by Da Capo Press
A Member of the Perseus Books Group
www.dacapopress.com

Da Capo Press books are available at special discounts for bulk purchases in the U.S. by corporations, institutions, and other organizations. For more information, please contact the Special Markets Department at the Perseus Books Group, 2300 Chestnut Street, Suite 200, Philadelphia, PA 19103, or call (800) 810-4145, ext. 5000, or e-mail special .markets@perseusbooks.com.

10 9 8 7 6 5 4 3 2 1

The Statue of Henry Clay stands in the Old House Chamber (now Statuary Hall) of the nation's Capitol, where he served as Speaker from 1811 to 1824. (Architect of the Capitol)

This Dust Was Once the Man

This dust was once the man,
Gentle, plain, just and resolute, under whose cautious hand,
Against the foulest crime in history known in any land or age
Was saved the Union of these States.

—WALT WHITMAN, 1871, BOOK XXII, *LEAVES OF GRASS*

Contents

List of Illustrations

Acknowledgements

My deepest thanks to Eric Brooks, curator at Ashland, the Henry Clay home in Lexington, Kentucky, for the valuable materials and information he provided me and, above all, for sharing his vast knowledge of Clay's life and times. My thanks as well to Robert Pigeon, a mentor and friend as well as executive editor at Da Capo Press of the Perseus Books Group. And although their names do not appear on the cover, the members of the wonderful publishing and editorial team at Da Capo Press are as responsible as I for this book. I am truly grateful for their help and honored by their support. In addition to Robert Pigeon, my thanks go to John Radziewicz, Publisher; Lissa Warren, Vice President, Director of Publicity; Kevin Hanover, Vice President, Director of Marketing; Sean Maher, Marketing Manager; Cisca Schreefel, Manager, Editorial Production; Justin Lovell, Editorial Assistant; Trish Wilkinson, Designer; and Josephine Mariea, Copy Editor. My warmest and most sincere thanks to you all and to the great sales team of the Perseus Books Group.

Chronology

April 12, 1777—Henry Clay born, Hanover County, Virginia.

1781—Father dies; mother remarries a year later.

1785–1790—Attends local log-cabin school.

1791–1792—Clerks in Richmond.

1792–1796—Reads law with Chancellor George Wythe.

1797—Admitted to Virginia bar, moves to Kentucky.

1798—Admitted to Kentucky bar.

1799—Marries Lucretia Hart.

1800—Daughter Henrietta born, first of six daughters, dies in 1801.

1802—Son Theodore Wythe born, first of five boys.

1803—Practices law in Lexington; elected to Kentucky legislature; son Thomas Hart born.

1805—Named Professor of Law, Transylvania University, Lexington; daughter Susan Hart born.

1804—Buys first part of Ashland plantation property; hired to defend Aaron Burr; fills unexpired term of US senator.

1807—Reelected to state assembly; chosen speaker; daughter Anne Brown born.

1809—Duel with Humphrey Marshall; fills unexpired term of US senator; daughter Lucretia Brown born.

1811—Elected to US House of Representatives; elected Speaker of the US House of Representatives; son Henry Clay Jr. born.

1812—Pressures President James Madison into war with Britain.

1813—Daughter Eliza Brown born.

1814—Serves on US Peace Commission, Ghent, Belgium.

1815—Negotiates trade agreement with Britain; reelected House Speaker.

1816—Helps found American Colonization Society; daughter Laura born, dies ten weeks later.

1817—Calls for Latin America independence; son James Brown born.

1819—Assails General Andrew Jackson in House speech.

1820–1821—Engineers Missouri Compromise; resigns as Speaker; son John Morrison born.

1824—Describes "American System" to bind the Union; loses presidential election.

1825—Appointed US secretary of state; accused of "corrupt bargain."

1826—Duel with John Randolph of Roanoke.

1831—Elected US senator; son Henry Jr. graduates second in West Point class; son Theodore committed to Lunatic Asylum of Kentucky.

1832—Loses campaign for US presidency; engineers tariff compromise, averts South Carolina secession; leads censure of President Jackson.

1837—Elected president of American Colonization Society.

1838—Involved in deadly Cilley-Graves duel.

1840—Assumes control of Senate; dubbed "The Dictator"; loses bid for presidential nomination.

1842—Resigns from Senate; resumes private law practice with son James.

1844—Loses US presidential election, despite support of Abraham Lincoln; opposes annexation of Texas.

1847—Son Henry Jr. killed in Mexican War; bid for presidential nomination rejected.

1849—Named US senator.

1850—Engineers Compromise of 1850, prevents secession and civil war.

1851—Resigns from Senate.

June 29, 1852—Dies in Washington, DC; Lincoln delivers eulogy, embraces Clay policies.

THE CLAY FAMILY

Parents

Henry Clay, 1777–1852
Lucretia Clay, 1781–1864

Children

Henrietta, 1800–1801
Theodore, 1802–1870
Thomas Hart, 1803–1871
Susan Hart, 1805–1825
Anne Brown, 1807–1835
Lucretia Hart, 1809–1823
Henry Clay Jr., 1811–1847
Eliza, 1813–1825
Laura, 1816–1817
James Brown, 1817–1864
John Morrison, 1821–1887

Note: The author has modernized spellings, punctuation, grammar, and syntax in nineteenth-century letters, manuscripts, and publications cited in this book without knowingly altering the intent of the original author. Readers may find the original language, spellings, and punctuation in the works cited in the notes. Unless otherwise noted, illustrations were obtained from the Library of Congress or sources in the public domain.

Introduction

On November 4, 1811, a fearless young lawyer from Kentucky threw open the doors of Congress and, like Hercules at the Augean Stables, began to cleanse it of corruption and barbarism and prevent the fracture of the infant American republic. With bold rhetoric and sheer will over the next forty years, he sowed the seeds of nationalism, preserving and strengthening the Union and lighting the way for Abraham Lincoln to guide the American Union through the Civil War intact.

Barely two decades after the Founding Fathers had formed their indissoluble Union, their heirs were unable to govern together and prepared to dissolve that Union, separating from each other as they had from Britain. In an era when congressmen debated with bullets as well as ballots, Kentucky's freshman congressman Henry Clay seized the Speaker's gavel and, outraged by the threat of separatism, stunned the nation's elected officials into order.

The youngest congressman—and only freshman—ever elected Speaker of the House, Clay spent his life in the House—and, later, the Senate—weaving historic political compromises that held the nation together and prevented civil war long enough to form an indivisible nation.

When Henry Clay became Speaker, the "United" States of America were a fast-unraveling association of semi-independent provinces and satraps. Although they had united in war against a common enemy, the former British colonies had few peacetime links. An absence of roads and waterways left transport and travel all but unmanageable, language and religious differences made cultural ties difficult and often impossible, and many of the nearly 900,000 slaves were ready to rise and slaughter their tormentors. The path to unity seemed blocked . . .

. . . until Henry Clay cleared the way to save the Union.

Exercising what Abraham Lincoln described as "power and influence which belonged to no other statesman of his age and times," Clay held the states together long enough for a new generation of Americans to emerge who embraced nationhood—and were willing to fight and die to preserve it.

Unlike the landed gentry of British subjects who founded the nation, Clay was the first *true* American leader. Born in Virginia in 1777 *after* independence, he began life with no birthright, no property, no standing among Virginia's fabled first families. Orphaned as a child, Clay worked his way through life with a quick wit, sharp tongue, remarkable political skills, and a deep understanding of and empathy for the disenfranchised, including slaves.

Like tens of thousands of other Americans, Clay moved west to improve his lot. He found fame and fortune in Kentucky—fame as a superb lawyer defending the defenseless, and fortune by marrying into Lexington's wealthiest family. Besides a generous dowry, marriage brought him prosperous clients, political influence, and a brilliant wife to lavish him with the love he lacked as a child and give him eleven children of his own.

Unlike many in the original thirteen colonies, Kentuckians and other settlers in the West had come from somewhere else, taming the wilderness with their own hands—usually without slaves. Mingling with settlers from states other than their own, they fought Indians together, prayed together, intermarried, and metamorphosed into "Americans." With only embryonic state and territorial governments to protect them, they looked to a "national" government to defend the frontier, develop public services, and strengthen links to their former homes. Henry Clay dedicated his life to meeting those needs, promoting what he called an "American System"—a nation-spanning network of roads, bridges, and canals to link every state and territory with each other.

Facing fierce opposition from southerners who feared open roads as escape routes for slaves, Clay used political wiles and promises of prosperity to weave ingenious political compromises that helped make his American System a reality, establishing physical, commercial, financial, and social links across the nation between families, friends, businesses, and state governments. As goods and people moved freely and swiftly in all directions, state barriers to trade and travel disappeared, fostering economic unity, unprecedented prosperity—and a union of more than twenty states that survived civil war.

Abraham Lincoln called Clay the "ideal" statesman—"the man for whom I fought all my humble life. His views and measures were always the wisest."[1]

In many ways Henry Clay grew more powerful than the President, reforming Congress and deciding—as House and Senate leaders still do—which bills emerge from debate to become the law of the land. A Quixotic champion of two irreconcilable political views—national unity *and* emancipation of slaves—his loathing of slavery cost him the presidency four times, but, as he put it, "I'd rather be right than president."[2]

Abraham Lincoln voted for Clay in 1832 and campaigned for him in 1844. Asserting that he "loved and revered" Henry Clay, Lincoln patterned his own political philosophy and life after Clay's. "I worshiped him as a teacher and leader," Lincoln said. "Mr. Clay's predominant sentiment was a deep devotion to the cause of human liberty—a strong sympathy for the oppressed and an ardent wish for their elevation. . . . I can express all my views on the slavery question by quoting Henry Clay."[3]

Despite Clay's failure to win the White House, his devotion to union never flagged. "If anyone desires to know the leading and paramount object of my public life," Clay proclaimed, "the preservation of the Union will furnish him the key."[4]

In his memorable eulogy, Lincoln said of Clay, "He loved his country. . . . He gave the death blow to fraternal strife . . . and peace to a distracted land." It was Clay who saved the union, Lincoln said, and the Civil War was a tragic confirmation of his work.

On the eve of that conflict Lincoln looked to heaven and mused, "I recognize his [Clay's] voice speaking, as it ever spoke, for the Union, for the Constitution and for the freedom of mankind."[5]

CHAPTER 1

Spitting in the Face of Congress

As torchlight parades feted Independence Day on July 4, 1791, a fourteen-year-old country boy lay alone in the attic of Richard Denny's general store in Richmond, Virginia. Disconsolate, Henry Clay wondered why his mother had abandoned him to a thankless job as an errand boy. Alone, he reached out for companionship, befriending and sharing his food with a young black runaway hiding in an alley near the store.

Henry Clay had been born in nearby Hanover County on April 12, 1777, about nine months after the United States declared independence from Britain. "The infant nation and the infant child began the race of life together," Abraham Lincoln explained. For Lincoln, Clay became a "revered teacher . . . whom I loved . . . during my whole political life."[1]

By the time Clay turned fourteen, years of tobacco plantings had sucked the nutrients from Hanover County's soil. Like many Virginia planters, Clay's stepfather, Captain Henry Watkins, sold the farm and moved to Kentucky to claim richer, unsettled ground in bluegrass country. He took Clay's mother, their own small children, and

Clay's two brothers, but he deemed the thin, tubercular Henry Clay unfit for backbreaking work clearing land and building a new home in Kentucky.

Hoping to steer the boy into a sedentary pursuit, Watkins tried placing young Clay as a clerk in the Richmond court system but found no openings, so he sent the boy to his friend Richard Denny in downtown Richmond.

"Left an orphan," Clay often lamented, "[I] never recognized a father's smile, nor felt his caresses—poor, penniless, without the favor of the great, with an imperfect and inadequate education, limited to the ordinary business and common pursuits of life."[2]

Henry Clay was born the seventh of nine children of the Reverend John Clay, a Baptist minister, whose 464-acre tobacco farm three miles from Hanover Courthouse included thirty-two cattle and sixteen slaves. The Clay home was large, handsome, and comfortable, if not luxurious—two stories, a chimney at either end, and three dormers jutting out from upstairs bedrooms under the roof.

Descended from inconsequential English gentry, the first of Henry Clay's forebears reached America just after the founding of Jamestown in the early 1600s; his mother's family arrived at the end of the same century. When Henry was only four, tragedy struck his family twice in quick succession: first, with his father's sudden death, then, a few weeks later, when Colonel Banastre Tarleton's British dragoons thundered across the family fields and burst into the house. As the terrified little boy hid in his mother's skirt, the soldiers smashed furniture, looted the larder, then rushed out to the yard and desecrated the graves of Clay's father and grandfather.

"I recollect in 1781 or '82 a visit made by Tarleton's troops," Clay related years later, "and of their running their swords into the newly made graves of my father and grandfather, thinking they contained hidden treasures. Though I was no more than four years of age, the circumstance of that visit is vividly remembered, and it will be to the last moment of my life."[3]

1. Henry Clay's boyhood home. The farm where Henry Clay was born, near Hanover Courthouse, Virginia, about twelve miles north of Richmond.

After his mother, Elizabeth, remarried, she and her husband sent Henry—eight by then—to the only school in the area, a one-room log cabin, or "field school," where, for the next three years he learned to read, write, and calculate. He expanded his knowledge by stopping on his way home from school at the doorway of Hanover Courthouse to listen to stirring oratory by Patrick Henry and other lawyers. Impassioned by what he heard, Clay memorized phrases and studied printed copies.[4]

"Mr. Clay's lack of a more perfect early education," Abraham Lincoln said of Clay, "teaches that in this country one can scarcely be so poor, but that if he *will*, he *can* acquire sufficient knowledge to get through the world respectably."[5]

Whatever may have been Henry Clay's ambitions at fourteen, however, he was unprepared when his stepfather delivered him to Denny's Richmond department store.

"In looking back upon my origin and progress through life," he recalled, "my father died in 1781, leaving me an infant of too tender years to retain any recollection of his smiles or endearments. My surviving parent removed to [Kentucky] in 1792, leaving me, a boy of fifteen [he was actually still fourteen] . . . in the city of Richmond, without guardian, without pecuniary means of support, to steer my course as I might or could."[6]

His stepfather had not forgotten him, though, and importuned a friend, the clerk of Virginia's High Court of Chancery,* to hire the boy as a clerical assistant. Clay went to work copying legal documents in the bowels of the breathtaking Virginia state Capitol. Former Virginia governor Thomas Jefferson had designed it, using as his model a Roman temple he admired in the southern French town of Nîmes.

Mocked for his country ways and homespun clothes, Clay applied his keen eyes and ears to adapt, and by the end of his first year at Chancery Court, he had transformed himself into a sophisticated young law clerk, with a command of courthouse legal jargon, a winning baritone voice, and a range of adolescent skills that included cards, gambling, drinking, a quick sharp tongue, and ears and eyes that absorbed every opportunity for advantage and advancement. Clay "conformed to customs," his biographer Calvin Colton explained, "as, for example, the custom of playing at cards with money at stake—a well-known fault of gentlemen in his sphere of society."[7]

"There were gentlemen attending the courts who studied Hoyle more than they did Blackstone," Kentucky congressman Micah Taul confirmed with a grin, "and generally won all the money."[8]

But Clay's quick mind absorbed far more than Hoyle. In addition to card skills, Clay perfected his penmanship, then an increasingly well-paid craft that risked none of the financial losses associated with cards. A dying breed by the end of the eighteenth century, writing masters were in great demand—by the nation's academies and

---

*Chancery court was a court of equity, which rendered judgments based on common law and whatever the judges considered "simple justice."

2. *The Capitol in Richmond, Virginia, built from 1783 to 1788, and designed by Thomas Jefferson, who copied plans of a Roman Temple, the Maison Carré, in Nîmes, France. (Library of Congress)*

universities, on the one hand, and, on the other, by the nation's courts, where evidence of declining literacy produced increased numbers of Xs in place of signatures on legal documents. Despite freedom of the press in America, a rising tide of immigration had raised illiteracy rates, with many wealthy Americans—especially women—unable to read or write to protect themselves in legal transactions.

Sensing opportunities for advancement in the legal world, Clay perfected his penmanship, and in 1793, when Virginia's ailing Chancellor (chief judge) George Wythe needed an amanuensis to take dictation and copy documents, the chief clerk of the court recommended young Clay.

A legendary patriot in early America, Wythe had signed the Declaration of Independence and attended the Constitutional Convention. Named the first professor of law at the College of William and

3. George Wythe. A signer of the Declaration of Independence, the Virginia chancellor (chief judge), trained Henry Clay in the law, as well as two future Presidents—Thomas Jefferson and James Monroe—and future Chief Justice John Marshall. (Library of Congress)

Mary in Williamsburg, he revolutionized American education for the law. To the standard study of law books he added classroom-style lectures, a moot court, and a mock legislature where students learned how to argue cases and to write, debate, and enact new laws. Among Wythe's law students were two future Presidents—Thomas Jefferson and James Monroe—and the future Chief Justice of the Supreme Court, John Marshall.

A lonely, sixty-six-year-old Quaker widower who had lost his only child, Wythe had moved from Williamsburg to Richmond to accept chancellorship of the Court of Chancery, Virginia's highest court. Subject to constant tremors in his hands by then, he needed someone to transcribe his decisions and correspondence into legible handwriting—and help fill lonely hours in his adopted city. Clay

4. After passing his bar examination, members of the Virginia Court of Appeals declared him "Henry Clay, Gentleman, duly qualified" to practice law. ('The earliest known image of Clay, from a miniature at Ashland)

too was far from family and friends and eager to embrace a paternal protector.

Clay moved into the judge's home, where Wythe became the boy's mentor, friend, and foster parent, imparting his Quaker beliefs, abhorrence of slavery, and social graces along with British and American law.

"To no man was I more indebted by his instructions, his advice, and his example," Clay said of Wythe. Clay would later name his firstborn son after Wythe.

Wythe gave Clay the run of his library, with its works of history, literature, and the arts, and coached him and sparked the boy's ambitions, inadvertently filling his own empty life with joy as he listened to the youngster's adolescent prattle. After four years, though, Wythe felt he had taught Clay all he could and sent the boy to his friend Attorney General Robert Brooke for a year's apprenticeship in the state attorney general's office. Brooke was already mentoring his younger brother Francis Brooke, who bonded with Clay and remained a close, lifelong friend. A year later Clay took his bar examination before members of the Virginia Court of Appeals, who declared "Henry Clay, Gentleman, duly qualified" to practice law.[9]

As capital of the nation's largest and wealthiest state, Richmond boasted some of the nation's most eminent attorneys—many of them connected by blood ties or long-standing friendships to the state's oldest, wealthiest families. Wythe and Brooke urged Clay to forego trying to practice in Richmond in favor of Kentucky, which had been part of Virginia and had only become a state five years earlier in 1792. Would-be settlers were streaming into Kentucky's bluegrass country to claim land—as his stepfather had done—but so many entangled themselves in conflicts over claims and titles that they created lucrative careers for lawyers. In November 1797 twenty-year-old Henry Clay set off across the Appalachian Mountains to Kentucky on the Wilderness Road through the Cumberland Gap that Daniel Boone had carved between the rugged hills twenty years earlier.

After reaching Kentucky, Clay stopped at Versailles, about twelve miles from Lexington, for a strained reunion with his mother and the rest of his family. By then his stepfather had expanded his holdings to about 1,000 acres, and Clay's two brothers had established a mercantile business in Lexington. None had anticipated Clay's appearance. None offered help of any sort.

"I established myself in Lexington in 1797 without patrons," Clay recounted, "without the favor or countenance of the great or opulent, without the means of paying my weekly board."[10]

Founded in 1775 by Mary Todd Lincoln's grandfather, among others, Lexington was named for the Massachusetts village near Boston where Minutemen had fired the first shots of the American Revolution. When Henry Clay arrived, Lexington's population was about 1,600; there were just over 200 houses—many of them built of logs—and twenty-four retail stores.

"I remember how comfortable I thought I should be if I could make one hundred pounds per year," Clay recalled years later, "and with what delight I received the first fifteen shillings fee. My hopes

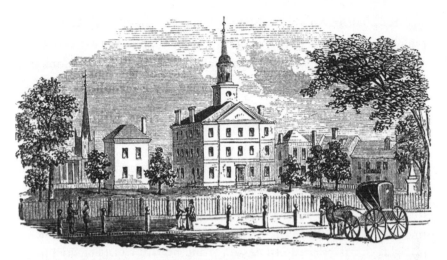

5. *Lexington, Kentucky, in 1797. Courthouse and Public Square in Lexington, Kentucky in 1797, when Henry Clay arrived to practice law. (Reproduced from John W. Barber and Henry Howe,* Our Whole Country or the Past and Present of the United States. *New York: G. F. Tuttle and H. M'Cauley, 2 vols., 1862–1863.)*

were more than realized. I immediately rushed into a successful and lucrative practice."[11]

Clay's flamboyance—derived largely by studying Patrick Henry's oratory and courtroom theatrics—earned him a sizable client base, as did membership in the Masons. A nonbeliever who had eschewed religion, Clay embraced the Masonic concept of "a greater power," or "Providence" as George Washington called it. But his primary motives for joining were camaraderie and the prospects of culling clients from the assembly of merchants and professional men.

He defended many farmers against land speculators and soon earned a reputation as a friend of the common man—a reputation he furthered by writing articles for the local press, demanding expansion of voter rights. In one he shocked rich and poor alike by calling for abolition of the state senate, which, like the US Senate, consisted of political appointees whose collective power could thwart the will of the popularly elected state assembly.

"The division of the legislature into two chambers," Clay complained, "has been founded upon the principle of two classes of men . . . the nobility and commonality. . . . These distinctions not existing in America, the use of the Senate has ceased."[12]

Apart from demands for popular control of government, Clay irritated political leaders by calling for changes in Kentucky's constitution, including abolition of slavery.

"Can any humane man be happy and contented," Clay posited in a letter to the local newspaper,

> when he sees near thirty thousand of his fellow beings deprived of rights . . . transferred like cattle . . . and hears the piercing cries of husbands separated from wives, and children from parents? . . . The sooner we attempt its destruction the better.[13]

Although his appeal for abolition failed, Clay gained statewide notoriety in Kentucky's political establishment as a radical firebrand. And after John Adams succeeded George Washington to the presidency, Clay's fame soared in Kentucky when he assailed the Alien and Sedition Acts that President Adams had rammed through Congress to criminalize spoken or printed criticism of the administration.

The Acts had climaxed a decade of constant congressional cession of its constitutional powers to the President. Lack of adequate roads and the absence of public transport across long distances had made it difficult for Congress to convene, and the President—first Washington, then Adams—found himself alone much of the year to run the government by himself. Ignoring the Constitution, President Washington borrowed funds, sent troops to war, issued proclamations with the force of law, and crushed constitutionally protected citizen tax protests—all without the authority of Congress required by the Constitution.

President Adams expanded presidential powers still more after the French navy tried blocking Anglo-American trade by seizing American cargo ships. Adams ordered the construction of a navy, the

6. *Debate in the House of Representatives. A cartoon entitled "Congressional Pugilists" shows Roger Griswold of Connecticut (right) fighting with Vermont Republican Matthew Lyon on the floor of the House of Representatives. The eccentric Virginia Representative John Randolph of Roanoke is depicted with his dog, rear left. (Library of Congress)*

arming of American cargo ships, and the call-up of troops to protect American shores against a French invasion. He ordered American ships to fire at will on French naval vessels, launching an undeclared naval war.

Although Clay did not object to America defending herself against the French, Vice President Thomas Jefferson, a fervent, longtime Francophile, called the President "insane," setting off vicious brawls in Congress between pro-war, Adams Federalists and pro-peace, Jefferson Republicans. After Federalist congressman Roger Griswold of Connecticut called Vermont Republican Matthew Lyon a coward, Lyon sprang across the floor and spat in Griswold's face. Griswold smashed his cane over Lyon's head, and Lyon grabbed a pair of tongs to parry. Griswold tackled him, and the two grappled until other congressmen pulled them apart by their legs.

The Lyon-Griswold free-for-all provoked a wave of anti-French frenzy that peaked on June 18, 1798, when President Adams demanded that Congress pass laws to crush public criticism of his government. Of the four Alien and Sedition Acts, the Sedition Act was the most oppressive, undermining the First Amendment by restricting freedom of speech and of the press. It imposed fines of up to $2,000 and prison sentences of up to two years for opposing or interfering with law enforcement or publishing "false or malicious writing directed against the President or Congress." Within a few weeks Federalist prosecutors filed sedition charges against a dozen journalists and against Representative Lyon—now dubbed the "Spitting Lyon." All were found guilty, fined, and imprisoned.*

The acts so outraged Vice President Jefferson that he drew up formal resolutions for state legislatures to restrict federal government powers and declare the Alien and Sedition Acts "void and of no force."[14]

He sent one to his acolyte, Virginia lawyer George Nicholas, who had moved to Kentucky, to present to the Kentucky legislature. As more than 1,000 Jefferson supporters gathered to protest dismantling of the Bill of Rights, Nicholas mounted a wagon to harangue the crowd. Henry Clay jumped aboard with Nicholas, and despite a smattering of hisses because of his stand on emancipation, Clay's deep, booming voice quickly "penetrated people's souls," according to George D. Prentice, editor of the *Louisville Journal*. "Mr. Clay came forward in defense of the rights of the people; and notwithstanding his youth and inexperience . . . he was soon regarded as one of the master-spirits of his party."[15]

Towering above the crowd, the six-foot-one Clay called Jefferson's Kentucky Resolution a cry of freedom and the Alien and Sedition

---

*The three Alien Acts were the Naturalization Act, which changed the period for naturalization from five to fourteen years; the Alien Act, which gave the President powers to deport aliens without trial if he deemed them "dangerous to the peace and safety of the United States"; and the Alien Enemies Act, which empowered the President to arrest, detain, and arbitrarily deport aliens in case of war—without trial or justification.

Acts nothing less than "federal government usurpation" of the people's constitutional rights.

Electrified by the young man's words, "the people took Clay . . . upon their shoulders . . . through the streets amid shouts and applause" and carried him in a triumphal procession through Lexington, according to witnesses.[16] Rallies followed across the state and elsewhere, and as torch-bearing protesters marched in defiance of President Adams and Congress, Kentucky's state legislature approved Jefferson's Resolution. After Virginia's legislature followed suit, Kentucky prepared to secede from the Union. Much of northern Virginia, western Pennsylvania, and parts of Ohio and Tennessee seemed ready to join Kentucky in a new Western Federation of American States. In Lexington, crowds hailed the former errand boy Henry Clay—barely twenty-one—as their choice to lead another American Revolution.

CHAPTER 2

No Fighting Here

Almost everyone in Lexington embraced Henry Clay—his name was on every lip, his words on every tongue. He was the center of every conversation, the object of invitations to every home of consequence, including the palatial Thomas Hart mansion—the crowning architectural gem of the town they would later call the "Athens of the West."

A Virginia native from Clay's (and Patrick Henry's) own Hanover County, Colonel Thomas Hart had fought in the Revolutionary War before moving to Maryland and reaping riches by manufacturing rope and nails under an exclusive contract with the US government. An early investor in the Transylvania Company, which owned 200,000 acres of northern Kentucky wilderness, he claimed his share in 1794 and moved with his wife to Lexington and its prosperous bluegrass country.

"You will be surprised to hear I am going to Kentucky," Hart wrote to his cousin, Governor William Blount of Tennessee. "Mrs. Hart who for eighteen years has opposed this measure has now given her consent, and so we go, an old fellow of 63 years of age seeking a new country to make a fortune in."[1]

A year later he wrote from Lexington: "Oh, if my old friend Uncle Jacob Blount [Gov. Blount's father] were here! What a pleasure we would have in raking up money and spending it with our friends. This is really one of the finest countries in the world."[2] Hart had not only reaped a second fortune selling thousands of acres of surplus land; he made a third fortune as a merchant and a fourth recreating his Maryland rope manufactory to process the endless supply of hemp that grew like weeds amidst the bluegrass.

Thomas Hart's success made his youngest daughter, Lucretia—plain, unmarried Lucretia—the target of every scheming Lexington suitor seeking a comfortable dowry and entry into Kentucky's wealthy power core.

Though Lucretia was "never a beauty," Henry Clay, with a caricature of a mouth that stretched from ear to ear, knew he was no Adonis. In the end both he and Lucretia found qualities in each other they believed would make for a long, comfortable, mutually beneficial, and extremely happy union. She saw beyond his evident faults—through the easy smile, glib chatter, and occasionally brash behavior that cloaked the residual sadness and loneliness of his youth. Indeed, Lucretia saw greatness in Henry Clay; she saw a brilliant political star on the rise with sparkling wit, a warm sense of humor, and an uncanny ability to win friends and bring friends and foes together. He, in turn, saw beyond her "plain," "unadmired" looks, embracing instead her astonishing intelligence, broad education, warm companionship, and evident business skills gleaned from her successful father.

On April 11, 1799, they were wed. Their marriage was perfect for both, each proving an ideal helpmate and lover for the other. Unflinchingly loyal, she excused his every misstep, ignored his occasional drinking bouts and flirtations with other women, and all but glorified his penchant for gambling.

What may well have started as a marriage of convenience, respect, and friendship blossomed into romance and deep love that would last more than fifty years and produce eleven children. Their love would not protect them from tragedy, however. Their first child, Henrietta, born about a year after their marriage, died after ten months. Their first son, Theodore Wythe Clay, was born the following year, and the couple would expand their brood for the next two decades, but more than half their children would meet untimely deaths.

Although only a handful of Henry and Lucretia's letters to each other remain (it was customary to burn such letters after a spouse's death), each began with the salutation, "My dear Wife" or "My dear husband." His usually ended, "God bless and preserve you, my dear Wife," while she closed with her prayer, "May God spare you to us. Do take care of yourself for our sakes."[3]

In addition to the love and family he had lacked during much of his childhood, Clay's marriage to Lucretia propelled him into Kentucky's highest circles of power and wealth. Assumption of his father-in-law's legal affairs expanded his practice, which quickly became the city's—and perhaps the state's—largest. When he married Lucretia, his personal wealth consisted of two horses and three slaves; by 1805, after four years of marriage, he owned more than 6,500 acres of land, eight slaves, fifteen livestock, and a town house where he and Lucretia had settled after their wedding. To his practice as a courtroom lawyer Clay added a successful career as a manager of legal affairs for businesses and well-to-do families. Among his clients were Andrew Jackson, who asked Clay to collect a loan, and lexicographer Noah Webster, who gave Clay power of attorney over his publications in the West.

But the heart of every law practice in the West was criminal law, and Clay became a master. "It is remarkable that no person, put in peril by process of the criminal code, invoked the aid of Mr. Clay without being saved," according to Calvin Colton, who, in 1844, went to Kentucky to become Clay's official biographer.*

---

*The official biographer of Henry Clay, Calvin Colton (1789–1857), wrote, assembled, and edited *The Private Correspondence of Henry Clay* (1855), *The Works of Henry Clay* (1856–1857), *The Life and Times of Henry Clay* (1846), and *The Last Seven Years of Henry Clay* (1846).

In one of his earliest criminal cases Clay defended a woman clearly guilty of having shot and killed her sister-in-law in a fit of passion. After admitting his client's guilt, Clay pleaded with the jury that his client was, after all, a woman "of a respectable family, the wife of a respectable man, who stands by her side. She has not before been accused of fault. . . . It was indeed a shocking crime," Clay shook his head in dismay. "No one has been more shocked than the perpetrator.

"But is there no exception to a general rule?" he cried out. "No rescue from a common law?" Clay then puzzled both judge and jury by introducing a new concept in criminal law—not guilty by reason of insanity:

"A dreadful crime was committed when reason was dethroned," he affirmed. "Passion is insanity—delirium."

The husband himself, Clay pointed out, was "forced to forgive the death of his own sister by the hand of his wife . . . and pleaded for mercy for his wife." He urged the jury to respond accordingly and restore "this unhappy woman to her husband and family."[4]

It did just that, establishing Clay's standing as one of the foremost criminal lawyers in the West and perhaps the nation.

Clay himself may have questioned some of his own courtroom antics. After winning acquittal for a murderer whose guilt was evident to all, Clay shook his head at his grinning client: "Perhaps I have saved too many like you who ought to be hanged."[5]

In Fayette County where he lived, however, he emerged as a folk hero. Voters elected him to the state general assembly, while Transylvania University, Kentucky's first institution of higher learning, named him Professor of Law and Politics. Asked to accept the politically important post of prosecuting attorney, he agreed, but he abandoned it abruptly after only one case: a slave had grabbed an axe to defend himself against a brutal beating by his white overseer and then killed his attacker. Clay sought to limit the charge against the black man to manslaughter—the usual definition of the same crime by a white man. But when a black man killed a white—even in self-defense—it was murder in Kentucky and the rest of the South, and the automatic punishment was summary death by hanging. Clay refused to handle the case and resigned from the prosecutor's office in disgust.

By then Virginia's Thomas Jefferson had won election as third President of the United States after an historic and controversial challenge by New York attorney Aaron Burr Jr. After garnering the same number of Electoral College votes as Jefferson, Burr reneged on a pre-election pledge to Jefferson to accept the vice presidency in the event of such a deadlock. Instead, he forced the House of Representatives to decide the outcome, and only after thirty-six ballots and days of tedious, bitter debate did Jefferson finally win the presidency.

Incensed by Burr's political about-face, the President grew obsessed with punishing the vice president, who in turn called on Clay to thwart the President.

Before Jefferson could act against Burr, however, Spanish authorities in New Orleans conspired with their French allies to close the port to American ships. A transit point for almost 2,000 American ships a year, New Orleans was essential to American commerce along the Ohio and Mississippi Rivers. As goods piled up on Ohio and Mississippi River docks, farmers gathered in Lexington, Louisville, and other western towns, demanding war. President Jefferson prepared to send 50,000 troops to attack New Orleans, including 5,000 from Kentucky. Outraged by the effects of the Spanish port closure on his fellow Kentuckians, Henry Clay was among the first to volunteer to fight for his country. Before Clay even picked up his weapon, however, President Jefferson sent his friend James Monroe to Paris to try to avert war by offering to purchase the island and port of New Orleans. Napoléon shocked Monroe and the world by selling not just New Orleans but the entire Louisiana Territory.

The surprising concession followed a series of savage rebellions in French-owned Santo Domingo (now Haiti), where slaves had butchered more than 10,000 French troops and 3,000 French civilians before declaring independence. Rather than risk further losses in far-off lands, Napoléon abandoned French holdings in continental North

America, selling to the United States the largest territory any nation had ever ceded peacefully to another in world history—almost 1 million square miles.

The Louisiana Territory doubled the size of the United States and offered prospects of untold wealth to tens of thousands of Americans eager to burst the confines of eastern states. At $15 million, the purchase proved a bargain for both the United States and thousands of its citizens, who were able to buy vast areas of rich wilderness lands for only four cents an acre, compared to the average price of $2 an acre for unsettled federal lands east of the Mississippi River. The Louisiana Purchase gave tens of thousands of disenfranchised Americans without property the chance to acquire land and wealth along with rights to vote, hold public office, and govern themselves.

Property owners in the East, however, absorbed huge losses with the availability of cheap land in the Louisiana Territory. Almost all of Henry Clay's neighbors in Lexington suffered, with Clay alone escaping the debacle. As it turned out, he had been so busy establishing his law practice during the first years of the century that he had had little time or money to invest in land, and, without any important investments, he suffered no losses.

By 1803, when land values fell, Clay had built a big, lucrative practice, won election to Kentucky's General Assembly, and accumulated enough capital to take advantage of plummeting prices with a number of sizable investments in rich, undeveloped lands across bluegrass country. In 1806 Clay purchased a one-hundred-acre farm a mile and a half from Lexington and his law office. A thick stand of magnificent ash trees embraced a modest house that Clay would transform into Fayette County's most beautiful residence. He called it Ashland, and, as its centerpiece, he built an elegant brick mansion two and a half stories high, with two wings on either side designed by the renowned American architect Benjamin Latrobe. Outbuildings included a smoke house, ice houses, a dairy, a carriage house, and slave quarters. The Clays had about two dozen slaves, some as household help and the rest to work the fields.

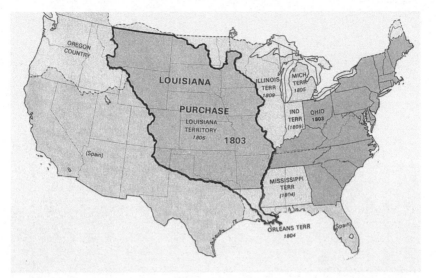

Map 1. The Louisiana Purchase added about 1 million square miles to the United States, allowing hundreds of thousands of Americans waiting to move westward. (Library of Congress)

Visitors described the surrounding gardens he installed as looking like an "English park." Lucretia and Henry Clay grew to love Ashland; they did much of the planning and planting in and about the house themselves, with Lucretia all but ecstatic inserting bulbs and flowering annuals and perennials into the rich soil, while Henry rejoiced digging holes and preparing the ground for ornamental shrubs and flowering trees. As additional acreage became available, Clay expanded his original Ashland property into a 400-acre estate and farm.

"I am in one respect better off than Moses," Clay exulted. "He died in sight of, without reaching, the Promised Land. I occupy as good a farm as any that he would have found, if he had reached it; and it has been acquired not by hereditary descent, but by my own labor."[6]

Over his lifetime Clay created a model farm, with corn, hemp, wheat, and other feed and cash crops. He was the first American farmer to buy and import Hereford cattle from England and expanded it into a herd of more than one hundred head. He raised goats and sheep, produced high-quality Merino wool, and bred some

7. Set in a grove of magnificent ash trees, Henry Clay's magnificent Ashland home had a central brick structure two and one-half stories high and two wings stretching to either side designed by famed architect Benjamin Latrobe. (From an engraving at Ashland)

of Kentucky's finest thoroughbred horses. His horses won so many races, in fact, that he built his own track at Ashland to train them. Lucretia was equally passionate about Ashland, and it was she who, during her husband's absences while in Washington, turned the farm into a thriving enterprise with the production and sale of milk, butter, eggs, cheese, cured hams, and other products.

Late in 1806 Clay received a letter from Louisville pleading for his legal assistance: "I shall insist, however, on making a liberal pecuniary compensation," the letter added. "I pray you to repair to Frankfort* upon receipt of this." It was signed by former Vice President Aaron Burr Jr.

---

*The Kentucky state capital, about thirty miles northwest of Lexington and fifty-five miles east of Louisville.

Wanted for murder in two states, Burr had shot and killed former US Treasury secretary Alexander Hamilton in a duel two years earlier in July 1804, in Weehawken, New Jersey. Although the two had been heroic comrades-in-arms in the Revolutionary War, their relationship soured after Burr unseated Hamilton's father-in-law from the US Senate in the 1791 elections and rose to the top ranks of the Republican Party. Just as Burr's political star was ascending, Hamilton's began to fall after the public disclosure of his involvement in a marital scandal forced him to resign as George Washington's Treasury secretary and most trusted cabinet aide.

Believing Burr responsible for exposing his marital indiscretion, Hamilton vowed to destroy Burr's political career, and when Burr challenged Jefferson for the presidency in the 1800 election, Hamilton helped engineer Jefferson's victory in the House. Burr then ran for the New York governorship, only to have Hamilton cost him the election with warnings to the public that Burr was "unfit to govern."[7] Although he faced as precipitous an end to his political career as Hamilton had suffered, Burr had done nothing to merit the assaults on his character, and he challenged Hamilton to a duel.

At sunrise on July 11, 1804, the two heroes of the American Revolution crossed the Hudson River from Manhattan Island to Weehawken, New Jersey (opposite present-day 42nd Street), where, just after 7 a.m., they prepared to kill each other for senseless reasons neither could fully explain.

Standing thirty feet from his opponent, Hamilton fired first—and missed. Burr fired next, intending only to wound Hamilton, he said, but the bullet penetrated Hamilton's right rib cage, tore through his liver and diaphragm, lodged in his spine, and killed him.

Encouraged by Jefferson, Republican prosecutors in New York City, with no jurisdiction in New Jersey, called a coroner's jury and badgered it into indicting Burr for violating New York's law against dueling. Although dueling was legal in New Jersey, that state's Republican prosecutor fabricated a murder charge, and Burr, still vice president of the United States, bid farewell to the Senate, resigned, and fled.

8. Hamilton-Burr Duel. In one of the most pointless confrontations in American history, Revolutionary War heroes Alexander Hamilton and Aaron Burr Jr. stand ready to kill each other for reasons neither man could fully explain.

"In New York I am to be disenfranchised and in New Jersey hanged," Burr wrote to his son-in-law. "Having substantial objections to both, I shall . . . seek another country."[8] (Most Americans still referred to each state as a "country.")

Burr eyed the wilderness in the newly acquired Louisiana Territory as a safe haven to begin life anew on vast tracts of vacant land anyone could claim for a pittance. Still a beloved—indeed, heroic— figure to many Americans, Burr found a warm welcome in the West. Nashville church bells pealed and cannons boomed a collective welcome to the former vice president. General Andrew Jackson staged a western-style parade in Burr's honor—urging Burr to settle in Tennessee and run for senator or President. Jackson invited him to stay at his home in Nashville, then publicly hailed Burr for defending his honor against Hamilton. Far from decrying duels, westerners and southerners saw dueling as an obligation of honorable men. A year later Jackson himself would kill a horse breeder in a duel that left a bullet lodged in Jackson's chest for the rest of his life as a painful memento of the encounter.

By the time Burr reached Ohio thousands of young men and women had boarded westward-bound wagons to begin new lives. Most sought—and needed—charismatic figures to lead them into the western unknown, and Aaron Burr, the grandson of the all-but-saintly churchman Jonathan Edwards, stepped into that role. Andrew Jackson urged his wife's nephew to join Burr in the new settlement.

Although Burr's boys intended nothing more aggressive than tilling land in northern Louisiana, increasingly sinister rumors dogged his movements. President Jefferson urged western governors "to have him strictly watched and on his committing any overt act unequivocally to have him arrested and tried for treason, misdemeanor or whatever other offense the act may amount to."⁹ The President's paranoia inflated Burr's young followers into an "army" of "fugitives from justice or from their debts . . . adventurers and speculators of all descriptions." Jefferson argued that "Burr's conspiracy . . . combined the objects of separating the western states from us, of adding Mexico to them, and of placing himself at their head. . . . He probably induced near a thousand men to engage with him. . . . The first enterprise was to have been the seizure of New Orleans."¹⁰

In November 1806 the President set loose the bulldog Federalist District Attorney Joseph Hamilton Daveiss to hunt Burr down and bring him to bay. Burr turned to Henry Clay, by then the most prominent defense lawyer in the West, pleading, "I have no design, nor have I taken any measure to promote a dissolution of the Union.

I have no design to intermeddle with the government or to disturb the tranquility of the United States. . . . I do not own a musket or a bayonet nor any . . . military stores nor does any person for me. . . . My views have been fully explained . . . such that every man of honor and every good citizen must approve. Considering the high station you now fill in our national councils, I have thought these explanations proper . . . to satisfy you that you have not espoused the cause of a man in any way unfriendly to the laws, the government, or the interests of the country.[11]

Burr convinced Clay.

"There was no ground for the prosecution," Clay concluded. "Such was our conviction of the innocence of the accused that when he sent us a considerable fee, we resolved to decline accepting and accordingly returned it."[12]

In taking Burr's case without charge, Clay cited Burr's status as "an eminent member of the profession [being] prosecuted without cause in a distant state."[13]

Clay appeared with Burr before the grand jury. Burr denied all charges, and after the prosecution failed to produce any witnesses, the grand jury discharged Burr. A crowd waiting outside burst into cheers when they learned the verdict, but their cheers turned into derisive hoots when the relentless prosecutor ordered Burr arrested as a traitor. Clay was incensed: "You have heard of inquisitions of Europe," he roared.

> You have heard of the screws and tortures made use of in the dens of despotism to extort confession; of the dark conclaves and caucuses for the purpose of twisting some incoherent expression into evidence of guilt. Is not the project of the attorney for the United States a similar object of terror?[14]

Clay went on to pledge his own "honor and innocence" as a state legislator on behalf of his client and again appeared with Burr when he made a second grand jury appearance. Burr remained unequivocal in denying any plot against the United States, and again, the prosecutor failed to produce witnesses or evidence. When he called several editors to testify, they admitted they had printed rumors as if they were truths and had no evidence of any Burr conspiracy.

9. Vice President Aaron Burr Jr. chose lawyer
Henry Clay to defend him against treason charges
leveled by President Thomas Jefferson. (From an
original painting by John Vanderlyn)

"When the grand jury returned the bill of indictment not true," Clay exulted, "a scene was presented in the courtroom which I had never before witnessed in Kentucky. There were shouts and applause from an audience, not one of whom . . . would have hesitated to level a rifle against Colonel Burr if he believed he aimed to dismember the Union or sought to violate its peace or overturn its Constitution."[15]

The prosecutor refused to yield, however, and summoned Burr to a third grand jury appearance. Although convinced of Burr's innocence, Clay had just won appointment to fill the last three months of a departing Kentucky senator's term, from December 29, 1806, to March 4, 1807. Apart from the opportunity of stepping onto the national political stage for the first time, the move to Washington would enrich him with an extra $3,000 in fees to handle three cases pending before the US Supreme Court—a common practice among congressmen.

Two weeks later Burr appeared before a third grand jury, but he did so without Clay, who had told the former vice president that further involvement in the case might "militate against my duty as a senator and therefore it would be improper for me to engage as his council."[16]

By then Clay was on his way to Washington, traveling by boat up the Ohio River to Pittsburgh, where he hoped to board a stagecoach to the East. To his dismay, "not a stage turned its wheels beyond Pittsburgh." As Clay worked his way eastward on horseback, he muttered to himself about the government's failure to install proper transportation to link the nation's regions commercially. He decided he would act to establish such a linkage when he entered the Senate.

Forced to use primitive transportation, he breathed easier about his decision to leave Lucretia and their children behind in Lexington. By then Lucretia had given birth to four: her firstborn, Henrietta, had died after only ten months in the spring of 1800. Although all three of the other Clay children—Theodore Wythe, four; Thomas Hart, three; and Susan Hart, one—were robust and healthy, none was fit for the long journey across the mountains to so primitive a city as Washington.

"Washington resembles those Russian towns in the deserts of Tartary [western Siberia], in whose enclosures we behold nothing but naked fields and a few groups of houses," wrote French ambassador Louis Felix de Beaujour. "With the exception of some public edifices appropriated for the use of government and of which the principle one . . . bears the pompous name of Capitol, nothing else has been hitherto built . . . because this country is not yet sufficiently rich to people such a town."[17]

In fact, the city was a gigantic marsh fringed by forests and perforated by islands of reclaimed land with clusters of shabby wooden boarding houses, inns, taverns, and stables near Capitol Hill. Clusters of squalid slave shacks added to the horror. Snakes slithered in and

10. *The US Capitol before the War of 1812, when Henry Clay became Speaker of the House of Representatives.*

out of low-lying houses; a heavy rain turned mud into a sea of ooze, the air into suffocating stench; and mammoth rats competed with pigs, cattle, and other livestock for footing and food on the few slime-coated islets of high ground. Clouds of insects swarmed through the air; disease was rampant; and influenza reached epidemic proportions in winter while small pox decimated the remnants of humanity without the means of escape in summer.

"We want nothing here," the witty New York senator Gouverneur Morris liked to tell visitors before he lost his seat in 1803, "nothing but houses, cellars, kitchens, well-informed men, amiable women, and other little trifles of the kind, to make our city perfect."[18]

Although only twenty-nine years old and constitutionally ineligible to serve as a US senator, Clay nonetheless took his seat amidst mutters of criticism for having defended Aaron Burr. After making the required courtesy call at the executive mansion, however, Clay began to change his opinion of Burr when President Jefferson showed him a so-called cypher letter. Sent by General James Wilkinson, commander of American troops in north Louisiana, the letter was in code, purportedly written by Burr. In it Burr elaborated plans to march southward with a force of 10,000 men to seize New Orleans and rendezvous with the British navy for a subsequent land-and-sea assault on Mexico.

A sly, smooth-talking intriguer, Wilkinson had climbed Army ranks from captain to brigadier general during the Revolutionary War and had prowled in the shadows of ambitious officers who plotted to oust George Washington as commander-in-chief at Valley Forge. When the plot failed and its authors were exposed, Wilkinson resigned and moved west to Kentucky.

During a trip to Spanish-held New Orleans Wilkinson made a secret agreement with Spanish authorities to lead a secessionist movement in Kentucky and incorporate the bluegrass state into what was still Spain's Louisiana Territory.

"Wilkinson is entirely devoted to us," the Spanish minister assured his foreign minister. "He enjoys a considerable pension from the King."[19]

In 1805 Jefferson appointed Wilkinson governor of northern Louisiana—even as Wilkinson was rousing Kentucky secessionists and promoting union with Spain. Spain gave Wilkinson title to 60,000 acres in Texas as a refuge in case the US government uncovered his plot and forced him to flee US territory. Wilkinson was convinced by then that a Spanish-American war was inevitable, and by establishing ties to both sides, he hoped to ensure his place in the winning camp, regardless of which side won.

To deflect suspicions of his involvement, Wilkinson whispered rumors he knew the President would eagerly embrace: Burr, whom Jefferson despised, was plotting against the President. As proof, Wilkinson forged the so-called cypher letter with Burr's signature, outlining the secession movement for which Wilkinson himself was responsible.

11. President Thomas Jefferson convinced Henry Clay to abandon former vice president Aaron Burr Jr., whom Clay had successfully defended before grand juries in the West. Convinced that Burr was guilty of treason, Jefferson ordered US attorneys to prosecute Burr again and showed Clay a letter in Burr's handwriting that discouraged Clay from continuing on the case. (From an original painting by Rembrandt Peale)

When the President showed Clay the cypher letter, the twenty-nine-year-old senator stood transfixed. A former department-store errand boy addressed by the President of the United States and author of the Declaration of Independence, Clay absorbed every word as gospel.

"On my arrival here [in Washington] in December 1806," Clay explained, "I became satisfied from . . . information communicated to me by Mr. Jefferson that Colonel Burr had entertained treasonable designs."[20]

After meeting with the President, Clay returned to the Capitol to pursue his own political agenda to improve the nation's transportation network. He won appointments to several prestigious committees and proposed three major federal projects that he called "internal improvements": a canal to bypass the Falls of the Ohio River near Louisville, Kentucky; a bridge across the Potomac from Washington to Virginia; and a canal connecting Chesapeake Bay and Delaware Bay. President Jefferson and Congress had combined to enact the Cumberland Road bill in early 1806, authorizing construction of a National Road from Cumberland, Maryland, to Wheeling, Virginia (later West Virginia). Clay, therefore, had high hopes of winning support for his projects.

"Mr. Clay, the new member from Kentucky, is quite a young man," remarked John Quincy Adams of Massachusetts, "an orator and a republican of the first fire." Adams might also have added gambler, bon vivant, philanderer, and politically ambitious lawyer to Clay's evident character traits, according to New Hampshire senator William Plumer. Plumer noted that Clay was "out every night," drinking heavily at times, sometimes gambling and attending "all parties of pleasure"—usually with a woman on his arm.[21]

Clay made a point of introducing himself to the Capitol's men of note—Secretary of State James Madison and Treasury Secretary Albert Gallatin, to name but two—and joining influential congressmen at card parties and other festivities. "But after all that I have seen," Clay was careful to write to his father-in-law, "Kentucky is still my favorite country."[22]

Before leaving the nation's capital, Clay fulfilled all his obligations to his Kentucky supporters, including those with cases before the Supreme Court. He applied for and won admission to practice before the High Court, winning all three cases—and $3,000 in fees.

When Congress adjourned in March, Clay returned to Kentucky, and President Jefferson resumed his relentless pursuit of Aaron Burr. Despite evidence that Wilkinson had forged the cypher letter, the President urged Wilkinson to continue his hunt for Burr. Wilkinson's troops arrested four of Burr's friends, a handful of lawyers who tried defending them, and a dozen public officials, including a sitting judge and a former Kentucky senator. At the same time, Wilkinson rejected all petitions for habeas corpus and shut down newspapers that printed even a word about the arrests.

"Never in the history of the United States did so powerful a combination . . . unite to break down a single man as that which arrayed itself against Aaron Burr," declared historian Henry Adams, whose grandfather John Quincy Adams was in the Senate at the time.[23]

Burr did not realize the enormity of the forces arrayed against him until, exonerated of all wrong-doing and set free by three grand juries, he set off down the Ohio River toward the Mississippi River and Natchez. On January 10, 1806, he learned of Wilkinson's ruthless roundup of his friends and the reward Wilkinson was offering for his capture. With a huge price on his head, dead or alive, Burr feared summary execution if captured.

As news of Wilkinson's illegal mass arrests reached Washington, President Jefferson's alter-ego in the Senate, William Branch Giles of Virginia, acted to legalize Wilkinson's actions. He proposed and won passage of legislation retroactively suspending habeas corpus for three months for anyone charged with "treason, misprision of treason, or other high crime or misdemeanor endangering the peace, safety, or neutrality of the United States."[24]

Eager to end the manhunt, Burr went voluntarily to the US territorial district court to testify before a special grand jury—his fourth—and again the jury refused to indict him. When Burr saw Wilkinson's thugs ride into the area, however, he feared for his life and fled into the Alabama territory. After a local official recognized him two weeks later, Alabama militiamen seized him and led him under guard to Richmond, Virginia.

On March 26 a heavy military escort led Burr into Richmond, where, after four days in jail, he appeared for arraignment before US Supreme Court Chief Justice John Marshall, who was riding circuit and sitting in the Richmond Circuit Court. Marshall concluded that no evidence of treason existed and dismissed the charge with a dose of ridicule for the prosecuting attorney for wasting the court's time. He did, however, hold Burr over for trial on the charge of leading an expedition against Spain.

By then Henry Clay had returned to Kentucky and won reelection to the state assembly. Out of touch and unconcerned with the Burr proceedings, he reacted with surprise to a letter from President Jefferson's attorney general asking him to assume prosecution of Burr in Ohio. Although flattered by the President's confidence, Clay refused, citing his public and private responsibilities at home in Kentucky, where the state supreme court and assembly were both in session. Appearing in Ohio would mean an extended leave from both his family—Lucretia had just given birth to another daughter—and clients who had cases pending before the state court. Moreover, he had just won election as Speaker of the Assembly, a powerful and prestigious post he was not about to abandon to prosecute a case that four grand juries had rejected for lack of evidence and that the Chief Justice of the US Supreme Court had ridiculed.

In December 1807 President Jefferson imposed a carelessly conceived—some said irrational—embargo that closed American ports to all foreign trade. The embargo was a response to years of British and French depredations on American shipping, including seizure of millions of dollars' worth of ships and cargoes and, in the case of the British, impressment of hundreds of American seamen into the British navy. For the British, impressment was a way to fill manpower shortages—caused in part by British seamen jumping ship to seek higher pay on American merchant vessels.

On June 22, 1807, a British naval assault devolved into atrocity when the British frigate *Leopard* hailed the American frigate *Chesapeake* in international waters and demanded the surrender of four seamen who, the British captain asserted, were British deserters. When the *Leopard*'s captain refused, the British ship opened fire, killing three Americans and wounding eighteen. British sailors boarded the American ship and removed the four sailors in question. The attack infuriated Americans—among them Henry Clay and other western leaders, who demanded action by the President.

Clearly unprepared, Jefferson stumbled on the idea of a trade embargo, but, fearful the British would consider it an act of war if he limited it to British goods, the President asked Congress to embargo all foreign trade. The President told puzzled Americans to do without imports, become self-sufficient, and rely entirely on American-made goods.

The embargo devastated New England, whose economy depended on trade with Britain, but enterprising westerners were quick to profit from it by establishing their own manufacturing plants—mills and looms to make textiles, furnaces to make iron products, and distilleries to make whiskey in quantities large enough to offset reduced shipments from Scotland and Ireland.

Henry Clay's father-in-law was quicker than most to exploit the embargo, and within a year he and Kentucky's other rope makers produced more rope than any state other than Massachusetts. Thomas Hart's super-productive hemp farms not only filled the needs of rope makers but also replaced cotton in the manufacture of cotton bagging. During the embargo Kentucky produced almost all the bagging for cotton bales in the United States.

The greater the market demand, the more Kentucky entrepreneurs worked to fulfill it. By 1808 Kentucky had the most gunpowder mills, ranked second in salt production, third in whiskey output, and fourth in cotton and wool cloth production, and, with no competition from imports, few Kentuckians raised a whisper of opposition to Jefferson's embargo. Henry Clay, an outspoken champion of free trade when Spain and France conspired to shut down New Orleans to American shipping, even defended the embargo, saying it was promoting the use of domestic manufactures.

New Englanders, however, depended heavily on trade with Britain for their economic well-being and rose up in defiance of Jefferson's embargo. Connecticut's legislature declared the Embargo Act "unconstitutional and despotic" and ordered state officials not to enforce it.[25] Connecticut governor Jonathan Trumbull taunted Jefferson with the President's own words from the Kentucky Resolution a decade earlier: "Whenever our national legislature is led to overleap the prescribed bounds of their constitutional powers," Trumbull mocked the President, "it becomes the duty [of state legislatures] to interpose their protecting shield between the right and liberty of the people and the assumed power of the federal government."[26]

In what grew into mass defiance of presidential and federal authority, New England's other state governments followed suit. Across New England a huge smuggling trade emerged, driving prices up uncontrollably as merchants openly defied the American government and engaged in illicit trade with England and her colonies, paying whatever prices smugglers demanded.

Ironically, the embargo had nothing but positive effects in Britain. In the absence of American vessels on world trade routes, British cargo ships filled the void in international commerce. Canada and South America replaced the United States as Europe's primary suppliers of lumber, grain, pelts, and other raw materials. American exports plummeted nearly 80 percent from $108 million in 1807 to $22.5 million in 1808, while imports fell nearly 60 percent from $138 million to less than $57 million. Government revenues from duties dropped from $16 million to a few thousand dollars. The Act marooned 55,000 sailors and left 100,000 other Americans— merchants, craftsmen, laborers, and others who depended on foreign trade—without work or income. American ships trapped in foreign waters when the Embargo Act went into effect fell prey to pirates as well as the British and French navies.

On March 1, 1809, only days before leaving office, Jefferson succumbed to anti-embargo protests in the East and reopened the United States to foreign trade. Imports of all shapes and sizes suddenly flowed into American markets, and Henry Clay did another turn-about, leading western demands for federal protection against foreign competition. After returning to Washington, he urged the secretary of the Navy to give preference to domestic hemp, cordage, and sail cloth. Then, in his first major speech in the Senate, he called on the government to help the nation evolve "from an agricultural to a manufacturing society:

> It is important to diminish our imports, to furnish ourselves with clothing made by our own industry, and to cease to be dependent . . . upon a foreign and perhaps inimical country. The nation that imports its clothing is but little less dependent than if it imported its bread.[27]

Clay went on to mock those who continued to patronize shops that sold imported British goods after victory in the War of Independence.

> Such was the partiality for [British] productions that a gentleman's head could not withstand solar heat unless covered with a London hat; his feet could not bear the pebbles or frost of the country unless protected by London shoes; and the comfort of his person was only [ensured] when his coat was cut out by the shears of a tailor "just from London."[28]

Clay's baritone voice boomed across the Senate Chamber: "American skills and ingenuity" were able to produce goods of equal quality and durability as imports, he insisted. "I entertain no doubt that, in a short time . . . the domestic manufactories in the United States, fostered by government . . . are fully competent to supply us with at least every necessary article of clothing."[29]

Clay's speech not only shifted Senate sentiment; it announced his emergence as a great American orator. Few members of Congress had heard Clay's moving summations in court—especially those in *United States v. Burr.*

"His voice filled the room as an organ fills a great cathedral," wrote historian George Bancroft, later secretary of the Navy and founder of the US Naval Academy. "[Clay's] voice was music itself, penetrating and far reaching, enchanting the listener."[30]

By then the case against Clay's former client Aaron Burr had come to an end. General Wilkinson had taken the stand under oath and admitted he had altered and forged parts of the notorious cypher letter and changed Burr's otherwise innocent missive into a blueprint for conspiracy. Chief Justice Marshall scolded the prosecution, saying it had charged Burr with levying war—an overt act that must be proved by two witnesses.

"It is not proved by a single witness," Marshall roared. He called the testimony that the jury had heard inadmissible, irrelevant and "incompetent to prove the overt act itself."[31] If Burr had, indeed, raised an army of 7,000 troops, Marshall asked, "what could veil his army from human sight? An invisible army is not an instrument of war."[32] A few minutes later the jury declared Burr "not proved guilty under this indictment by any evidence submitted to us. We therefore find him not guilty."[33]

Freed by the court, Burr nonetheless faced assault by lynch mobs, and when former friends proved unwilling to shelter him, he fled to England in June 1808 and found both safe haven and friendship at the home of philosopher Jeremy Bentham. He busied himself with Bentham's various projects—abolition of slavery, women's suffrage, prison reform, and Latin American liberation—until Jefferson left office and allowed most Americans to forget about Burr.*

One of Kentucky's most ardent Hamiltonians was Humphrey Marshall, the leader of Kentucky's Federalist party and a state-assemblyman with Clay. A cousin of Chief Justice John Marshall and brother-in-law of prosecuting attorney Joseph Hamilton Daveiss, Humphrey Marshall was as crazed as Daveiss with hatred for Burr for having killed Hamilton. He repeatedly assailed Henry Clay in

---

* Burr returned to New York in early 1812, only to learn that his grandson, ten-year-old Aaron Burr Alston, had died in Charleston, South Carolina. The boy's distraught mother, Theodosia—Burr's only child—boarded a boat to rejoin her father in New York but never arrived. The ship, passengers, and crew were lost at sea. Burr remained in New York, shunned politics, and practiced law in relative obscurity for the rest of his life.

the state assembly for defending Burr. When Humphrey Marshall criticized the President's embargo on foreign trade, however, Clay fired back, defending the President in a resolution that called the embargo "a measure highly judicious and the only honorable expedient to avoid war."[34]

Humphrey Marshall exploded with rage, denouncing Clay and his resolutions but encountering humiliation by casting the only vote against them. Never one to withdraw from a political battle when he held the initiative, Clay called Marshall's attacks "base malice," then goaded Marshall with another resolution that called on "members of the general assembly to clothe themselves in productions of American manufacture and restrain themselves from the use of cloth or linens of European fabric until the belligerent nations respect the rights of neutrals by repealing their orders and decrees as relates to the United States."[35] Once mocked as a boy for wearing homespun in Jefferson's Richmond statehouse, the former court clerk now insisted that his tormentors dress as he.

Clay not only humiliated Marshall; he dictated the clothes Marshall was to wear in public, winning an overwhelming 57-to-2 vote for the resolution. That was too much. Marshall stormed into the assembly the following day dressed in garish English imports and cited Clay's resolution as that of "a demagogue." Clay, wearing homespun with pride, shouted back, questioning Marshall's love of country. The two traded increasingly angry insults until Marshall called Clay "a liar," and Clay leaped at the Federalist, fists raised to pummel his opponent into submission. Fortunately, a giant German-born assemblyman, General Christopher Riffe, who sat between the two, intervened. Grasping both combatants by their collars and separating them, he triggered gales of laughter across the state as he told his squirming captives in German-tinged English, "Come poys. No fighting here. I vips you both."[36]

After Clay cooled and apologized to his colleagues, Marshall shouted, "It is the apology of a poltroon."[37] Clay saw little choice but to challenge Marshall to a duel, or, as he put it in his letter, "the ceremonies proper to be observed."[38] Two weeks later Clay, Marshall, their seconds, and surgeons crossed the Ohio River near Louisville and reached a spot near the mouth of Silver Creek, Indiana, where Kentuckians, barred by law from dueling in their home state, routinely traveled to settle differences. Unlike Marshall, Clay was unfamiliar with guns or rifles, having spent his adolescence in a department store and a courthouse basement while most American boys were practicing sword play and hunting small game in fields and woods.

Clay and Marshall were to have three shots each. Marshall fired first and missed; Clay fired and grazed Marshall. Marshall's second shot missed, and Clay's "damned pistol snapped" without firing—but it counted as a shot, and they prepared for the third and final round.

Marshall fired first, and his shot hit home.

CHAPTER 3

~

An Imperious Despot

In the afternoon a courier galloped into Ashland with a note for Lucretia Clay. She read it and looked up at her sister, who had come from Lexington to comfort her.

"Thank God," Lucretia cried, "he is only slightly wounded!"

"My wound is in no way serious," Henry Clay had assured his physician, "a flesh wound in the thigh."[1]

Clay's flesh wound, however, elevated him onto a hero's pedestal in the eyes of most Kentuckians.

"Worthy Friend!" wrote State Senator James Johnson, later a Kentucky congressman. "Your firmness and courage is admitted now by all parties. I feel happy to hear of the heroism with which you acted . . . this will serve to stop the mouths of all the snivel faced Tories. . . . I disapprove of dueling but it seems necessary sometimes for a man's dignity."[2]

Most Kentucky legislators agreed. Although they censured both Clay and Marshall for dueling, they acknowledged Clay as their new leader, and, on the same day, voted to send him to the US Senate again—this time to fill the unexpired term of Kentucky senator

Buckner Thruston, who had resigned to accept a federal judgeship. By then James Madison, the longtime secretary of state under Jefferson, had won election to the presidency, with Clay's support ensuring him Kentucky's Electoral College votes.

Again traveling without his family, Clay rode overland to the Ohio River and took the boat to Wheeling, where a series of brutal stagecoach rides over the mountains carried him to Washington. Thoroughly familiar with Senate procedures by then, Clay took his seat on February 5, 1810, and, less than three weeks later, erupted in anger when Senator Nathaniel Macon of Georgia proposed a bill to reopen trade with Britain and France.

"I am for resistance by the sword," Clay thundered.

> No man in the nation desires peace more than I. But I prefer the troubled ocean of war . . . to the tranquil, putrescent pool of ignominious peace. . . . Has not Congress solemnly pledged itself to the world not to surrender our rights? . . . I am for war with Britain . . . her injuries and insults to us were atrocious . . . her violation of the sacred personal rights of American freemen, in the arbitrary and lawless impressment of our seamen—the attack on the *Chesapeake*—the murder . . . the wrongs & disgraces . . . the nation is benumbed by dishonorable detail.

Clay called for immediate retaliation, saying, "Conquest of Canada is in your power . . . the militia of Kentucky alone are competent to place Montreal and Upper Canada [Ontario] at your feet. . . . I call upon the members of this house . . . to acquire the entire fur trade . . . and to destroy the temptation and the opportunity of violating your revenue and other laws."[3]

Although western senators stood to cheer, they were a minority; the full Senate easily ratified the bill reopening trade with Britain and France—subject, however, to their ending their depredations against American shipping.

But Clay's words echoed across the West and along the southern and northern frontiers. In the summer of 1810 American settlers in

Spanish-held West Florida took Clay's words to heart and rebelled. After seizing Baton Rouge, they declared independence from Spain and asked the United States to annex their new state. President Madison agreed, and Congress supported him, with Clay calling for still greater US expansion: "I hope to see, ere long, the new United States . . . embracing not only the old thirteen states, but the entire country east of the Mississippi, including East Florida and some of the territories to the north of us also."[4]

Roused by Clay's nationalistic fervor, his home district of Fayette County, Kentucky, a center of manufacturing and industrial development, elected him to the House of Representatives, making him simultaneously both a senator and representative from his state.

In contrast to the quiet solemnity and decorum of the Senate, lunacy gripped the House. Members walked in, out, and about at will, shouting to (or at) each other, shoving each other, oblivious to cries for order from the Speaker and appeals from colleagues to support legislative proposals. Unlike the dignified elite portrayed in history tomes and stately oil paintings, frontiersmen in buckskins chewed tobacco and shot spittle toward brass spittoons—sometimes hitting their mark. Big-bellied Philadelphia bankers pushed their way to their seats, and high-hatted southern slave masters snapped at prune-faced New England abolitionists. Many wore pistols—loaded and ready to fire. Philadelphia gunsmith Henry Derringer had invented a small pistol that fit into a man's pocket and allowed many congressmen to enter the Capitol armed without wearing holsters. The unpredictable Representative John Randolph of Roanoke, who ruled a vast Virginia plantation with 400 slaves, gained notoriety for his theatrical entrances in boots, spurs a-jingle, whip in hand, a retinue of slaves on his coattails, and two ferocious hunting dogs bounding at his side.

Every congressman knew the legendary Randolph warning to a debt collector: "Sir, had it not been for your exceedingly genteel appearance, my dogs would have torn you to pieces."[5]

Ironically, those who filled the House of Representatives were the very men the framers of the Constitution had envisioned when they designed the American government. They began the Constitution with the words "We the People" and gave more powers to the House of Representatives than to any other branch. The only popularly elected branch of the federal government, it alone reflected the entire spectrum of voters, with all their stark differences and conflicting local interests.

"Not the rich more than the poor," wrote James Madison, an author of the Constitution, explaining the intent of the framers. "Not the learned more than the ignorant; not the haughty heirs of distinguished names more than the humble sons of obscurity and unpropitious fortune. The electors are to be the great body of the people of the United States."[6]

But the result was chaos: barbarism, corruption, and vicious brawls—often on the House floor, sometimes on dueling grounds outside the capital—between the high born and low, farmers and bankers, frontiersmen and townsfolk, abolitionists and slaveholders, northerners, southerners, westerners, easterners. Far from a single nation, the "United" States were a loose association of semi-independent nations with few ties to hold them together, and when a congressman spoke of "my country," he spoke not of the United States but of his state—with good reason.

Few roads or waterways linked East to West across the rugged Appalachian Mountains, swamplands and hills separated South from North, foul winter weather and spring floods isolated vast regions of the country for weeks or months, and the distances that separated Americans were enormous. In the best of weather Washington lay more than five days' travel from New York, ten days from Boston, and all but inaccessible from far-off Charleston, South Carolina.

In addition to geography, language and religious differences made cultural ties among Americans tenuous at best. The South—and southerners—were as foreign to most New Hampshiremen as China and the Chinese. Across the country only 60 percent of Americans had English origins. The rest were Dutch, French, German, Scottish, Irish, Scotch-Irish, and Scandinavian. Although English often served as a common tongue, German prevailed in much of eastern Pennsylvania, Dutch along the Hudson River Valley north of New York City, and French in northern Vermont and parts of New Hampshire and in what would become Maine. Southerners were Episcopal or Baptist; New Englanders, Puritan/Congregational or Roman Catholic; and middle-staters, Lutheran and Roman Catholic. Newport, Rhode Island, harbored a pocket of Jews, while the South held nearly 900,000 black people in slavery—many ready to rise and slaughter their white tormentors. Members of the House reflected all the regional and ethnic—if not racial—differences of the nation and erupted in bitter arguments and violent confrontations on the House floor and dueling grounds across the Potomac River in Virginia.

It was into this maelstrom that thirty-three-year-old Henry Clay entered in the fall of 1810 with a small army of fresh, young, newly elected representatives from the nation's frontiers. Many had already been aroused by his calls for protection of homemade products, internal improvements to expand commerce, and impregnable national defenses to fend off the nation's enemies—Indian and foreign.

The raucous behavior of the House puzzled Clay and his followers at first—they were political novices, after all. Initially Clay said he found "the turbulence of a numerous body" more stimulating than "the silent stillness of the Senate chamber," but he soon changed his mind.[7] Indeed, he grew outraged at what he saw as desecration of the democratic American political system.

In fact, the system had all but collapsed in Washington years earlier—for evident reasons. The hardships of traveling great distances on trails and primitive roads and the impossible living conditions in the Washington swampland discouraged even the hardiest of congressmen from frequenting the national capital. So Congress met only twice a year for as short a time as possible, leaving Presidents alone to govern as they saw fit, without the congressional restraints the Constitution provided.

With Congress absent and the nation under attack from within and without, Presidents Washington and Adams each sent troops to war to protect American citizens. In doing so, however, each assumed quasi-tyrannical powers not granted by the Constitution. Thomas Jefferson flirted more openly with dictatorial rule by emasculating the Supreme Court, suspending habeas corpus, and sending political enemies to prison without trial. Jefferson thwarted challenges to his one-man rule by sending the Supreme Court into exile for two years, forcing justices to ride to circuit courts far from the national capital without opportunity to convene.

When James Madison succeeded Thomas Jefferson as President in 1809, America's enemies stepped up their assaults. Just after Henry Clay arrived in the House, Indian raiders laid waste the western and southern frontiers, burning American homes and settlements, while the British navy increased the number of attacks on American cargo ships. By 1812 they had seized 300 to 400 vessels and impressed some 6,000 seaman. As their war with Napoleonic France gained momentum, the British seized every ship bound for France, declaring even nonmilitary supplies such as foodstuffs to be contraband that could help the French war effort.

After eight years as secretary of state under President Jefferson, Madison preferred negotiations and sanctions over war. Clay, however, grew incensed at what he viewed as British outrages and American failure to retaliate. He organized a core group of frontier congressmen and young members from the original thirteen states to wrest power from senior colleagues.

"The majority [in the House] had, for years, wavered and hesitated to act decisively," Abraham Lincoln explained years later.

> Mr. Clay, more than any other man . . . aroused and nerved and inspired his friends and . . . bore down all opposition. He appealed to the . . . pride, the honor and the glory of the nation. He pleaded the cause of the injured sailor . . . invoked the genius of the Revolution. Mr. Clay bearded and defied the British Lion . . . [and] sounded the charge.[8]

12. *The youngest representative and only freshman ever elected Speaker of the House in American history, Kentucky Representative Henry Clay faced chaos on the House floor as he took command. (From an original painting by Matthew Jouett)*

On November 4, 1811, "war hawks" in the new 12th Congress elected Clay the seventh Speaker of the House of Representatives, making him the youngest man ever to hold that office and the only freshman congressman ever to do so.

With Clay's elevation to national leadership, his wife, Lucretia, and their children came to Washington, braving the uncomfortable steamboat ride up the Ohio and bone-jarring stagecoach rides across the Appalachian Mountains to the East Coast. The trip was especially brutal for children. The Clays had six by then. The youngest, Henry Clay Jr., had been born the previous April and was his father's pride and joy. The other youngsters were Theodore Wythe, nine; Thomas

Hart, eight; Susan Hart, six; Anne Brown, four; and Lucretia Hart, two. Theodore was all but unmanageable. He had fractured his skull several years earlier, and a surgeon had trepanned his skull, drilling through the bone to drain fluid that was collecting beneath the injury site and compressing the boy's brain. Although Theodore survived the operation, the injury left him subject to periodic delusional behavior and uncontrollable rages. The doctor predicted—correctly—that Theodore would inevitably decline into insanity.

With so many children to care for, Lucretia found social life in the national capital difficult. "She is a thousand times better pleased sitting in the room with all her children round her, and a pile of work by her side, than in the most brilliant drawing room," commented Margaret Bayard Smith, wife of *National Intelligencer* editor/publisher Samuel Harrison Smith. Mrs. Smith chronicled Washington social life for the first forty years of the nineteenth century, listening to every word in every drawing room—and many bedrooms. If she didn't see or hear it, it probably never happened.[9]

When Lucretia accompanied her husband to Washington parties, he usually deserted her for the card tables, where he gambled while she waited patiently. Shocked by the sums that changed hands one evening, a Boston matron asked Lucretia whether her husband's gambling didn't worry her.

"Sometimes, yes," Lucretia conceded with a casual toss of her head. "But really—he most always wins."[10]

Although Margaret Smith was a ubiquitous presence in the city's drawing rooms, she especially enjoyed Lucretia and her children—even helping Lucretia organize parties for the youngsters. At one the two ladies "decked themselves out with flowers, drank punch, ate sugar plums and cakes and oranges and then, while Lucretia played the piano, the children romped rather than danced till a late dinner."[11]

While Lucretia was controlling her children's behavior, her husband tried controlling the behavior of the people's representatives, who often acted like children. He brought the Speaker's gavel crashing down on the sound block like Thor's hammer, his deep, resonant voice demanding order, declaiming like God what thou shall and shall not do and when thou shall and shall not speak. The House had never seen or heard anything like it.

Clay, however, had served as Speaker in Kentucky's Assembly; he was a consummate performer and had learned to wield the gavel and voice its power. "Decide! Decide promptly!" he later counseled Massachusetts representative Robert C. Winthrop before Winthrop himself took the Speaker's chair. "There will always be men to cavil and quarrel about your reasons, but the House will sustain your decisions."[12]

Young as he was, Clay's baritone voice boomed authority, to which he added rapier-like wit and an astonishing command of the law. Seizing control of the Rules Committee, he created a new set of strict—if byzantine—procedures that gave him and future Speakers command of the entire legislative process. Clay named committee chairs and members and, through them, indirectly decided whether and when a bill could come to the floor for a vote. He selected which members could speak for or against it on the floor, when they could speak, and for how long. One veteran congressman who spoke beyond his allotted time heard the thunder of Clay's gavel and felt the sting of his lightning tongue.

"I speak to posterity!" the old man protested.

"Yes," Clay shot back, "and you seem resolved to continue speaking until the arrival of your audience."[13]

The ensuing roar of laughter sent the old man slumping into his seat in a red-faced funk.

A hard-drinking card player, Clay often played until morning's light reminded him to run to the Capitol and call the House to order. Questioned once whether he felt well enough to do so after a night of cards and whiskey, he snapped, "Come up, and you shall see how I will throw reins over their necks."[14]

In one of his first—and at the time most daring—decisions, Clay challenged Virginia's explosive representative John Randolph, who had first entered the House in 1799 and proceeded to write his own

13. *The eccentric, explosive Virginia representative John Randolph owned a 900-plus-acre plantation, 400 slaves, and a pack of hunting dogs, two which he regularly led onto the floor of the House of Representatives—until Henry Clay seized the Speaker's gavel. (Library of Congress)*

rules of conduct. Randolph owned the 900-acre Roanoke Plantation in Charlotte County, Virginia, along with some 400 slaves. Originally a firm supporter of his cousin Thomas Jefferson's campaign for the presidency, Randolph broke with the President over the Louisiana Purchase, which he deemed unconstitutional—as indeed it was. As Randolph pointed out correctly, nothing in the Constitution gave the President or Congress powers to acquire foreign territory and annex it to the United States.

"Everything and everybody seem to be jumbled out of place," Randolph complained, "except a few men who are steeped in supine indifference, whilst meddling fools and designing knaves are governing the country."[15]

Many "old" Republicans and Federalists agreed and coalesced into a new political group of strict constitutionalists. "Presently we shall be told we must have . . . the gold mines of Mexico," Virginia senator S. T. Mason grumbled, "then Potosi—then Santo Domingo, with their sugar and coffee and all the rest. . . . But what have we to do with the territories of other people? Have we not enough of our own?"[16]

Unable to thwart Jefferson's foreign ventures, Randolph devolved into a disruptive presence in the House, shrieking opposition to legislative proposals in an abnormally high-pitched voice—the result of a childhood illness. His girlish squeal would have provoked laughter had it emanated from a less intimidating figure. When North Carolina representative Willis A. Alston complained about Randolph's dogs, the Virginian pounced on Alston and beat him savagely with a cane. Clay's predecessor as Speaker, Massachusetts representative Joseph Varnum, looked away, pretending not to see or hear.

Clay—standing as tall as his six-foot-one-inch stature permitted—would have none of it, and, as other House members gasped at his audacity, he ordered the sergeant-at-arms to remove Randolph's dogs. Rendered all but apoplectic by Clay's impertinence, Randolph waited for Clay to leave the chamber, then blocked his way, snarling, "I never sidestep skunks."

"I always do," Clay smiled as he stepped nimbly around Randolph and walked away—postponing the inevitable duel that would climax their festering enmity.[17]

Evicting Randolph's dogs from the House was the least important of Clay's House reforms. During his twelve years as Speaker he used wit, wiles, charm, tact, political skills, and personal courage to transform the House from an impotent discussion group into the legislative institution the framers of the Constitution had intended it to be. In doing so, he converted the Speaker's role from that of an impartial moderator to a powerful political leader—as powerful, at times, as the President himself. Even Clay's enemy John Randolph conceded that as Speaker, Clay had become "the second man in the nation."[18] A bill could become law without the President's signature, but not without the Speaker's.

Not everyone in the House admired Clay or his methods. The Harvard-educated Boston Brahmin, Representative Josiah Quincy, despised Clay. He called Clay "bold, aspiring, presumptuous, with a rough, overbearing eloquence . . . which he had cultivated and formed in the contests with the half-civilized wranglers in the county courts of Kentucky. . . . He had not yet that polish of language and refinement of manners which he afterwards acquired by familiarity . . . with highly cultivated men."[19]

In fact, the Founding Fathers had never expected the Speaker to emerge from the ranks of Quincy's "highly cultivated men." They had designated him the "elect of the elect"—the elected head of the only governmental body directly elected by the unwashed electorate: "We the People of the United States."

As no predecessor had done, Clay recognized the powers the Constitution had vested in the House, and as Speaker, he seized and used those powers to pack committees with chairmen and members who would further legislation he considered to be in the interests of the people. Although he usually appointed close allies such as South Carolina's John C. Calhoun to the most important committees, Clay was too savvy a politician to ignore potential opponents such as Daniel Webster, who entered the House in 1813 representing his native state of New Hampshire. By placing Webster on the powerful foreign relations committee, he converted a potential political foe into a loyal friend.

His powers cascaded into every area of legislative life, controlling which legislation committees considered and which reached the floor of the House or were tabled into oblivion. Knowing that the Constitution required his signature for any measure to become law, members soon knew better than to propose legislation that he opposed. In the end Speaker Henry Clay—and those of his successors strong enough to embrace his tactics—determined much of the legal structure of the United States and earned Clay the title of "Dictator."[20]

"There has never been a more imperious despot in political affairs than Mr. Clay," journalist Benjamin Perley Poore asserted. "He regarded himself as the head-center of his party—*l'état c'est moi*—and he wanted everything utilized for his advantage."[21]

To inflate his powers, Clay often injected his influence on important legislation by dissolving Congress into a "committee of the whole"—a committee consisting of the entire congressional membership. By appointing someone other than himself as chairman, he could then argue his views before the entire Congress—something the rules did not permit him to do as Speaker. As leader of his political party, his words and vote often determined the fate of legislation—no more so than in 1812.

Early that year the British navy stepped up seizures of American ships at sea. As revenues from foreign trade plunged, the American economy followed suit. Adding to the nation's woes, the British army command in Canada was providing arms and ammunitions to Indian raiders in the West to assault and massacre American settlers.

"All hope of honorable accommodation with England is at an end," Henry Clay proclaimed to the committee of the whole.

> It is by open and manly war only that we can get through the present crisis with honor and advantage to the country. Our wrongs have been great; our cause is just: and if we are decided and firm, success is inevitable. Let war be forthwith proclaimed against England.[22]

With Clay's war hawks in command of committees, Congress offered the Speaker little opposition. By then President Madison had replaced his insubordinate Secretary of State Robert Smith with fellow Virginian James Monroe. A Revolutionary War hero who had become a client and friend of Henry Clay, Monroe intensified the spreading war fever by echoing Patrick Henry's call to arms more than three decades earlier: "Gentlemen, we must fight," Monroe announced. "We are forever disgraced if we do not."[23]

Although reluctant to go to war, President Madison realized he could not let British depredations on American ships continue

14. *President James Madison had served eight years as Thomas Jefferson's secretary of state, but hesitated to confront the British over depredations to American ships until 1812, when Speaker Henry Clay convinced him to ask Congress to declare war. (Library of Congress)*

unanswered if he hoped to win reelection in the fast-approaching presidential elections. Federalist congressman Josiah Quincy of Massachusetts charged that Clay told the President that his support in the elections "depended upon his screwing his courage to a declaration of war."[24]

On June 1, 1812, the President capitulated and asked the House to declare war against Britain. It did, and the Senate followed suit two weeks later; for the first time in American history Congress exercised its constitutional power to declare war.

With no military experience and unsure how to be commander-in-chief, Madison asked Clay to be secretary of war, but instead was met with a sharp, albeit confidential, rebuff and a reminder about the constitutional obligations of the President of the United States. Clay pledged to soldier for the President on the floor of the House.

"Henry Clay," Josiah Quincy charged, "was the man whose influence and power more than that of any other produced the War of 1812 between the United States and Great Britain."[25]

From the opening salvo the war was both a political and military disaster. What Clay and his war hawks did not—and could not— know was that the American trade embargo had brought British industrial production to a near-halt just as England's long war with Napoléon's France was raging. English forces desperately needed American raw materials—powder, iron, ship timbers, textiles, and the like—and on June 23, 1812, Parliament voted to restore good relations with the United States by ending impressment and other depredations against American ships. The Americans had, at last, won their thirty-year dispute with Britain.

But victory came too late to benefit either side: Clay and Congress had already declared war on Britain. It took a month or more for messages to cross the Atlantic before the laying of the first trans-Atlantic communications cable in the 1850s, and neither Madison nor Clay nor Monroe were aware that Parliament was considering peace overtures to the United States. When they found out, it was too late.

America's maritime and commercial states—Massachusetts, Connecticut, New York, New Jersey, and Delaware—demanded that the federal government rescind its declaration of war and resume negotiations with the British, but fighting had already started, and from the first, American forces embarrassed themselves so badly that a ceasefire would have been tantamount to surrender.

US troops crossed into Canada on three fronts that stretched from Detroit in the west to Lake Champlain in upstate New York. Although one force managed to burn public buildings in a surprise raid on York (now Toronto), the capital of Upper Canada (now Ontario), it quickly retreated back to the United States after British troops counterattacked. Undermining the American military effort was the refusal of New York and New England states to participate in the war, saying terms of troop enlistments in their militias did not permit them to cross state lines.

With New England unaffected by fighting, a huge smuggling trade developed, driving prices up uncontrollably as merchants openly defied the American government and traded illicitly with England and her colonies, paying whatever prices smugglers demanded.

In contrast to Army humiliations on land, America's little navy scored significant victories over the vaunted British fleet with twelve fast and highly maneuverable ships. The forty-four-gun frigate *Constitution* demolished Britain's thirty-eight-gun *Guerrière* off the coast of Nova Scotia, and other American ships defeated Britain's navy off the coasts of Virginia and Brazil. On Lake Erie Captain Oliver Hazard Perry's fleet engaged the British for three hours off the Ohio coast at Put-in-Bay on September 10, 1813. Although the encounter left Perry's ship in splinters, he inflicted even more damage on the enemy and emerged from the wreckage to send his famous message: "We have met the enemy and they are ours."[26]

When news of America's naval victories reached London, the British prime minister sent an offer to Secretary of State James Monroe to begin peace negotiations at a neutral site in Gothenburg, Sweden. President Madison decided against sending Monroe, who had been an outspoken Francophile and Anglophobe during the Washington administration. Instead, the President named the dean of his foreign service, John Quincy Adams, to lead negotiations. American ambassador to Russia at the time, Adams was the son of former President John Adams, and Madison hoped his presence would symbolize the importance the President placed on the peace talks.

In a startling move to calm congressional war hawks and ensure political peace at home, Madison asked Henry Clay, the congressional architect of the war, to join Adams. Madison's request surprised Clay; the decision to cede his power as Speaker of the House was not easy.

"You will see that I am going to Europe," Clay wrote to a friend in Lexington.

Having a decided preference for a seat in the House of Representatives over any other station under the government, I vacated it with great reluctance. But I did not feel myself at liberty to decline a service, however delicate and responsible, which the President, without solicitation on my part, has been pleased to assign me.[27]

At a dinner party shortly before leaving Clay displayed his gift for compromise with a toast conceived to please the broadest range of political thought in Congress: "To the policy which looks to peace as the end of war—and to war as the means of peace."[28]

Early in 1814 Clay resigned the Speaker's chair and his seat in Congress, and after embracing his wife and children in Washington, rode to New York where, on February 28, he set sail for Europe on the *John Adams*. Their separation devastated Lucretia.

"My Dear Husband," she wrote,

> The children that I have with me are all well, and [three-year-old] Henry is always talking of you. He comes up and kisses me for his papa. I long very much to be at home with my family, for I am very dreary here, as I do not pay visits. Indeed I found I could not go out without you in the evening, but I do all in my power to keep me from being melancholy. . . . You need not make yourself the least uneasy on our account. Susan [ten] and Anne [seven] send their love to you. May God spare you to us. Do take care of yourself for our sakes.[29]

As Clay crossed the Atlantic, John Quincy Adams traveled overland from Russia. By then the Russian, Prussian, and other armies allied against Napoléon Bonaparte had captured Paris and forced the French army to surrender. Bonaparte, who had crowned himself Emperor Napoléon I, abdicated and accepted exile on the tiny isle of Elbe, off the Italian west coast in the Mediterranean Sea. French King Louis XVIII acceded to the French throne and signed a treaty of peace with his nation's European neighbors and with Great Britain.

The peace freed 14,000 British troops to sail for North America for a massive land-and-sea attack against the United States.

When Clay reached Sweden for the peace talks, he learned to his dismay that the British wanted to move the talks to London. Clay refused, saying his appearance in the enemy capital would be tantamount to recognizing a British victory. The British government then agreed to hold the peace talks at a neutral site in Ghent, Belgium, and Clay took full advantage of the change to tour Sweden, Denmark, Germany, and Holland before arriving in Ghent.

As British and American peace negotiators gathered in Ghent, British ships shelled US cities along the entire East Coast, devastating the entrance to the Connecticut River, Buzzard's Bay in Massachusetts, and Alexandria, Virginia, just across the Potomac River from Washington.

In mid-August 1814 4,000 battle-hardened British troops landed along the Patuxent River near Benedict, Maryland, routed a force of Americans, and marched on the capital. Bent on avenging the burning of public buildings by American troops in York, the British began an all-night spree of destruction in Washington on August 24, setting all public buildings ablaze, including the Capitol and the President's mansion. As the Americans had done in York, the British spared most private property, although they set fire to four homes whose owners repeatedly shot at passing redcoats. By then Lucretia and the children had returned home to Kentucky.

The British also spared the Patent Office, which contained models of inventions and records that the British commander deemed private property and that might well belong to British as well as American patent holders.

A storm the following morning brought bursts of heavy winds that sent flames flying erratically in so many directions that they forced the British to withdraw—for their own safety. By September 12 they had sailed down the Patuxent River into Chesapeake Bay, then northward toward Fort McHenry, which guarded the entrance to the port of

15. Burning of the Capitol in 1814. British troops capture Washington, DC, on August 24, 1814 and burn all public buildings, including the presidential mansion (seen here in flames). The thick white paint with which workers covered scorch marks on the stone exterior gave the building its name "The White House." (Library of Congress)

Baltimore. While troops stormed ashore to besiege the fort by land, British ships sailed northward to lay siege from the water.

As the bombardment continued throughout the day and into the night, a prominent thirty-five-year-old attorney and amateur poet Francis Scott Key watched "the rockets' red glare" and "bombs bursting in air" from a nearby ship, where he was negotiating a prisoner exchange with the British. To Key's amazement, "by dawn's early light . . . our flag was still there," its tatters fluttering over the fort and inspiring his poem "Defense of Fort McHenry." A newspaper published it a few days later with a new name, "The Star-Spangled Banner."*

---

*Although set to music almost immediately, "The Star Spangled Banner" did not become the national anthem until 1931.

On September 14 the British abandoned their fruitless assault, withdrew their troops, and sailed out of Chesapeake Bay for the British West Indies. Their departure ended the fighting, but after a month of talks at Ghent, negotiators had no solutions to the war in sight. John Quincy Adams, who led the American delegation, grew impatient—not with British negotiators but with his American colleague, Henry Clay. Adams complained about the Kentucky congressman's penchant for lingering at the table after dinner "to drink bad wine and smoke cigars, which neither suits my habits nor my health and absorbs time which I cannot spare."[30]

Making matters worse, Adams's room at the Hotel des Pay-Bas was next door to Clay's, which became the site of card parties and drinking bouts that often continued until dawn. By then Adams was rising to read his Bible. For some time Clay and Adams considered each other insufferable—the one an insufferable libertine, the other an insufferable Puritan. Ironically it was the neophyte Clay, not the seasoned diplomat Adams, who held the American delegation together. While the Harvard intellectual Adams filled his spare hours poring over impenetrable texts on history, art, and philosophy, the other American delegates had reached the end of their patience with British negotiating tactics, which aimed at wearing down the Americans with delays by reexamining and questioning every punctuation mark. All but Adams were ready to break off the negotiations and return home to their families. They had toured Ghent's monuments to the point of boredom. Only Clay's ebullience, entertaining chatter, card games, and drinking parties made life tolerable enough for the other American delegates to remain. He was a master at calming frayed nerves and uniting people.

Nonetheless, formal negotiations seemed ready to dissolve when the Swiss-born American secretary of the Treasury, Albert Gallatin, proposed a path around the impasse: they would simply declare the war ended and relegate demands of both nations to an arbitration commission to be set up at a later date.

16. *Agreement at Ghent. Admiral Lord Gambier, Britain's chief negotiator, holds the treaty ending the Anglo-American War if 1812 and shakes hands with John Quincy Adams, America's chief negotiator. Henry Clay is seated on the right at the rear. (From* The Signing of the Treaty at Ghent, Christmas Eve, 1814, *a painting by Sir Amèdée Forestier, 1914; Smithsonian American Art Museum, gift of the Sulgrave Institution of the United States and Great Britain.)*

Although the treaty they signed represented a satisfactory compromise for the exhausted negotiators, it was a stinging defeat for both the British and American governments. A costly two-year war had ended with a return to the status quo ante bellum, releasing all prisoners and restoring all conquered territories to prewar status except for West Florida, which fell under American sovereignty.

On Christmas Eve 1814, as John Quincy Adams, Henry Clay, and other negotiators signed the Treaty of Ghent with Britain's Lord Gambier, a fleet of fifty British ships landed 7,500 troops on Louisiana's southeastern coast near New Orleans. To their shock, General Andrew Jackson awaited in ambush with 5,000 Tennessee and Kentucky woodsmen—all crack marksmen. After a spectacular but indecisive artillery battle on January 1, the British pulled back and regrouped to attack again a week later. As redcoats advanced in the traditional linear style of European warfare, Jackson's men opened fire. The British troops stepped forward mechanically into a rain of American fire, toppling one by one, then by dozens. Bodies piled higher and higher until the "horror before them was too great to be withstood: and they turned away, dropping their weapons and running to the rear."[31] After only thirty minutes the battle was over; the British commanding general and two other generals lay dead along with more than 2,000 British troops. British survivors limped back to their ships and, on January 27, sailed away from what was the last battle of the war and the last hostile incursion by British troops onto American soil.

A few days later Secretary of State Monroe called members of Congress into the Patent Office building in Washington, the only public building the British had spared from flames. They unleashed a chorus of sustained cheers when he delivered the news of Jackson's victory. Federalists, Republicans, hawks and doves alike, exchanged handshakes and adjourned to soak in the news with appropriate drinks.

What they did not know, however, was the utter uselessness of Jackson's victory. Two weeks earlier John Quincy Adams and his American negotiators had signed the treaty ending the war, but like Parliament's concessions when the war began, news of the settlement did not arrive until weeks later when a British sloop sailed into New York Harbor flying a flag of truce. The war the United States could have won without firing the first shot had ended before they fired the last.

Nonetheless, Americans—almost unanimously—deluded themselves into calling the war a glorious triumph over the world's most powerful nation—a "second war of independence." The national delusion stemmed from a series of chronological coincidences: the victory at New Orleans had come just before Americans received news of peace, and in the public mind the chronology of events made the battle seem decisive in forcing the British to sue for peace and end depredations on American shipping. In fact, it was Napoléon's defeat that allowed Britain to harbor her warships and end the need to impress seamen and seize ships with contraband.

17. *The Battle of New Orleans. The battle at New Orleans on Christmas Eve 1814 had no impact on the outcome of the war. American and British negotiators had signed a treaty of peace in Ghent, Belgium, ending the war two weeks before the battle. (National Archives)*

Adams, Clay, and the others had signed the peace treaty with England on December 24, 1814, and although Clay longed to return home, the President asked him to remain overseas and join Adams and Treasury Secretary Gallatin in London for negotiations scheduled for April of a new commercial treaty with the British. Clay spent the next three months exploring and carousing in Paris and parts of France with American ambassador William H. Crawford, a former Georgia senator.

Virginia-born like Clay, Crawford had grown close to Clay while they were members of the Ghent peace commission—often irritating Puritan John Quincy Adams with their raucous all-night drinking bouts. Crawford took pleasure introducing Clay to Paris life—by day and night. Clay met Paris luminaries at the court of Louis XVIII and at fashionable salons. Far from Denny's Department store in Richmond, Virginia, the former errand boy displayed the gallantry of Kentucky's storied land barons by kissing the hand of French writer Madame de

Staël, the daughter of the renowned Swiss banker-statesman Jacques Necker. Clay met her extensive social set, including the Duke of Wellington, by then legendary as victor over Napoléon at Waterloo. When Madame de Staël told Clay the British had contemplated sending the duke to America during the War of 1812, Clay tried to be clever. "I am very sorry, Madam, that they did not send his grace."

"And why, Sir?" Madame de Staël asked.

"Because if he had beaten us, we should only have been in the condition of all Europe, without disgrace. But if we had been so fortunate as to beat the duke, we should have added greatly to the renown of our arms."

Later, when Madame de Staël introduced Wellington to Clay and repeated the American's remark, the equally glib Wellington had a ready riposte: "If I had been sent on that errand and been so fortunate to be successful against so gallant a foe as the Americans, I should have regarded it as the proudest feather in my cap."[32]

After three months in Paris Clay left for London to join Adams and Gallatin at the negotiations with the British government. After signing a commercial agreement giving each nation limited most-favored-nation trading privileges with the other, Clay left for home. He arrived in America in September 1815 and immediately returned to his wife and family—and a hero's welcome in Lexington, Kentucky.

Like most Americans, Kentuckians believed the United States had scored a stunning victory over Britain in the War of 1812 and shouted Clay's name as their choice for President. Clay did not try to dissuade them, accepting all the honors heaped upon him and quite ready to return to Washington and march triumphantly into the fire-gutted presidential mansion. Henry Clay believed he was not only ready to be President but would also win election to that office. The only question was when.

CHAPTER 4

❧

"They Will Foment War No More"

In December 1815 Henry Clay returned to Washington with Lucretia and the younger children. When, after settling his family into their quarters, he walked into the public room a hotel had set aside for Congress to reconvene, the Republican majority stood to cheer, then climaxed its acclaim by reelecting him Speaker.

A few days later President and Mrs. Madison celebrated the presumed American victory over Britain by staging "the most brilliant reception ever held in Washington," according to one capital resident:

> Rejoicing in the assurance of peace and of her husband's restored popularity, Mrs. Madison received her guests with smiles, and . . . radiated an atmosphere of happiness and good will. . . . The Peace Commissioners to Ghent—Gallatin, Bayard, Clay and Russell— were there. Mr. Adams alone was absent. The heroes of the War of 1812 . . . all in full dress.[1]

The gaiety of the reception, however, barely masked the devastation that surrounded them. With the presidential mansion a blackened shell gutted by fire, the Madisons had taken refuge in Octagon House, the magnificent town house of Virginia planter John Tayloe III, a few hundred yards west of the presidential mansion. With the Capitol gutted, Congress had been cramming members into a hotel, while the Supreme Court met in a private home.

In January 1816 Speaker Clay startled Congress by proposing the reopening of the Bank of the United States, whose closure he himself had engineered only five years earlier before the start of the War of 1812. Chartered in 1791 at the behest of then secretary of Treasury Alexander Hamilton, Congress had created the Bank of the United States as the federal government's own bank to deposit and withdraw funds for day-to-day government operations. The bank also printed currency and sold bonds to the public when the government needed extra cash.

By 1811, when Congress needed to renew the bank's charter, English bankers rather than Americans had snapped up two-thirds of the bank's outstanding bonds *and* stock—just as sentiment for war against Britain had reached explosive proportions. Adding to resentment of British control over the national bank was the growth in the number of state and local banks—more than one hundred—each printing its own currency. Few had enough specie—if any—to back their currency and compete with the Bank of the United States.

Henry Clay had used every power of his House speakership to defeat rechartering the national bank, even leaving the Speaker's chair to argue—as Jefferson had in 1791—that the national bank was unconstitutional and that the Constitution did not give the federal government power to establish its own bank or any other private corporations. Brilliant orator that he was, Clay triumphed.

Five years later he reneged. For anyone but Clay it would have been a public humiliation. By then, however, eighteen state banks had flooded markets across the nation with various currencies—all of them worthless on international markets—and without a bank of its own to issue a national currency, the Treasury defaulted. Rather than risk ridicule and hear his own earlier arguments against a national bank hurled at him, Clay remained aloof during the House debate and let one of his original war-hawk allies, South Carolina's John C. Calhoun, lead the struggle to reestablish the national bank. Unlike Clay, the stern-faced Calhoun had favored rechartering the First Bank of the United States in 1811, and he now won the day in establishing the Second Bank of the United States.

Like Clay, Calhoun was born a country boy, growing up on a prosperous 2,000-acre farm in western South Carolina, one hundred miles from the nearest settlement. Thirty slaves tilled the corn and wheat fields and tended the cattle, hogs, and sheep. Calhoun's father died when the boy was still in his teens, but at six-feet-two inches and with the strength of someone twice that height, John joined his brothers in running the farm. Eighteen years old in 1780, he came under the influence of a brilliant itinerant teacher and, with financial support from his older brothers, traveled north to New Haven, Connecticut, to enroll at Yale College. After earning his degree he went to Litchfield, Connecticut, to study law at Tapping Reeve's law school—the first such school in America. Unlike Clay, Calhoun was blunt and direct in his speech, whether to an individual, a jury, or his colleagues in the House. An intimidating figure with an intimidating face, he never relied on histrionics and rarely smiled. He was a perfect political ally for the theatrical Clay, whose wide mouth seemed locked in a perpetual grin.

Clay tried staying aloof during the debate, but so few House members understood the financial complexities of a national bank that they demanded an explanation for Clay's change of heart. With his usual bravado, Clay insisted that, as a senator in 1811, he had had no choice but to follow the Kentucky legislature's instructions to vote against rechartering the bank to protect the state-chartered Bank of Kentucky against competition by the national bank. Furthermore, as Thomas Jefferson had claimed when Congress chartered the first national bank in 1791, the Constitution had not authorized the federal government to create a corporation nor did it authorize Congress to continue the bank in 1811. But in one of the most important declarations in congressional history, Clay now insisted that

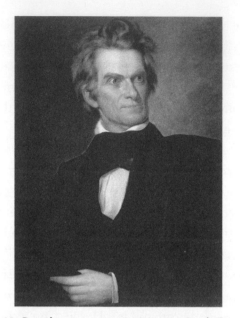

18. *Raised on a prosperous 2,000-acre South Carolina plantation, Representative John C. Calhoun had gone north to Yale College for his education and law degree before entering Congress and becoming a staunch ally of Speaker Henry Clay for nearly twenty years. (National Portrait Gallery)*

the Constitution gave Congress "implied powers" unmentioned in the actual language of that document. Alexander Hamilton had presented the same argument nearly forty years earlier.

Hamilton had cited Section 8 of the Constitution giving Congress power "to make all laws . . . necessary and proper for carrying into execution" its constitutional powers. "A bank is . . . an essential instrument in the obtaining of loans to government," Hamilton insisted.

Clay now expanded Hamilton's argument:

The Constitution vests in Congress all powers "necessary and proper" . . . to put into motion and activity the machinery of government which it constructs. The powers that may be so necessary are deductible by construction. They are not defined in the Constitution.

They are from their nature indefinable. When the question is in relation to one of these powers, the point of enquiry should be, is its
exertion necessary to carry into effect any of the enumerated powers
and objects of the general government?[2]

In effect, Clay broadened Hamilton's interpretation of the Constitution, declaring Congress ruler of the nation, with the "necessary
and proper" clause giving the legislature all but supreme power.

Clay's dictum officially embraced constitutional activism. Like
Hamilton, he insisted that "a total change in circumstances" and
"events of the utmost magnitude" had changed the obligations and
powers of government.

Under Speaker Clay, Congress authorized capitalization of the
Second Bank of the United States with $35 million, to be raised with
the sale of stock. The bank would then buy outstanding government
paper (bonds), thus driving its market value higher and, gradually,
restoring the value of US currency. Although offered the presidency
of the bank, Clay refused, believing that his colleagues and, indeed,
his supporters in Kentucky might question his motives for supporting recharter. He nonetheless purchased five shares in the bank and
told its president, William Jones, that "I will cheerfully render any
service in my power to an institution whose prosperity I consider
indissolubly connected with that of the country."[3]

Clay's embrace of extended federal government powers into banking did not sit well with voters in Kentucky and other western and
southern states. Clay added to their displeasure by supporting a bill
to raise congressmen's salaries from $6 a day (about $900 a year) to a
new flat rate of $1,500 a year, regardless of hours spent on the floor
of the House. The Speaker's salary, already $12 a day (about $1,800
a year), would climb to $3,000 a year. Far from being the "salary
grab" that many critics called it, the shift from daily to annual pay
was a response to criticisms that, as life in Washington had improved,
Congress was unnecessarily stretching the days it remained in session
to collect as many pay days as possible.

When he returned home to campaign for reelection in the summer of 1816, Clay found many once-adoring supporters infuriated by the pay increase. His opponent was Federalist John Pope, who had lost an arm as a youth. Pope charged Clay with having voted for the "salary grab" to pay for the luxurious way of life he had acquired while in Europe and imported to Kentucky to enjoy in his lavish mansion at Ashland.

Many voters agreed. One longtime friend and loyal political supporter shocked Clay by declaring, "Mr. Clay, I have concluded to vote for the man who has but one arm to thrust into the treasury."[4]

Clay's European stay and his intimate contact with the high-born— British prime minister Lord Castlereigh, Lord Gambier, Madame de Staël, the Duke of Wellington, and the like—had indeed changed his outward personality. No longer the clumsy country boy who stumbled into Richard Denny's Richmond department store, he had traveled through western Europe invariably addressed as "Your Excellency." He had dined with Europe's nobility and its most celebrated figures in the arts, sciences, and government. By now he had embellished the interior of his Ashland home to rival chateaux of European nobility. It included arched doorways, an octagonal entry hall, an octagonal library with ash and walnut paneling, and a domed skylight to augment the light.

"His disgusting vanity and inordinate ambition," Virginia senator Armistad Thomson Mason grumbled, "were fast destroying his influence and his usefulness as a public man."[5]

The changes in Clay were evident to neighbors, friends, and voters—even his family. Unable to cope with the unruly behaviors of his two oldest sons, fourteen-year-old Theodore and thirteen-year-old Thomas, he sent them away to a boarding school so he could focus on his campaign.

His wealth and new tastes had not dulled his wit, however. After a former supporter voiced his displeasure and said he would vote for Pope, Clay retorted, "Have you a good rifle, friend?"

"Yep."

"Did it ever flash?"

"It did, once."

"And did you throw it away?" asked Clay.

"No. I picked the flint, tried it again, and it was true."

"And will you throw me away?"

Flustered by Clay's question, the voter thought for a few seconds, then agreed he would not vote against Clay.[6]

Clay only barely won reelection to the House, however, and, indeed, garnered no support—not one vote—in his not-so-subtle appeals for consideration as a presidential candidate. He suffered an even more devastating political—and, indeed, personal—setback after James Monroe won the presidential election. Though a longtime client of Clay, Monroe named John Quincy Adams of Massachusetts as his secretary of state, a post considered a stepping stone to the presidency.

"Mr. Adams's claims, by long service in our diplomatic concerns, entitle him to the preference," Monroe explained before offering to appoint Clay secretary of war.[7]

Although Adams had won national and international recognition as America's outstanding foreign diplomat, Clay's vision was too clouded by his personal ambition not to view Monroe's appointment of Adams as a personal affront. When the President-elect repeated his offer of the War Department, Clay spurned the gesture "in the most decided manner" and refused to attend Monroe's inauguration.[8] The President appointed South Carolina's John C. Calhoun secretary of war but continued wooing Clay by offering him the appointment as ambassador to Britain. Clay again scorned the President's offer, calling it "the leavings" of John Quincy Adams.

Monroe's inauguration was the first open-air presidential inauguration in American history, made all the more poignant by the ruins of the Capitol looming in the background. The British had burned much of the Capitol, but American democracy remained standing, albeit on a temporary wooden platform outside the Senate building.

President Madison and associate justices of the Supreme Court greeted the President-elect as marines and army artillerymen and riflemen fired explosive military honors. In his inaugural address

19. *James Monroe Inauguration. With the Capitol ruins looming in the background, Chief Justice John Marshall swears in James Monroe as the nation's fifth President. The destruction by British troops in the War of 1812 forced the presidential inauguration outdoors for the first time in American history.*

Monroe pledged that "harmony among Americans . . . will be the object of my constant and zealous attentions. . . . Discord does not belong to our system. The American people . . . constitute one great family with a common interest."[9]

At Monroe's request, Chief Justice John Marshall, Monroe's close friend since childhood, administered the oath of office in a ceremony fraught with emotions for both. From the time they were boys in the Virginia woods Monroe and Marshall had led lives in tandem, attending the same little backwoods school together as boys, going off to the same college in Williamsburg, enlisting and fighting heroically in the Revolutionary War, shivering through a bitter winter in the same log hut at Valley Forge, and leading the charge into British lines at Monmouth with the commanding general they revered, George Washington. Both Marshall and Monroe had become dedicated public servants, and now, at Monroe's presidential inauguration, they stood together as the last Revolutionary War veterans in high office and, together with outgoing President James Madison, the last of Virginia's Founding Fathers still leading the infant nation's federal government.

Speaker Henry Clay was the only official of note not present at the historic ceremony, and although Clay had rebuffed President Monroe's offer of a cabinet post, the President opened the door to the presidential mansion and all cabinet meetings to the Speaker. Clay refused to attend, however, and seemed intent on challenging the new President for power. Clay believed that the nation's first three Presidents—Washington, Adams, and Jefferson—had usurped powers the Constitution had specifically assigned to Congress. The Constitution, after all, opened with the words "We the People" and devoted four of its seven articles to the powers granted to the nation's directly elected representatives in Congress. Only one, relatively brief article defines the limited powers of the President and clearly subjects him to the overriding powers of Congress—in appointing members of his cabinet and in making treaties with foreign nations. Clay intended to reestablish those limits on executive power and make the Speaker's chair the most important seat in government—akin to that of a prime minister.

Although the Constitution gave the President power to veto acts of Congress, Congress could override vetoes, and in the end, laws could take effect without the President's signature or approval—but not without the Speaker's.

Chastened by voter anger at what the press called the "salary grab," Clay returned to the Speaker's chair and called for repeal of the bill that had increased congressional pay. The pay raises had cost many of his colleagues their seats, and the extraordinarily large number of freshmen congressmen in the new House supported Clay by repealing the raises and returning to per-diem remuneration.*

Clay had only just returned to Congress when his two-month-old baby, Laura, came down with whooping cough. Contracted during the long ride from Kentucky, it was almost always fatal in infants then.

---

*During the succeeding session in 1818, however, Congress again voted themselves a pay raise, from six to eight dollars a day, or $1,200 a year.

Lucretia's sister Nancy, Elizabeth Lowndes, the wife of South Carolina congressman William Lowndes, and Margaret Smith sat vigil with Lucretia and Henry, taking turns day and night cradling the child in their arms as it hacked and gasped. Margaret Smith described Clay's reaction.

"He has from nature a fund of tenderness and sensibility, which even ambition, that all-absorbing passion, has not had power to dry up.

> Henry Clay is not a thorough politician, for on many occasion I have witnessed the irrepressible tenderness of a feeling heart. Never can I forget the tears he shed over his dying infant as it lay on my lap, and he kneeled by my side . . . he impressed a long tender kiss on its pale lips, murmuring, "Farewell, my little one."[10]

The next morning, Mrs. Smith said, Clay paced the floor "as if struggling to compose his feelings."

"My only difficulty," he sobbed, "is to decide what is my duty. I would fain remain at home this morning, but I have no right to allow private concerns to interfere with public duty. No. I must go to the House."[11]

As it turned out the House sergeant-at-arms presented the official condolences of the members when Clay arrived and presented an offer from them all to attend the funeral.

"Thank the gentlemen for me," he replied after collecting himself, "and tell them I am truly grateful for their indulgence in excusing my attendance this morning. I beg they will not put themselves to inconvenience . . . I wish only the presence of my family and the few friends who are with us."[12]

Laura's death changed Clay noticeably, replacing arrogance and personal ambition with altruism. "Instead of depression of spirit," Mrs. Smith remarked, "his mind seemed inspired with new vigor and animation.

> New scenes, new projects opened on his view—like a wrestler who had been thrown but not disabled. He started up, shook off the dust,

and wiped off the sweat of the first conflict, gathering up new strength and resolution, prepared for another combat for the prize of glory . . . more elastic, more vigorous, more high spirited. And I verily believe he is actually happier than if calmly and securely seated in the presidential chair. . . . Henry Clay was meant for action—not for rest.[13]

After Laura's death Clay went into action as never before, launching a legislative juggernaut to enhance the economy of Kentucky and other western agricultural areas. Indeed, Clay planned nothing less than an economic and social revolution that would change American society.

Oddly enough, he ignited the first sparks of his revolution in the temporary House Chamber before a body of men other than congressman: Almost all were slave owners like himself, gathered to form the American Colonization Society and buy uninhabited territory in West Africa where freed American slaves could settle in a land of their own as free men and women.

Although not as radical as emancipation, which some in the audience favored, the Society would nonetheless ease the plight of former slaves, whom their masters had freed but were left to fend for themselves. "They are not slaves, and yet they are not free," Clay pointed out. "The laws, it is true, proclaim them free, but prejudices, more powerful than any laws, deny them the privileges of freemen."[14]

At the time Clay owned twelve slaves and would soon own fifty. Although he would free some before he died and more in his will, his purchase, sale, and ownership of slaves exposed the conflict between the private and public man—as it did for many southern leaders. Publicly he called slavery "a deep stain upon the character of our country," but privately he insisted that slaves were better off under his care than anywhere else—as, indeed, they probably were.

The society elected Associate Justice Bushrod Washington, George Washington's favorite nephew, as its president. Clay would remain a lifelong member and become society president in 1836, retaining the post for sixteen years until his death.

When the American Colonization Society ceded the House Chamber back to its members, Clay fired the next shot in his political revolution with a call to Congress to subsidize and oversee construction of a vast network of roads and canals to link the nation commercially and ensure "the cementing of the Union." Although Madison's last act as President had been to veto a similar bill as an unconstitutional federal intrusion into state prerogatives, Clay again called for a new, more liberal interpretation of the Constitution.

"In interpreting the Constitution," Clay explained, "We must look at the history of the times when it was adopted and . . . at the great aim and object of its framers . . . the preservation of this Union." A network of roads and canals along with other internal improvements, he argued, were essential to national defense and economic growth as well as binding the states into a permanent union.

"Is it possible that a mere military officer might order a road and construct it [in time of war] and yet that power should be denied to the legislative branch of the government?" he asked. "The friends of state rights contest every inch of ground [as if] Congress were about to introduce some plague or pestilence . . . which was to destroy the liberties of the country.

> And of what power was such language used? Of a power to promote social intercourse; to facilitate commerce between the states; to strengthen the bonds of our Union; to make us really and truly one family—one community in interest and in feeling. . . . The power was not of an offensive nature.[15]

President Monroe, however, had made it clear that he, like Madison, believed federal government construction of local roads was unconstitutional. Eastern leaders agreed. New England traded more with Britain than with the American West, and almost all its leaders opposed spending federal tax dollars in the West without clear benefits for the East. Using President Monroe's constitutional argument to bolster their opposition, they united in voting down Clay's bill by a substantial majority.

Ironically, President Thomas Jefferson, the strict constitutionalist and father of the dominating Republican Party, had coaxed Congress into authorizing federal funds in 1806 to build the nation's first "interstate" roadway—the so-called National Road from Cumberland, Maryland, to Wheeling, (West) Virginia, and the easternmost navigable section of the Ohio River.

Construction had started in the spring of 1811 and was still under way when Clay proposed expanding it into a national transportation network. The network was a key element of what Clay now called his "American System" to bind the Union commercially, politically, and socially. Other elements were a tariff wall to protect American products against foreign competition and the application of revenues from the sale of federal lands for internal improvements. He was particularly concerned about protecting Kentucky's thriving new industry of weaving local hemp into cotton bagging. In addition to higher tariffs on inexpensive Scottish bagging, he sought higher tariffs on English and Swedish iron, which threatened the survival of Pittsburgh's new iron smelters.

To the consternation of westerners, President Monroe rejected Clay's road construction bill, leaving farmers, manufacturers, and consumers in Kentucky, Tennessee, and other western areas with only primitive ways to ship goods to and from eastern markets and coastal gateways to Europe. The setback came at a time when industry was rapidly expanding to meet the needs of the increased number of settlers crossing the Appalachians into the West. Clay, however, saw the defeat as part of a power struggle between the executive and legislative branches of government, with the executive attempting to dictate the course of local government. Clay prepared to strike back by intruding into the President's domain over foreign affairs.

While Americans were still fighting the War of 1812, Napoléon's army had invaded Spain, and Spain's South American colonies took advantage by rebelling, with Argentina declaring independence. When Monroe took office, he opened negotiations with Spain for cession of East Florida but ignored events in Latin America so as to avoid alienating Spain and reiterated America's long-standing policy of neutrality in foreign affairs.

In the House, however, Speaker Clay challenged the President, demanding a more aggressive American stance. He called Latin American rebellions the off-springs of America's own War of Independence. Although he supported the President's ambitions in Florida and won approval of a bill authorizing the President to seize East Florida by force, he added resolutions to send an ambassador to Argentina and to recognize Latin American colonies that declared independence.

"Not a Spanish bayonet remains within . . . La Plata [Argentina] to contest the authority of the actual [revolutionary] government," he told Congress.

> It is free! It is independent! It is sovereign! Are we not bound, then, upon our own principles, to acknowledge this new society? If we do not, who will? At the present moment, the patriots of South America are fighting for liberty and independence—for precisely what we fought for.[16]

Secretary of State John Quincy Adams, who backed the President's policy of "impartial neutrality," warned that, far from espousing liberty, South America's rebel leaders had been guilty of "execrable outrages" against opponents of the revolution.

"If so," Clay argued, "it was because execrable outrages had been committed upon them by the troops of the mother country.

> Could it be believed if the slaves had been let loose upon us in the South as they had been let loose in Venezuela . . . that General Washington would not have resorted to retribution? . . . The only means by which the coward soul which indulges in such enormities can be

reached is to show to him that they will be visited by severe but just retribution.[17]

Clay charged the Spanish with having pledged the "destruction of every principle of liberty. . . . Do we know whether we shall escape their influence?" Clay then called on the House to exercise control over foreign policy, adding his "hope that submission to the executive pleasure would not characterize this house."[18]

Although Latin American rebel leaders hailed Clay as a champion of liberty, a majority of the House decided Clay had carried his challenge of presidential policies too far and that, as representatives of local districts, they lacked both the competence and constitutional authority to determine foreign policy. With that, they handed Henry Clay a stinging defeat, 115 to 45, to go with his previous defeat in the road-construction issue.

President Monroe took full advantage, deploying troops on three fronts without consulting Congress. He sent one detachment to seize Amelia Island in the Atlantic Ocean near the Florida-Georgia border; pirates had used the island as a base from which to attack American shipping. The President sent a second military expedition to Galveston Island in the Gulf of Mexico off the Texas coast; the United States had claimed Galveston as part of the Louisiana Purchase but had never planted its flag there. Finally, President Monroe dispatched a third contingent of troops to Spanish Florida, a haven from which renegade Seminole Indians and runaway slaves had been raiding and burning farms and settlements across the border in Georgia.

The President told Secretary of War John C. Calhoun to order military commanders to pursue and attack the Indians and blacks "unless they should shelter themselves under a Spanish post."[19] Knowing Speaker Henry Clay stood ready to pounce if they overstepped constitutional bounds, the President and his war secretary acknowledged that, in Monroe's words, "an order by the government to attack a Spanish post would . . . authorize war, to which, by the principles of our Constitution, the Executive is incompetent. Congress alone possesses the power."[20]

Two weeks later Monroe sent commanding general Andrew Jackson an enigmatic message that the Seminoles had "long violated our rights and insulted our national character." He told Jackson that "great interests are at issue, and until our course is carried through triumphantly . . . you ought not to withdraw your active support from it."[21]

Well aware that carrying out his mission "triumphantly" would mean attacking Spanish troops and, thus, represent a de facto declaration of war without congressional consent, Jackson sought to avoid personal responsibility. He sent the President a cryptic request: "Let it be signified to me through any channel (say, [Tennessee congressman] Mr. J. Rhea) that the possession of the Floridas would be desirable and in sixty days it will be accomplished."[22]

Because of constitutional constraints, the President could not— and did not—reply. To tell one congressman of his warlike intentions would have revealed them to the entire Congress and risked censure. When Jackson received no response from the President, however, he followed his original instructions from the secretary of war and led 1,000 troops across the border into Florida. After seizing Spanish posts at St. Marks, about forty miles south of the Georgia border, he and his men swept eastward to the Sewanee River, where they captured the Seminole village of Bowleg's Town and burned 300 houses. He then reversed course, marching his force westward across the panhandle, leaving every Seminole or black village and fort he could find in ashes. To terrify the population into submission, he hanged two captured Creek chieftains.

"They will foment war no more," Jackson proclaimed.[23]

On May 24 Jackson's troops stormed into Spanish-controlled Pensacola, on the Gulf of Mexico near the border with Alabama, effectively taking control of the entire Florida panhandle. He also captured two British traders, one of them a ship owner, whom he accused of aiding the enemy and summarily hanged from the yardarm

20. *A bitter enemy of Henry Clay, General Andrew Jackson dodged a Clay-led effort to censure him for invading Spanish-held Florida without congressional authorization. Later, Clay's resolution made Jackson the only President in American history to be censured by the Senate. (Library of Congress)*

of his own ship in front of a group of terrified Indians. He ordered a firing squad to execute the other Britisher.

On June 2 Jackson sent a message to Monroe that he had won the Seminole War. If the President would now send the Fifth Infantry, Jackson wrote, he would deliver Fort St. Augustine. "Add another regiment and one frigate, and I will ensure you Cuba in a few days."[24]

Spanish ambassador Juan de Onis expressed outrage when he heard of Jackson's exploits. He fired a vicious protest to the State Department, all but declaring war. More embarrassed than intimidated, the President ordered Jackson to retire and cede Spanish towns back to the Spanish. Nonetheless, the President defended his military commander, calling his invasion of Florida "an act of patriotism, essential to the honor and interests of your country" and declaring,

> The United States stand justified in ordering their troops into Florida in pursuit of their enemy. They have this right by the law of nations, if the Seminoles were inhabitants of another country and had entered Florida to elude pursuit. It is not an act of hostility to Spain. It is the less so, because her government is bound by treaty to restrain . . . the Indians there from committing hostilities against the United States.[25]

The President warned the Spanish ambassador that Spanish troops would have to maintain peace along the frontier with America or else American troops would do the job for them.

Henry Clay was furious at the President and his evident contempt for Congress in sending troops to Amelia Island and Galveston without congressional authorization. And he grew apoplectic at Jackson's usurpation of congressional and, indeed, presidential authority.

"Beware how you give a fatal sanction . . . to military insubordination," Clay warned the President in a speech to Congress. "Remember that Greece had her Alexander, Rome her Caesar, England her Cromwell, and France her Bonaparte, and if we would escape the rock on which they split, we must avoid their errors."[26]

Subdued somewhat by his earlier failure to win control over foreign policy decisions, Clay did not ask the House to censure the President, but he had no such hesitation in demanding condemnation of Andrew Jackson. Jackson had, on his own, invaded foreign territory without presidential or congressional authority and murdered Indian chiefs and British captives.

In contrast to Clay and other constitutionalists, the general public hailed Jackson as a hero for his Florida adventures, including his

21. British officer strikes young Andrew Jackson. Captured by the British during the Revolutionary War, the 13-year-old volunteer trooper Andrew Jackson refused to clean a British major's boots and received a sword cut and scar for his defiance. (Library of Congress)

murder of the Britishers and Indian chieftains. Westerners especially saw Jackson as one of their own. Born in 1767 of Scotch-Irish immigrants in a remote frontier area along the border between the western Carolinas, he was orphaned at birth, his father having died three weeks earlier. Like Clay, Jackson's only formal education was in a local field school. He took a job in a saddle-maker's shop before enlisting in the militia as a courier when he was thirteen.

Captured by the British with his older brother Robert, he nearly starved to death, and when he refused to clean the boots of a British officer in exchange for food, the officer slashed him with a sword, permanently scarring the boy's head and left hand. He and his brother both contracted small pox, and after their mother obtained their release, both she and Robert died of the disease, leaving Andrew alone in the world at fourteen. He later studied law in North Carolina and won admission to the bar in the Western District of North Carolina, which would become Tennessee.

In the face of overwhelming public support for Jackson, Congress rejected Clay's censure proposal. President Monroe not only lauded Jackson's conquest; he told Secretary of State Adams to instruct the American minister in Madrid to defend Jackson's invasion and present the Spanish government with an ultimatum: either prevent further attacks on American territory or cede Florida to the United States and let Jackson's troops do the job. Faced with revolts across South America and terrified of again confronting the man they called "the Napoléon of the woods," the Spaniards capitulated.[27]

In the negotiations that followed, Adams let the Spanish government save face by withdrawing American troops and restoring nominal sovereignty over Florida to Spain. Spain then signed a treaty ceding both East and West Florida to the United States and renouncing all claims to both territories. The United States, in turn, renounced all claims to Texas.

In addition to ceding the Floridas, the Adams-Onís, or Transcontinental, Treaty defined western limits of the Louisiana Territory, with the Spanish ceding all claims to the Pacific Northwest and extending nominal US sovereignty there to the Pacific Ocean. In sending Jackson to seize Florida, Monroe had seized almost the entire continent for the United States. He rewarded Jackson by naming him governor of Florida.

The public hailed the acquisition of Florida as a great victory for Jackson and America, but Jackson was seething with anger at Clay's attacks, and armed as usual with pistols, he rode across the mountains to Washington to confront Clay. An adoring public intervened, however, and prevented what might have been a bitter, even bloody confrontation by welcoming Jackson so warmly that he decided to avoid a public encounter.

"Whenever the General went into the streets," one newspaper reported, "it was difficult to find a passage through, so great was the desire of people to see him. . . . Among the people . . . [Jackson's] popularity is unbounded—old and young speak of him with rapture."[28]

To try to bridge the rift he had created, Clay went to Jackson's hotel to apologize, but the general snubbed the Kentuckian, made a show of checking out in advance, and left for New York.

"The hypocrisy and baseness of Clay make me despise the villain," Jackson wrote to a neighbor in Tennessee. "I hope . . . you will see him skinned here [in Washington], and I hope you will roast him in the West."[29] Jackson's snub marked the beginning of a bitter, lifelong feud that would see Jackson wreak revenge and all but shatter Clay's personal political ambitions.

Together with the Louisiana Purchase, acquisition of Florida expanded the small nation George Washington had created into a vast, rich, and powerful empire (See Map 2, page 92). It set off a wave of westward migration that sent tens of thousands—many of them slave owners with their slaves—into the Missouri territory and provoked demands for statehood.

In February 1819 Clay obliged with an enabling bill. New York representative James Tallmadge Jr., however, proposed a rider banning further entry of slaves into Missouri and emancipation at age twenty-five of all slave children born in the state. The amendment would have ensured Missouri's entry into the Union as a free state and given free states a big enough majority in both House and Senate to emancipate slaves in the entire nation.

Georgia's Thomas W. Cobb exploded with anger. "If you persist," he warned Tallmadge, "the Union will be dissolved!"

"If a dissolution of the Union must take place," Tallmadge fired back, "let it be so! If civil war . . . must come, I can only say, let it come!"[30] A colonel in the Revolutionary War, the fiery New Yorker had helped capture British general John Burgoyne at Saratoga, New York, and went on to fight the British again in the War of 1812.

The exchange between Cobb and Tallmadge awakened Clay to the task that lay ahead if he was to keep the Union whole. Reflecting the North's popular majority, abolitionists passed the Talmadge amendment in the House. In the Senate, however, every state had two votes, regardless of population, and the number of slave states equaled that of free states. As it turned out, the Senate rejected the Talmadge Amendment by a wide margin, when several northern senators expressed fears that emancipation would provoke social upheaval comparable to that in Haiti.

At the time only the New England states had emancipated slaves. Although New York, New Jersey, and Pennsylvania had abolished the slave trade, they had not approved emancipation, and many African Americans remained in bondage. Senators from those states opposed any federal action that would strip owners of their "property" without proper compensation.

"We have a wolf by the ear [sic]," former President Thomas Jefferson commented from his home at Monticello, "and we can neither hold him nor safely let him go. Justice is in one scale, and self-preservation in the other."[31]

The debate over Missouri statehood raged for months, with hot-tempered slave-state radicals and fanatic New England Free Soilers all threatening to secede from the Union rather than yield to their political opponents. For the first time in his tenure as Speaker, Clay was unable to "throw reins over their necks" and bring opposing interests together. Fittingly, the divisions in the House reflected the divisions among the American people. The Union faced dissolution unless Clay could conceive a compromise on slavery that most Americans could accept.

"The Missouri question is a most unhappy one," Clay lamented to a friend in Kentucky, "awakening sectional feelings and exasperating them to the highest degree. The words civil war and disunion are uttered almost without emotion."[32]

Even Clay was unable to reconcile the contradictions of slavery in a land that proclaimed all men created equal. President Washington had failed to resolve the problem, as had Presidents Adams, Jefferson, Madison, and, now, Monroe. Like all of them, Henry Clay despised slavery, but owned slaves. Like all of them, Henry Clay did not believe that abrupt abolition was an answer—especially in the South. Unlike the North, the South had no towns or cities to absorb slaves in industries and apprenticeship programs. The South was agricultural. The road out of one plantation led only to the road into the next; unskilled slaves had no recourse but to work the land. Emancipation would leave untold thousands of unskilled men, women, and children without work, without homes, with no place to go or means of survival.

As Clay had warned the American Colonization Society, even when slaves obtained their freedom, "prejudices, more powerful than any laws, deny them the privileges of freemen" in American society.[33]

With no evident solution to the deadlock in Congress, Clay for once kept silent. Although he is said to have delivered a four-hour address on February 8, 1820, it went unrecorded in the *Annals of Congress* and was either lost, destroyed, or ignored and apparently had no impact on the House debate.

Indeed, Congress was on the verge of dissolution when Clay saw an opportunity for compromise appear suddenly when Maine petitioned to join the Union. In what became the first compromise to save the Union, Clay leaped at the opportunity to end the Missouri controversy by linking Maine's admission with that of Missouri, without restrictions on either state. Moreover, Missouri's geography gave Clay a second opportunity for compromise that would resolve future conflicts when other western territories applied for statehood.

Until then the Ohio River had been the unofficial north-south dividing line between free states and slave states. The second element of the Missouri Compromise extended the line along Missouri's southern border at latitude 36°30'—not far from where the Ohio River ended and dumped into the Mississippi River. Although Missouri sat above the line, it would be the sole exception to the Free Soil rule, which would ban slavery in all future states above 36°30' and permit it in states below it.

As the clerk tallied the final vote, Virginia's eccentric John Randolph of Roanoke moved for reconsideration. After weeks of bitter

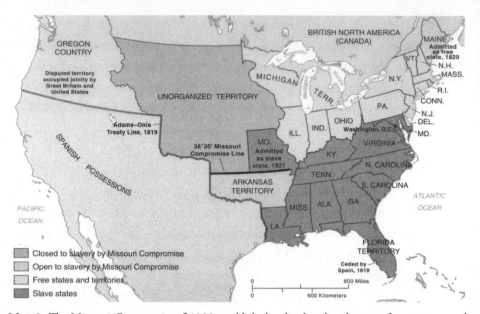

Map 2. The Missouri Compromise of 1820 established a dividing line between free territory and slave territory, with slavery illegal in any new states established north of the line, but permitted in states formed to the south. The map also shows the results of the 1819 Adams-Onís Treaty, ceding Florida to the United States and fixing western borders of the Louisiana Purchase.

debate, Speaker Clay—like most members—was exhausted and not about to allow a man whose sanity he questioned disrupt so fragile a compromise by restarting the debate. As Randolph spoke in favor of reconsideration, Clay kept his eyes fixed on the Virginian while moving his fingers imperceptibly and signing the Missouri Compromise. He slipped it to a clerk who stood by to take it to the Senate for final approval.

When Randolph finished speaking, Clay nodded his head politely, then expressed his deepest regrets that the clerk had already delivered the bill to the Senate, ending all opportunity for reconsideration in the House. Randolph raged in protest but was overruled and could do little but brood and plan his revenge. Missouri would become a state after presenting a constitution satisfactory to the Congress. Clay's parliamentary ruse had saved the Missouri Compromise—and the Union for at least another generation.

Although Congress—and much of the nation—hailed Clay for the Missouri Compromise, his effort left him exhausted and longing to return to Ashland. In the spring of 1821 Henry Clay gave up his chair as Speaker of the House of Representatives and ceded his rule as congressional dictator.

CHAPTER 5

※

The Great Pacificator

James Monroe won reelection for a second term as President in 1820 without opposition. With the disappearance of opposition, political parties in the United States dissolved—for a while at least. In Congress, however, the absence of party affiliations did not mean harmony. Indeed, when Henry Clay returned in the winter of 1821—no longer the Speaker—he found the House on the verge of the same disorder he found when he first entered a decade earlier. The new Speaker, John W. Taylor of New York, maintained close ties to both President Monroe and Secretary of State Adams, but without political parties to maintain member discipline, he was unable to muster voting majorities.

When the day came for Congress to meet in joint session to count Electoral College votes, Taylor lost all control. Although Monroe had run away with the election, few congressmen could agree on whether to include Missouri's Electoral College votes in the final count.

"Missouri is a state!" shouted some.

"Missouri is not a state!" came the reply.

As Taylor gaveled in vain, senators rose from their seats and left rather than lend their presence to (or suffer injury in) the disorder. Gradually Clay collared enough of his former political allies and convinced them to count Electoral College votes twice—with and without Missouri's votes. In another classic Clay compromise, he demonstrated that Missouri votes would have no impact on Monroe's victory either way.

After Clay had calmed the House, senators returned and confirmed what everyone already knew—that Monroe had won reelection—the only President to win without opposition since Washington. Monroe won 231 of 235 of the Electoral College votes, with three electors abstaining and a fourth, legend has it, casting his vote for John Quincy Adams to ensure George Washington's place in history as the only presidential candidate ever elected unanimously.

The balloting did nothing, however, to resolve Missouri's unexpectedly shaky status in the Union. Irate over attempts by out-of-state abolitionists in Congress to influence them, Missouri legislators had written a constitution that made it "the duty of the [Missouri] General Assembly to pass such laws as may be necessary to prevent free Negroes and mulattoes from coming to and settling in this state under any pretext whatever."[1]

Although the US Senate let it pass, Free Soilers in the House called it a violation of Article IV, Section 2 of the US Constitution that declared "citizens of each state . . . entitled to all privileges and immunities in the several states." A majority of the House agreed and turned it down. Southerners rose to protest, and as fighting broke out and Derringers appeared in some parts of the chamber, senators again pushed their way out of the spreading melee.

Again Clay edged between and around angry disputants, finally convincing enough of them, one by one, to put their Derringers back in their pockets and appoint a committee to resolve the dilemma. They did, and with Clay as chairman, the first committee issued a report that the House rejected. Clay organized a second committee. He was indefatigable—terrified that the Union might fall apart.

22. *The Chamber of the House of Representatives where Henry Clay made his impassioned plea for the Missouri Compromise that preserved the Union. Rebuilt after the British destruction in the War of 1812, the chamber served the House of Representatives until 1857, when that body moved into a new, larger chamber. The old chamber seen here now serves as Statuary Hall to house 100 statues of great Americans—two from each state. [See frontispiece.]*

In concert with a Senate committee, Clay's committee composed a new resolution calling for Missouri's admission to the Union, subject to its state legislature passing a law pledging never to deprive any citizen of rights guaranteed by the federal Constitution. Missouri's legislators complied a few months later but added a last-minute addendum stating that it had no power to bind future state legislatures to its pledge.

On August 10, 1821, President Monroe issued a proclamation admitting Missouri to the Union, after which Missouri's state legislature reasserted its sovereignty; without notifying federal officials, it banned Negroes and mulattoes from settling in the state.

By then Congress had adjourned, its members exhausted. Before leaving the Capitol, they extolled Clay as "the great pacificator" for his contribution to the second Missouri Compromise and preservation of the Union. To her husband's triumph in Congress, Lucretia added more joy with the birth of their eleventh child, John Morrison Clay.

It was clear to all, however, that Clay's compromise in preserving the Union had come at a price. No one really knew what Missouri's new constitution would mean for slaveholders, their slaves, free blacks, or mulattoes. Slavery remained firmly in place elsewhere in the South, whose laws were incompatible with northern statutes, with the Declaration of Independence, and with constitutional guarantees of individual rights and equality before the law.

Henry Clay, however, had done all he could to keep the nation whole. As fatigued as everyone else in Congress—more so—he resigned his seat, intending to end his congressional career, return home, and focus on his own and his family's affairs after years of neglect.

Although the fields on his farm had gone to seed and its buildings—including the main house—had fallen into various states of disrepair, Clay and his family found the rest of Fayette County— and, indeed, the rest of Kentucky—immersed in unprecedented prosperity. Jackson's seizure of Florida had left America's southern frontier invulnerable to attack for the first time since the nation declared independence. With Jackson's rifles cocked and ready to fire at the nation's enemies, the US minister in London, former attorney general Richard Rush, negotiated an amendment to the Treaty of Ghent and ended years of skirmishes along the Canadian frontier. For once the United States signed an agreement that favored itself more than Britain, ending the flow of British arms from Canada to American Indians and fixing the boundary between the United States and British North America along the 49th parallel, from Lake of the Woods to the crest of the Rocky Mountains (See Map 2, page 92).

The end of Indian raids in the West provoked a land rush that generated scores of new villages and towns and endless fields of grain. New homes sprouted as fast as corn and, with them, banks that loaned money with few or no questions of anyone who said he planned to buy and build. Recognizing the economic sense of Clay's American System, some state governments cooperated with each other by connecting roads, turnpikes, and canals at state lines and linking inland regions to coastal outlets and overseas shipping routes. Clay's American System began to materialize via state rather than federal initiatives, with the Union growing more interconnected and interdependent, despite opposition by proponents of state sovereignty.

In 1818 workers completed a 130-mile stretch of the great National Road, a twenty-foot-wide stone-surfaced route stretching between Cumberland, Maryland, on the Potomac River, and Wheeling, Virginia (later West Virginia), on the Ohio River. Completion of the road fulfilled George Washington's and Henry Clay's dream to link the great western rivers and eastern waterways to the Atlantic with a modern overland highway to carry grain and other goods in bulk across the Appalachian Mountains. The road opened Kentucky and the rest of the West to large-scale farming, mining, forestry, and hunting.

Clay hailed "the effect of internal improvements in cementing the Union—in facilitating internal trade, in augmenting the wealth and population of the country."[2] As he had predicted, thousands of tons of grain, furs, pelts, and other products began to stream over the Appalachians to eastern manufacturers and onto cargo vessels bound for Britain, Europe, and the West Indies. By then steamboats had lowered transportation costs and increased the speed with which goods traveled along the Atlantic Coast and on the Mississippi and Ohio Rivers and other waterways large enough and deep enough to float them.

In the most spectacular engineering scheme the world had ever seen, the first 15 miles of the 360-mile long Erie Canal opened between Utica and Rome in upstate New York. The canal would eventually link the Great Lakes with the Hudson River and the Atlantic Ocean, generating new towns and transforming old towns like Utica, Syracuse, and Rochester into prosperous cities.

"At no period of our political existence," President Monroe rejoiced, "have we had so much cause to felicitate ourselves at the prosperous and happy condition of our country. The abundant fruits of the earth have filled it with plenty."[3]

Determined to refill his own home with plenty and with family love, Henry Clay set aside his ambitions for high office and began to transform Ashland into a profitable enterprise, practice law, and reassert his role as the caring father he had lacked as a boy.

Missing from the family when Clay returned was Laura, of course, who had died in Washington and jolted Clay into recognizing the importance of a close-knit family to his own happiness as well as to his wife and children. Clay's long absences in Washington and Europe had exacted a toll on his children. To Clay's dismay, the two oldest boys had turned wild and undisciplined, and the oldest girls lacked command of the decorative and ornamental arts (pianism, singing, table settings, etc.) essential for marriage in American society. To his even greater chagrin, he found himself an all-but-forbidding stranger to his surviving children. He and Lucretia had occasionally taken some of the children to Washington, and Lucretia had remained home with all of them during her husband's stay in Europe. But Henry Clay had been away too much, and the Clays had often left their oldest in the care of others.

A tutor had stayed with the two oldest boys for two years before Clay sent them off to boarding school. Although nineteen-year-old Theodore Wythe had enrolled at Harvard, he remained subject to uncontrollable rages, and the college expelled him. Thomas Hart, eighteen, had completed his studies at Transylvania University in Lexington and enrolled at the US Military Academy at West Point, but he failed academically. The Academy dismissed him, and he came home—drunk. When, therefore, Henry Clay returned to Ashland in 1821, he came home to a family in disarray.

"The truth is, and I say it with infinite pain," the distraught father wrote of Thomas to the family's doctor, "I have lost all confidence in his stability. . . . In short . . . he fills me with inexpressible distress."[4]

In contrast, ten-year-old Henry Clay Jr.—then in nearby Transylvania University's preparatory school—was, like most ten-year-olds, craving for fatherly attention. Determined to become the father he himself had craved, Clay reached out to Henry Clay Jr., and the two bonded, growing all but inseparable in the weeks—indeed, years— that followed. As for the girls, they were pleasant, if appropriately shy. They didn't know their father, and he knew even less about them, but he all but humbled himself in his efforts to embrace them and demonstrate his love. Susan, soon to be seventeen, would marry before the year was out, and fourteen-year-old Anne would follow suit about eighteen months later, but both grew close to their father before embarking on married life. He would never have a chance to know then-twelve-year-old Lucretia, however. She died just before Anne's marriage.

Clay's absences had also taken their toll on his house and property. Although willing and able, his slaves—all deeply loyal—didn't have the initiative or direction to maintain Ashland in his absence. With the irrepressible Henry Clay Jr. at his side, Clay set slaves to work. A carpenter and painter restored the house and outbuildings while others worked on lawns and gardens—mowing, weeding, planting, or transplanting dogwoods, hollies, and a small forest of flowering trees and ornamental shrubs.

Clay also added to his acreage, expanding feed crops such as corn and cash crops such as tobacco, wheat, and rye. But his main crop was hemp, to feed Lexington's (and his father-in-law's) rope-making facilities. As he increased his crops, he doubled the number of his slaves to about two dozen, buying some, selling others, leasing a few, and trading less capable slaves for stronger or smarter ones.

He studied articles on soil quality in agricultural journals and the effects of light and wind on different crops. With what he learned, he explored surrounding areas, buying twenty-five acres from two neighbors, one hundred from another, and swapping plots of land with others to create fields that were perfect for growing hemp.

"Ashland never looked better than it does," he wrote to one of his brothers-in-law after a few months, "and I never was so well satisfied with the state of my preparations for a good crop. . . . I am getting a passion for rural occupations, and feel more and more as if I ought to abandon forever the strife of politics." He admitted, however, that "friends at Washington keep me well advised as to all that is passing there and worth knowing."[5]

Clay's law practice had deteriorated more than his farm during his Washington years. Fortunately, the president of the Bank of the United States (BUS) had recalled Clay's offer two years earlier "to render any services in my power" to the bank: he appointed Clay legal counsel for the bank in Ohio and superintendent of the bank's legal services in both Ohio and Kentucky, with a then-handsome annual retainer of $6,000. The prestige of his ties to the nation's bank drew many new clients to his office.

Lexington had changed dramatically by then. Its original settlers had prospered—replacing log cabins with stately brick and clapboard homes that sprawled beneath huge stands of shade trees along the road to town. An eighty-foot-wide main street, paved with a new material called macadam,* stretched through the center. Twelve-foot-wide walkways on either side carried shoppers past an array of elegant stores with goods from around the nation and the world. Transylvania University boasted almost as many students and faculty as Harvard and had transformed Lexington into what townsfolk legitimately called "the Athens of the West."

As in other growing western towns, the land rush spawned new banks to finance land purchases. Anyone with enough funds could start one—and too many did, often lending to borrowers who had no personal assets and nothing but raw land as collateral. Bankers didn't seem to care, reasoning they could seize the lands of borrowers who failed to repay their loans. As land values kept rising—and there was no reason to doubt that they would—bankers stood to profit handsomely, whether borrowers repaid their loans or not.

---

*Invented in 1820 by Scottish engineer John Loudon McAdam, the macadam process used a binder such as tar to cement a layer of small stones on roadways and congeal into a smooth hard surface.

Certain they couldn't lose, local bankers financed loans by borrowing from state banks, which, in turn, borrowed from BUS until 1819.

In 1819 all the banks ran out of money.

The collapse of American banking set off a national financial panic. Clay's friend William Jones, the president of BUS, made the collapse worse by losing a large amount of national bank funds by speculating in the bank's own stock. Although the available land in the West had seemed infinite after the War of 1812, the money to pay for it was not. Subject to the same laws of supply and demand as other commodities, properties lost value in the East with the increased availability of low-cost land in the West. Banks had often loaned money without screening clients. Apart from losses on loans to charlatans, bankers lost enormous amounts loaned to prospective land buyers who gambled away the money before buying a square inch of land, leaving bankers with worthless paper.

Henry Clay, however, managed to profit handsomely from the economic turmoil. Although the panic left him $40,000 in debt at first, contingency fees from lawsuits he filed on behalf of BUS earned him substantial multiples of that amount in cash and left his properties intact.

The case of *Osborne v. Bank of the United States* in September 1819 thrust him back into the national spotlight after he recovered $98,000 that Ohio's state treasurer had collected in state taxes from BUS. In effect, Clay restated the arguments of the landmark case of *McCullough v. Maryland* that the Supreme Court had adjudicated the previous March. As it had ruled in the Maryland case, the High Court declared the federal government sovereign over states and ruled it unconstitutional for any state to tax the federal government or its agencies. As it had ordered Maryland to do after the earlier case, the Supreme Court ordered Ohio to refund the taxes it had collected—$100,000—to BUS, which, in turn, would pay Henry Clay the appropriate commission.

Kentucky voters responded to Clay's brilliant legal performance by returning him to the House in August 1822, and when he arrived in Washington, the House overwhelmingly voted him back into the Speaker's chair.

"I would have preferred remaining a year or two longer in private life," he grumbled to a friend, "but my friends everywhere concurred in thinking my presence [in Washington] might be material in relation to another object." The other object was the presidency.

Not long after Clay returned to the House the President sent his seventh annual message to Congress, and to Clay's immense satisfaction, he adopted as national policy what Clay had advocated for years: support for Latin American independence.

Mexico had declared independence a year earlier, in September 1821, and by the end of 1822 Venezuela, Ecuador, and Colombia had joined Argentina and Chile in severing ties to Spain. A year later, in December 1823, President Monroe climaxed his presidency by embracing independence for all the Americas.

In what became the most important political manifesto in American history after the Declaration of Independence, Monroe proclaimed an end to foreign colonization in the New World and warned the Old World that the United States would no longer tolerate foreign incursions in the Americas. His words—later dubbed the Monroe Doctrine—shaped the future of US foreign and military policy for a century thereafter.

Monroe called the years of his presidency "the golden age of this republic"—a time in which the United States had maintained "peace and amity with all the world."[6] He said that although his government intended to maintain those relations in the future, it would consider any European attempts to extend its system anywhere in the Western Hemisphere a threat to the United States. The United States, he said, sought nothing but peace, had never meddled in Europe's internal affairs, and would not do so in the future. But he declared it "a principle in which the rights and interests of the United States are involved" that "the American continents, by the free and independent condition which they have assumed and maintain, are henceforth not to be considered as subjects for future colonization by any European powers."[7]

Five years earlier Clay had called on Congress to recognize the independence of Latin American republics then in rebellion against Spanish rule. "The patriots of the South are fighting for liberty and independence; for precisely what we fought for," Clay had said.[8] With his new doctrine, the President agreed with Clay and aligned the nation's foreign policy accordingly.

Clay jumped to take advantage of the shift in Monroe's thinking, hoping it would apply to domestic as well as foreign policy. He introduced a bill promoting his American System for internal improvements with a $30,000 appropriation to conduct surveys and draw up plans for roads and canals essential to national defense, commerce, and postal service. Like President Madison, President Monroe had vetoed legislation assigning federal moneys to extend the National Road beyond Wheeling, (West) Virginia, as an unconstitutional federal intrusion in state prerogatives.

Fresh from arguing constitutional law before the US Supreme Court, Clay presented a different interpretation. All but waving the document in the President's face, Clay called it "treachery" for a public official to defy the popular will and "refuse to exercise a power which has been fairly conveyed to promote the public prosperity.

> The Constitution vests in Congress the power . . . to raise a public revenue and pass "all laws necessary and proper" to employ the public money . . . to establish post offices and post roads, to regulate commerce. . . . The President seems to contemplate as fraught with danger the power . . . to effect internal improvement of the country. . . . Roads and canals are in the nature of fortifications . . . they enable to bring into rapid action the military resources of the country. They are better than any fortifications because they serve the double purpose of peace and of war.[9]

Clay's nemesis John Randolph called Clay's interpretation a ploy of lawyers—he called them "word shufflers"—and questioned Clay's educational credentials.

"I know my deficiencies," Clay replied softly. "I was born to no proud patrimonial estate. From my father, I inherited only infancy, ignorance and indigence."

"The gentleman might continue the alliteration and add 'insolence,'" Randolph shot back at no one in particular.[10]

Much as he had yielded to Clay on Latin American independence, President Monroe finally embraced Henry Clay's "American System" by signing the Survey Bill to fund surveys of—if not build—the national network of roads and canals that Clay envisioned binding East and West commercially, economically, politically, and even socially. Clay believed that interstate migration would establish strong family ties across state lines and make it unthinkable for states to separate and war with each other as Europeans had done.

Protective tariffs, however, were as integral a part of Clay's American System as internal improvements, and, flush with his Survey Bill victory, Clay called for a tariff wall to protect domestic production of iron, hemp, woolens, cottons, and wool and cotton bagging against imports. Congress agreed, and President Monroe signed it into law, winning Clay the cheers of westerners along with the Kentucky legislature's nomination for President—by unanimous vote—in the 1824 election.

Others, however, were as fired with ambition as Clay to succeed Monroe to the presidency: Treasury Secretary William Crawford of Georgia, Secretary of War John Calhoun of South Carolina, Secretary of State John Quincy Adams of Massachusetts, and General Andrew Jackson of Tennessee. Together they set off one of the most vicious political campaigns in American history.

"I have never known such a state of things," President Monroe lamented to former President James Madison, "nor have I personally ever experienced so much embarrassment and mortification.

> Where there is an open contest with a foreign enemy . . . the course
> is plain and you have something to . . . animate you to action, but
> we are now blessed with peace . . . so that there is no division of that

kind. . . . There being three avowed candidates in the administration is a circumstance which increases the embarrassment. The friends of each endeavor to annoy the others. . . . In many cases the attacks are personal, directed against the individual.[11]

With no political parties to nominate candidates, state legislatures did the job in six states, while qualified voters in other states simply cast ballots for electors who pledged to vote for certain candidates in the Electoral College. Before Kentucky nominated Henry Clay, the Tennessee legislature nominated Jackson, and Massachusetts, John Quincy Adams. A group of Republicans in Congress nominated Crawford, and Calhoun nominated himself. With little national support, however, Calhoun withdrew from the presidential race and nominated himself for vice president—a post he knew no one else would seek. To ensure his election, he placed himself on both the Adams and Jackson tickets.

In September 1823 Crawford suffered a paralyzing stroke, leaving Adams, Jackson, and Clay as the only active presidential contenders.

Clay did not help his chances after he returned to Washington in the fall of 1824. With Lucretia adamant about staying home with the children, he reverted to habits of earlier years—drinking to excess, gambling, and parading about with the most attractive women he could find. Clay's after-hours conduct at Ghent had appalled John Quincy Adams, and he now called Clay "void of good morals and . . . a reckless demagogue—ambitious and regardless of truth when it comes in the way of his ambition."[12]

Clay realized that New England's opposition to his American System precluded his chance of winning a majority of votes in the Electoral College. But it was just as unlikely that any of his opponents would win the needed majority. The House of Representatives, which he had controlled for many years as Speaker, would have to make the final decision.

Although the election campaign consumed most of the nation's attention, Congress was planning to celebrate the fiftieth anniversary of

23. Lafayette. Congress invited sixty-seven-year-old Marquis de Lafayette to tour America as the "guest of the nation," to celebrate the fiftieth anniversary of the victory at Yorktown. (Library of Congress)

the victory over the British at Yorktown. President Monroe thought the nation would benefit from the presence of the last of the heroic leaders in that battle—the beloved French Marquis de Lafayette. Congressional leaders agreed, and the President sent Lafayette a congressional resolution inviting him to be "the Nation's Guest."

The effect of Lafayette's arrival fulfilled all the President's hopes—and more. America threw him the biggest celebration in its history, with huge parades, banquets, and receptions. In celebrating Lafayette, they were celebrating themselves and their nation—as they never would again in their lifetimes.

"As if by magic," wrote Auguste Levasseur, Lafayette's private secretary and companion on his trip to America, "for nearly two months, all the hostilities . . . excited by this election, which were to have delivered the most terrible convulsions . . . were forgotten, and one could only think of Lafayette and the heroes of the Revolution."[13]

Lafayette traveled east, west, north, and south, visiting historic places, former comrades in arms, and everyone of note—governors, mayors, and others. He stopped at Lexington (Massachusetts), Brandywine, Monmouth, and Yorktown; he visited Washington's grave at Mount Vernon with Washington's nephew, Supreme Court Justice Bushrod Washington, and Washington's beloved step-grandson, George Washington Custis; he visited Andrew Jackson and his wife at their home in Nashville; and he went to Lexington, Kentucky, in Fayette County, to see Ashland, "the charming country home where Mr. Clay's family resided." Although Clay was not home, "Mrs. Clay and the children performed all the honors of the house in his name," Levasseur reported.[14]

On December 10 Lafayette returned to Washington for an official congressional presentation of a gift on behalf of "more than ten million people"—$200,000 and title to a township of land near present-day Tallahassee, Florida. After breakfast together, Clay presented Lafayette with the gift, citing him as "a faithful and fearless champion of liberty, ready to shed the last drop of your blood . . . which you freely and nobly spilt here in the same holy cause."[15]

Lafayette's reply "appeared to come from the heart," according to witnesses, but a Jacksonian newspaper charged that Clay had written both his own words of welcome and Lafayette's acknowledgment.[16] Lafayette's secretary Levasseur was shocked by "the immoderate and perhaps even unthinking attacks directed at him [Clay] by some partisan newspapers at the time of the election."[17]

After the ceremonies Clay and everyone else in Congress turned their collective attention to the election results. Andrew Jackson, who had won election to the US Senate, won far more popular votes for the presidency than his rivals—just under 153,000, compared to 114,000 for Secretary of State Adams and about 47,000 each for Clay and Crawford. None of the candidates had a majority of Electoral

College votes, however. Jackson won 99, John Quincy Adams 84, Crawford 41, and Clay 37. Under the Constitution, the House of Representatives had to decide the election between the top three vote-getters, with each state casting one vote under a unit rule.

Although Clay won more popular votes than Crawford, the three states he won had fewer Electoral College votes, and Clay had to quit the race. He nonetheless retained enough political influence in the House to throw the votes of the states he won to the candidate of his choice. Supporters of the remaining candidates swooped down on him, showering him with promises of high posts and other emoluments in their administration.

Bemused by "the unction applied to me by all the returned candidates for the presidency, or rather their friends," Clay described how he was "touched gently on the shoulder by a friend of General Jackson, who thus addressed me: 'My dear sir, all our dependence is on you; don't disappoint us.

> Immediately after, a friend of Mr. Crawford will accost me: "The hopes of the Republican Party are concentrated on you. For God's sake preserve it." Next, a friend of Mr. Adams comes with tears in his eyes. "Sir, Mr. Adams has always had the greatest respect for you and admiration for your talents. There is no station to which they are not equal.

"Really," Clay laughed, "the friends of all three gentlemen are so very courteous and affectionate that I sometimes almost wish that it was in my power to accommodate each of them."[18]

But it was not, as he explained to his friend, Virginia judge Francis T. Brooke, the younger brother of Virginia attorney general Robert Brooke, who had mentored Clay when Clay was a young man. "Mr. Crawford's state of health appears to me to be conclusive against him," Clay wrote. "And, as a friend of liberty," he said of Jackson, "I cannot consent to the election of a military chieftain."[19]

Clay had been at odds with Jackson, of course, since his unsuccessful effort to censure the Tennessee general for violating the Constitution by invading Florida without congressional consent. Clay explained his position in great detail to his friend Francis Preston Blair,* circuit court clerk and sometime-newspaperman in Frankfort, Kentucky. He called it "a dangerous precedent" to elevate "a Military Chieftain [Clay's capitalizations], merely because he has won a great victory. . . . I cannot believe that killing 2500 Englishmen at New Orleans qualifies for the various, difficult, and complicated duties of the Chief Magistracy."[20]

Well aware of Clay's criticisms, Jackson fired back, pointing out that no less a man than George Washington was "a military chieftain" and that "Mr. Clay has never yet risked himself for his country."[21]

In public Clay made light of the decision he would have to make. At a dinner for Lafayette he saw Jackson and John Quincy Adams sitting on either side of an empty chair, their eyes fixed forward, averting all contact with the other. Always the wit, Clay approached the two with a broad grin:

"Well, gentlemen. Since you are both so near the chair, but neither can occupy it, I will slip in between you and take it myself."

As everyone other than Jackson and Adams roared with laughter, Clay sat down between the two dour-faced candidates.[22] Always quick to find humor in the most complex human entanglements—even at his own expense—he announced plans for "the funeral solemnities of his own candidacy."[23]

He asked for a private meeting with Adams, however, and arrived at John Quincy Adams's house at 6 p.m. on January 9, 1825.

---

* Francis Preston Blair would later move to Washington, take over the *Globe*, a DC newspaper, and, with his wife and three children, move into a house across the park from the White House, which became known as Blair House and now serves as the official guest house for the White House.

According to Adams, the two men "spent the evening . . . in a long conversation."

> He said that the time was drawing near when the choice must be made in the House of Representatives of a President . . . that he had been much urged and solicited with regard to the part in that transaction that he should take. . . . He wished me as far as I might think proper to satisfy him with regard to some principles of great public importance, but without any personal considerations for himself. In the question to come before the House between General Jackson, Mr. Crawford and myself, he had no hesitation in saying that his preference would be for me.[24]

Clay had good reasons for supporting Adams. Although the grim-faced Adams had scorned Clay's card games and all-night drinking bouts in Ghent, they had worked together harmoniously in the diplomatic sector, and Clay had an intimate knowledge of Adams's thinking. Both were fervent nationalists with a deep belief in the nation's "manifest destiny," and Adams favored Clay's "American System." Clay, in turn, had always supported Adams's foreign policy of American neutrality, of noninvolvement in foreign wars, and the principles of the Monroe Doctrine. Moreover, Clay saw an Adams-Clay alliance as a perfect blending of eastern and western political interests that would promote national unity and the Union.

And neither wanted to see a man as reckless and ill qualified as Andrew Jackson in the White House.

In contrast to Jackson, John Quincy Adams had been trained from birth to be President. The son of Abigail and John Adams, he had witnessed the Battle of Bunker Hill as a boy, traveled to Europe with his diplomat father, learned to speak six foreign languages besides classical Latin and Greek. He had earned a bachelor's degree from Harvard College and became one of Boston's most accomplished lawyers. He had been American minister to five European countries, had headed peace negotiations at Ghent to end the War of 1812, and had been a brilliant secretary of state for eight years, helping draft the Monroe Doctrine.

Although Adams had intended to retain the entire Monroe cabinet, he would have to name a new secretary of state to replace himself and a secretary of war to replace William Crawford. Even if he and Clay, as they claimed, did not discuss filling the two posts, there was no need for them to do so. Clay had made it clear when he rejected the War Department post eight years earlier that the powerful State Department was the only cabinet-level position he sought or would ever accept.

On January 24, at Clay's behest, the Kentucky delegation in the House announced it would cast its vote for Adams, despite express instructions from the state legislature to vote for Jackson. Jackson had scored an overwhelming popular victory in Kentucky's popular election. All the votes had gone to Clay and Jackson; Adams had not won a single vote. Clay's directive to give Kentucky's votes to Adams added to the political price he would pay for supporting Adams. Clay also convinced congressional delegates from Ohio and Missouri— the other states he had won—to cast their votes for Adams, and on February 9, after only one House ballot, John Quincy Adams won election as the nation's sixth President. In doing so, he became the first non-Virginian to win the presidency since his father thirty years earlier in 1796. He also became the first son of a Founding Father and President to become the nation's chief executive.

For the first time in three decades northerners flocked to Washington to attend the inauguration of one of their own.

"The city is thronged with strangers," complained the southern-born socialite Sarah Seaton, whose brother published the *National Intelligencer*, "and Yankees swarm like the locusts of Egypt in our houses, our beds, and our kneading troughs!"[25]

John Quincy Adams was more enthusiastic than Mrs. Seaton and wrote to his "dear and honored father" John Adams to tell him of "the event of this day, upon which I can only offer you my congratulations and ask your blessings and prayers," and he signed it, "Your affectionate son."[26]

24. President John Quincy Adams. Henry Clay finished fourth in the presidential election of 1824 and threw his votes to John Quincy Adams, who named Clay as secretary of state and provoked a national outcry against what political opponents called a "corrupt bargain" between the two. (Library of Congress)

The ailing former President answered immediately:

Never did I feel so much solemnity as upon this occasion. The multitude of my thoughts and the intensity of my feelings are too much for a mind like mine, in its ninetieth year. May the blessing of God Almighty continue to protect you to the end of your life, as it has heretofore protected you in so remarkable a manner from your cradle. I offer the same prayer for your lady and your family and am your affectionate father, John Adams.[27]

Five days after his election victory John Quincy Adams appointed Henry Clay secretary of state. The appointment appalled American political leaders, who called Adams's election victory "a mockery of representative government."[28]

"So you see," Andrew Jackson wailed in outrage, "the Judas of the West has closed the contract and will receive thirty pieces of silver.

> His end will be the same. Was there ever witnessed such a bare-faced corruption in any country before? I weep for the liberty of my country. The rights of the people have been bartered for promises of office. . . . The voice of the people of the West have been disregarded, and demagogues barter them as sheep in the shambles for their own views and personal aggrandizement.[29]

The nation's press charged John Quincy Adams and Clay with a "corrupt bargain" that undermined the election process and stripped voters of their chosen candidate. Philadelphia's *Columbian Observer* printed a letter said to have been written by an anonymous congressman detailing the "the most disgraceful transactions that ever covered with infamy the Republican ranks.

> For some time past, the friends of Clay have hinted that they . . . would fight for those that pay best. Overtures were . . . made by the friends of Adams to the friends of Clay offering him the appointment of secretary of state for his aid to elect Adams. And the friends of Clay gave the information to the friends of Jackson . . . but none of the friends of Jackson would descend to such mean barter and sale. . . . It is now ascertained . . . that Henry Clay has transferred his interest to John Quincy Adams. As a consideration for . . . this unholy coalition . . . Clay is to be appointed secretary of state. I am clearly of opinion . . . there is an end of liberty.[30]

Clay exploded, calling "the member, whoever he may be, a base and infamous calumniator, a dastard, and a liar." In a letter to the *National Intelligencer* Clay challenged the man to a duel, "if he dare unveil himself."[31]

The more Clay protested, however, the more frequently the charges against him appeared—to the point at which his protests provoked mockery and laughter, adding jokes to the pervasive disbelief.

"Why is Adams on tricky ground?" one newspaper cartoonist asked. "Because he's standing on slippery Clay."

Others mocked Clay's large mouth or his boorish advances toward women—or both. "When men crowd around him for a shake of his hand, and women beset him for a kiss," wrote editor Edward G. Parker, "his capacity for gratifying both was unlimited, for the ample dimensions of his kissing apparatus enabled him to *rest* one side of it completely, while the other side was upon active duty."[32]

New York senator Martin Van Buren, who had backed Crawford's candidacy, warned a Kentucky congressman who had voted for Adams that, in signing his ballot, "you signed Mr. Clay's political death warrant."[33] Delaware representative Louis McLane predicted that "irretrievable ruin" would be Clay's "inevitable fate." Calling Adams's appointment of Clay a "monstrous union," McLane—who would later become a secretary of state—predicted that "all the waters of the sweet heavens cannot remove the corruption."[34]

The friends of Jackson "have turned on me," Clay admitted, "and agree to vituperate me: I am a deserter from democracy. A giant at intrigue, have sold the West, have sold myself, defeating General Jackson's election to leave open the western pretensions that I may hereafter fill them myself. . . . The knaves cannot comprehend how a man can be honest. They cannot conceive that I should have solemnly interrogated my conscience and asked it seriously what I ought to do."[35]

Clay admitted in retrospect, "It would have been wiser and more politic to have declined the office of secretary of state. Not that my motives were not as pure and as patriotic as ever carried any man into public office." Indeed, Clay had not jumped precipitously at Adams's offer. He sensed it might have negative repercussions but believed that the only hope for establishing the American System and cementing the

Union was as secretary of state. Then the most powerful executive post after the presidency, the secretary of state in the 1820s wielded powers variously held in the twenty-first century by the secretaries of Interior, Agriculture, Commerce, Labor, Transportation, and Energy—as well as State. In addition, Clay feared critics would call it political treason to refuse to serve the President he had helped elect. Little wonder he believed the "calumny" that followed his acceptance to be "as gross and unfounded as any that was ever propagated.

"But my error in accepting the office," he said pensively, "arose out of my under-rating . . . the force of ignorance. Of that ignorance, I had a laughable example . . . traveling in Virginia. We halted at night at a tavern kept by an aged gentlemen . . . who had four sons . . . divided in politics, two being for Adams and two for Jackson. He said he wished they were all for Jackson.

"'Why?' I asked him.

"'Because,' he said, 'that fellow Clay . . . cheated Jackson out of the presidency.'

"'Have you ever seen any evidence of that?' I asked.

"'No,' he replied. And he wanted to see none.

"'But suppose Mr. Clay were to assure you upon his honor that it was all a vile calumny. Would you believe him?'"

"'No.'"[36]

Few members of the Washington political scene doubted that John Quincy Adams had promised, tacitly or otherwise, to reward Clay for his support. Knowing how Clay lusted for the presidency, all assumed that Adams would appoint him secretary of state as a stepping stone to higher office. Presidents Jefferson, Madison, Monroe, and John Quincy Adams had all served as secretaries of state before stepping up to the presidency. Rumors of "bargain and sale" spread across the political landscape, with some Jackson supporters even mumbling about Tennessee's secession.

"What a farce," cried Andrew Jackson Donelson, Andrew Jackson's nephew and soon-to-be private secretary, "that Mr. Adams should swear to support the Constitution of the United States which he has purchased from representatives who betrayed the Constitution and which he must distribute among them as rewards for the iniquity."[37]

The mood in the White House turned tense a few days after the House vote as President Monroe hosted a reception for the President-elect. The rooms were so crowded, "they could scarcely move," according to Margaret Smith. "General [Winfield] Scott was robbed of his pocket-book containing 800 dollars. The idea of pick-pockets at the President's drawing room occasioned much mirth."[38]

Mrs. Smith reported several Jackson supporters sneering and "pointing to A [Adams], saying 'There is our Clay President. He will be molded at that man's will and pleasure as easily as clay in a potter's hands.'"[39]

"It was impossible to win the game, gentlemen," John Randolph of Roanoke fumed. "The cards were stacked."

Clay walked about "with a fashionable belle hanging on each arm," according to Mississippi senator Thomas H. Williams, who called Clay "a villain. . . . When Prometheus made a man out of clay, he stole fire from heaven to animate him. I wonder where our Speaker will get the fire with which to animate his Clay President."[40]

President Monroe was chatting with a guest when Andrew Jackson, recovering from a debilitating illness, suddenly thrust his gaunt scowl through the doorway. All knew that Jackson carried pistols and was a veteran of more than a dozen duels—some said more than a hundred. Jackson still carried a bullet in his chest from the 1806 duel over cheating in a horse race. Now Jackson's hawk eyes hunted for John Quincy Adams, whom many charged with cheating the Tennessean out of the American presidency. Adams, Monroe, Lafayette, and others held their collective breaths, some expecting gunfire, as they watched Jackson step into the room.

He stared at President-elect John Quincy Adams like a bird of prey on the hunt, then broke into a broad grin and bounded forward, his hand outstretched.

Monroe and Lafayette breathed sighs of relief and beamed with satisfaction as they watched the two former opponents fulfill the promise of American liberty and republican self-government. For a moment America remained secure.

"General Jackson shook hands with Mr. Adams and congratulated him very cordially on his sweep," Mississippi senator Thomas H. Williams gleamed. He called Jackson's handshake "honorable to human nature, but it was not very honorable to human nature to see Clay walking about with exultation and a smiling face. . . . He looked as proud and happy as if he had done a noble action by selling himself to Adams and securing his election."[41]

For Henry Clay, appointment as secretary of state meant the end of his career as the greatest Speaker of the House of Representatives in American history. Although he had not won all his debates, he scored landmark victories that restored the constitutional stature of the House of Representatives and powers of its Speaker. When he first entered its chamber, the House was a body of unruly presidential servitors; when he left, he had transformed it into the separate, powerful, independent branch of the federal government as defined by the Constitution. The only government body directly elected by "We the People," the House, under Clay's leadership, reasserted its parity with the indirectly elected executive and the appointed judiciary. Although Presidents would continue to test the limits of their authority—as Washington, Adams, and Jefferson had done—Clay established ways and means for future Speakers to rein them in and prevent executive flirtations with tyranny.

CHAPTER 6

Corrupt Bargain

The end of Clay's career as Speaker of the House did not launch a brilliant new career as the nation's top diplomat. Although he became secretary of state in name, he could not shake off charges of having made a corrupt bargain with John Quincy Adams to secure his post.

"Poor Mr. Clay," Mrs. Smith reported, "The *Telegraph* gives him no rest. . . . We have not seen Mrs. Clay for three weeks. . . . She says when Mr. Clay dines at home, he never dines alone, but always has a social company. . . . She is obliged to go to other people's parties, sick or well, for fear of giving offense, a thing more carefully avoided now than ever."[1]

Jackson and his supporters were relentless—determined to ensure Jackson's victory in the next presidential election by destroying Adams and Clay professionally and personally along with the Adams-Clay administration.

"Clay voted for Adams and made him President," Jackson repeated over and over, "and Adams made Clay secretary of state. Is this not proof as strong as holy writ of the understanding and corrupt coalition between them?"[2]

Jackson encouraged press attacks. "Would it not be well," Jackson asked his campaign manager, "that the papers of Nashville and the whole state should speak out with moderate but firm disapprobation of this corruption—to give a proper tone to the people and draw their attention to the subject?"

Far from moderate disapprobation, however, Jackson fostered unrestrained fury in the crowds he addressed, calling Clay and the Adams administration "the rascals at Washington" and condemning their "cheating and corruption and bribery.

> There is no other corrective of these abuses but the suffrages of the people . . . [to] preserve and perpetuate the liberty of our happy country. If they do not, in less than twenty-five years, we will become the slaves not of a military chieftain, but of such ambitious demagogues as Henry Clay.[3]

Jackson and his supporters split the Republican Party, with Jacksonians calling themselves Democrat-Republicans, or, more simply, Democrats. Clay tried desperately to hold the remaining Republicans together: "I think your party is wrong," he pleaded, urging a Kentucky Jacksonian to "forget the past and unite for the future in advancing the true interests of the state."[4] His efforts failed, as did his efforts to dispel notions of a "corrupt bargain" between him and President Adams.

Clay escaped his political woes for a while in the spring of 1825, when he packed up his family and went home to Ashland for several weeks. On the return trip, however, twelve-year-old Eliza developed a fever, and when they reached Lebanon, Ohio, not far from Cincinnati, a doctor advised them to put the girl to bed. After several weeks Eliza improved, and the doctor assured Clay he could go on to Washington, that Eliza would soon recover. Leaving Lucretia in Lebanon with Eliza and the two youngest boys, Henry Clay resumed his journey to take up his duties as secretary of state. Several days later, only twenty miles from Washington, he sat for breakfast, opened the

Daily National Intelligencer, and all but collapsed as he read that his daughter Eliza was dead.

"I wish, my dear wife, I could offer you some consolation," he wrote to Lucretia after reaching the capital. "I cannot describe to you my own distressed feelings, which have been greatly aggravated by a knowledge of what yours must have been in the midst of strangers, and all your friends far away." He searched for the right words, but there were none, and he concluded, "We must bow, with religious resignation, to decrees which we have no power to revoke."[5]

For Lucretia, the loss of Eliza was devastating. "Our little daughter was the only unmarried one that we had," Henry Clay explained to his friend, Methodist Pastor Henry B. Bascom, whose appointment as chaplain to Congress Clay had arranged. "Her mother had anticipated much gratification from her society and from completing her education in this city."[6]

Adding to Clay's distress was the difficulty in finding a home for his family in the still-primitive city of Washington. They lived in uncomfortable quarters at a boarding house for a month until Clay found a beautiful brick house that a State Department official rented to him for the family's exclusive use for $500 a year. A spacious three-story brick home, it stood on F Street between 14th and 15th Streets in view of the White House. But the Clays had no sooner settled into their new quarters when tragedy struck again: Their daughter Susan, only twenty, had died of yellow fever in New Orleans, leaving behind her husband and two infants, one a newborn.

"Our last affliction has almost overwhelmed us," Clay sobbed to a friend.

We were beginning to be composed, by reflection, by occupation, and by time, as to that which preceded it. But this new, unexpected, and severe blow! Is it not cruel, of six daughters, to be deprived of all but one? Age, grief, and misfortune make us feel a great want, and God alone can supply that.[7]

The loss took its toll on both Clay and his wife. She withdrew, turned to prayer and the church, and eschewed society generally. Her husband tried smothering his despair with work, often spending sixteen or more hours at his desk. He developed a severe cough and looked unwell. "You must let me admonish you to take care of your health," Massachusetts senator Daniel Webster scolded him in a friendly note.

Webster and Clay had not started off as friends. When they first met in the House in 1813, Clay was already Speaker, and Webster, five years younger, was a combative freshman congressman from his native New Hampshire. It was not until he moved to Boston to practice law that Massachusetts became his home state and elected him senator. Born and raised on his family's farm, Webster—unlike Clay—had obtained the finest formal education his state could offer, first at Philips Exeter Academy and then Dartmouth College. He graduated Phi Beta Kappa and went on to study law and gain renown as one of New England's finest orators. Federalist son of a Federalist father in a staunchly Federalist state, Webster railed at President James Madison for declaring war against Britain, New England's vital trading partner.

"Give us but to see that this war hath clear justice . . . on its side," Webster demanded of President Madison, "and we are ready to pour out our treasure and our blood in its prosecution."[8] Elected to Congress, Webster stormed into the House intent on embarrassing the President with resolutions demanding information on the events that provoked Madison's decision to go to war. Henry Clay's "war hawks" dominated Congress, however, leaving Webster all but alone in opposition to the Speaker on every issue during his two terms in the House. But Speaker Clay was too skilled a politician to ignore the New Englander. He appointed Webster to the Committee on Foreign Relations—an appointment that flattered him until he faced its chairman: Clay's chief ally among the war hawks, South Carolina's John C. Calhoun.

To Webster's initial surprise, Calhoun approved Webster's resolutions on the President's prewar deliberations, but it was a parliamentary ruse. Instead of letting Webster stir up antiwar sentiment with oratory, Calhoun asked the House to pass the resolution without debate, leaving Webster victorious without having said a word—and thoroughly deflated.

Although Webster delivered the resolutions to the White House, Secretary of State Monroe prepared a report so vague and evasive that it left Webster with no ammunition to pursue his campaign against the war. And because it was marked "Secret," he could not even cite it publicly for what it was: executive obfuscation and evasion.

Having learned his lessons in House politics, Webster returned to New England after only two terms and moved his practice to Boston, where he became America's greatest (and arguably wealthiest) constitutional lawyer. From 1816 to 1824 Webster won a series of cases before the US Supreme Court that effectively rewrote the Constitution, expanding federal powers, limiting state sovereignty, and protecting private property and industry against arbitrary government seizure.*

Webster's courtroom triumphs won him national acclaim and reelection to Congress in 1822 by the people of Massachusetts, a far more powerful constituency than tiny New Hampshire. Clay had also returned by then. Reelected Speaker, Clay paid tribute to Webster's legal achievements before the Supreme Court by appointing him to the important House Judiciary Committee. Clay himself had

---

*In 1919 Webster represented his alma mater in *Dartmouth College v. Woodward*, with the Court ruling New Hampshire's state takeover of the private college as unconstitutional. Two weeks later Webster won the case of *McCulloch v. Maryland*, declaring unconstitutional a state's effort to tax a federal entity and introducing the constitutional concept of "implied powers." In 1821 he won a court declaration in *Cohens v. Virginia*, giving citizens federal court protection in every jurisdiction, including state courts and local criminal courts. In *Gibbons v. Ogden* in 1824 he won a court ruling declaring state-run monopolies that interfered with interstate commerce unconstitutional. (See Unger, *John Marshall*, 321–325).

used Webster's Supreme Court victories as precedents for winning cases of his own before the High Court, including his personally lucrative victory over the State of Ohio for having taxed the Bank of the United States. More worldly and less doctrinaire by the time they entered the Senate, the two reconciled their political differences and became close political allies and personal friends.

The warm-hearted Webster tried to console his friend:

"Knowing the ardor and intensity with which you may probably apply yourself to the duties of your place," Webster told Clay, "I fear very much you may overwork yourself." With characteristic wit, Webster described an Austrian official who "never did anything today, which he could put off till tomorrow; nor anything himself which he could get another to do for him. I think you ought to be . . . governed by the same rules," he told Clay.[9]

Clay's spirits picked up a bit when the ministers of Mexico and Colombia approached him to attend a congress of American nations that Simón Bolivar was organizing in Panama for June and July 1826. Bolivar had led Venezuela, Colombia, Panama, Ecuador, Peru, and Bolivia to independence from Spain, and he now called on all the Americas to cooperate economically, politically, and militarily. In addition, he hoped the congress would establish a League of American Republics, with a common military and a supranational parliament to effect political and economic union among American nations.

Having championed South American independence from Spain, Clay embraced the Bolivar Congress and American participation, and he urged John Quincy Adams to send emissaries. The President hesitated, suspicious of the ambitious Bolivar's motives and the pervasive influence of the Roman Catholic Church in Latin America. But Clay's newfound enthusiasm proved contagious, and Adams agreed to propose US participation in Panama in his state of the Union address to the US Congress in December 1825. Pleased to see Clay buoyant again, Adams went a step farther and agreed to add Clay's cherished "American System" to the proposals in his annual message.

Unfortunately the President had a penchant for rocking the political boat, and before he delivered his address, he fell overboard—literally. Intent on remaining physically fit, the President took a daily swim across the Potomac River, with his valet rowing him one way and the President swimming back. "Before we got half across," the President reported in his diary, "the boat had leaked itself half full and . . . I jumped overboard."[10]

The President stripped and swam ashore, where his son John Adams II pulled him from the water while the valet scampered out and ran to the Adams house to get a carriage. "While Antoine was gone," the President said, "John and I were wading and swimming up and down on the other shore, or sitting naked basking on the bank at the margin of the river. . . . The carriage came and took me home, half dressed."[11]

Although the President escaped physical injury, he did not escape political injury. His political enemies and the press peppered him with ridicule. Congress greeted his State of the Union message with sneers, snickers, and laughter, and the Tennessee legislature publicly humiliated the President by nominating Andrew Jackson for the presidency—three years in advance of the next presidential election in 1828. To deepen the political wound, Jackson resigned his Senate seat and began a national campaign to discredit and unseat the President.

Adams unwittingly marred his own public image in other ways. Instead of addressing the needs of ordinary citizens, Adams appealed to the most educated. Speaking in language most ordinary Americans—and even some congressmen—could not understand, he issued philosophical pronouncements that "the great object of civil government is the improvement of the condition of those who are parties to the social compact.

Roads and canals . . . are among the most important means of improvement. But moral, political and intellectual improvement are duties assigned by the Author of our existence. . . . Among the first . . . instruments for the improvement of the condition of men is knowledge, and to the acquisition of much of the knowledge adapted to the wants, the comforts and enjoyments of human life, public institutions and seminaries of learning are essential.[12]

In what he considered—and, indeed, was—a brilliant, forward-looking address to advance the nation, he called on Congress to promote "the improvement of agriculture, commerce and manufactures, the cultivation and encouragement of the mechanic and of the elegant arts, the advancement of literature, and the progress of the sciences." Among the sciences he cited astronomy as the most important and called for federal construction of astronomical observatories, or "lighthouses of the sky," to study the heavens. He warned that failure to do so "would be treachery to the most sacred of trusts."

Turning to Clay's American System, Adams went on to make one of the most politically inept statements of his career by asking Congress to ignore public opposition and appropriate federal funds to extend the National Road.

While foreign nations . . . are advancing with gigantic strides in . . . public improvement, were we to slumber in indolence . . . and proclaim to the world that we are palsied by the will of our constituents, would it not be to . . . doom ourselves to perpetual inferiority?[13]

Even the President's most loyal supporters misunderstood his phrase "palsied by the will of our constituents." North Carolina congressman Nathaniel Macon charged that "the message of the President seems to claim all power to the federal government."[14] And General Edmund Gaines, whom former President Monroe had sent to rid Amelia Island of pirates, predicted that "the planters, farmers and mechanics of the country" would see the next presidential election as "a great contest between the aristocracy and democracy of America."[15]

Jackson thundered a reply that devastated the President: "When I view . . . the declaration that it would be criminal for the agents of our government to be palsied by the will of their constituents, I shudder for the consequence. . . .

"The voice of the people . . . must be heard," Jackson proclaimed. "Instead of building lighthouses in the skies, establishing national universities, and making explorations round the globe," Jackson called out to the President, "pay the national debt . . . then apportion the surplus revenue amongst the several states . . . leaving the superintendence of education to the states."[16]

While newspapers ridiculed the President's "lighthouses in the skies," Jackson addressed the needs and concerns of ordinary people. He called for an end to debtors' prisons, citing a blind man in a Massachusetts prison for a debt of $6 and a Rhode Island woman behind bars for a debt of sixty-eight cents. There were five times more debtors than criminals in prisons, Jackson complained. Most were indigent, with debts of less than $50 and forced to pay for their food in jail—or starve.* Jackson also called for reform of bankruptcy laws to prevent employers from declaring bankruptcy to avoid paying wages.

Although many of the President's proposals were a century or more ahead of their time, he was out of touch with his own time. In what was clearly a clash of cultures—indeed, a clash of generations—Adams saw man in general and Americans in particular as having unlimited talents, restrained by lack of educational opportunities that he believed the federal government could and should provide.

In fact, Americans were largely a society of farmers and laborers tilling the soil and accepting their lot as all but predestined and, for the most part, were content with meeting physical rather than intellectual needs. Far from thinking about school or college, the average American man yearned to own property, work its soil, plant, and harvest enough to feed himself and his family, selling any surplus at market. And above all he wanted to be left alone on his land with

---

*Private charities emerged in most of the North to feed them. There is little documentation of their fate in the South.

his family—free from intrusions by hostile British troops, marauding Indians, squatters, or government tax collectors.

John Quincy Adams's proposals were so alien to then-current American thinking that his programs—along with his presidency—met nothing but ridicule and rejection. His chance for leadership spent, he saw his dream for advancing the nation culturally and economically shattered—along with Clay's hopes for a quick establishment of the American System to bind the nation in a firm, lasting union.

Congress rejected the American System and refused to approve American participation in the Panama Conference. Southerners united against it to protest the Latin American embrace of abolition and recognition of the black-run Republic of Haiti. Several congressmen warned of plans to seat black and mulatto delegates beside white delegates at the Panama meeting. One congressman cited Washington's Farewell Address that warned against "the insidious wiles of foreign influence."[17]

President Adams, however, ignored Congress and sent two delegates to Panama, one of whom died en route. By the time the second arrived, the conference had ended. Britain's observers left with a satchel full of lucrative trade agreements, whereas the United States had nothing but another policy failure for the Adams administration.

The President's dispatch of delegates to Panama against the wishes of Congress infuriated and alienated his and Clay's political friends as well as enemies. Quarrels erupted in the President's cabinet. Jackson and a group of supporters bought a newspaper, the *United States Telegraph*, to attack Clay and Adams and promote Jackson's candidacy in the next presidential election.

On March 26, 1826, the *Telegraph* published a vicious full-page editorial entitled "Bargain, Management and Intrigue," detailing the alleged Clay-Adams "corrupt bargain." Voters everywhere—even in Henry Clay's once-loyal state of Kentucky—responded by sending an army of Jacksonians to Congress in the off-year elections of 1826.

Meanwhile Virginia elected Clay's longtime nemesis, the eccentric John Randolph, to the US Senate, where he leaped at every opportunity to attack the President and his secretary of state. Vice President John C. Calhoun, the former senator from South Carolina who presided over the Senate, lacked the powers of the House Speaker to call a member to order.

"When he was engaged in debate, his high-toned and thin voice would ring through the Senate Chamber like the shrill scream of an angry vixen," Benjamin Perley Poore, the Washington correspondent for the *Boston Journal,* remarked of Randolph. "Every fifteen minutes, when he occupied the floor, he would exclaim in a low voice, 'Tims, more porter,' and the assistant doorkeeper would hand him a tumbler of potent foaming malt liquor, which he would hurriedly drink, and then proceed with his remarks, often thus drinking three or four quarts in an afternoon."[18]

The *Telegraph* article on the Adams-Clay "corrupt bargain" provoked a vicious Randolph attack on the administration. In a bizarre squeal that approached hysteria, he charged Clay with being "an evil genius" and likened the Adams family to the Roman Catholic "House of Stuart," plotting to overthrow Britain's Protestant king.

"That moment," Randolph screamed, "did I put, like Hannibal, my hand on the altar and swear eternal enmity against him and his, politically."

As puzzled senators looked at one another, trying to understand the connection between Hannibal and the House of Stuart, Randolph rambled on, demanding to know, "What made him [Clay] a judge of our usages? Who constituted him? He has been a professor, I understand. Who made him the *censor morum** of this body?"[19]

He snorted as he screamed.

"Will anyone answer this question?" He wheezed.

"Yes or no?" He paused again.

"Who?

"Name the person!

---

* Latin: critic or censor of morals.

"Above all, who made him the searcher of hearts and gave him the right, by an innuendo black as hell, to blacken our motives?"

Nothing Randolph said made sense. Some senators whispered their suspicions that he had crossed into insanity.

"Here I plant my foot!" Randolph squealed. "Here I fling defiance right into his teeth before the American people. Here I throw the gauntlet to him."[20]

After charging Clay with having forged the Mexican minister's invitation to the Panama Conference, Randolph repeated charges of a "corrupt bargain" between President Adams and Clay. South Carolina senator Robert Young Hayne tried to restrain Randolph but only provoked more venom. Randolph called the Panama mission "a Kentucky cuckoo's egg laid in a Spanish-American nest" and condemned what he called the marriage of "old Massachusetts and young Kentucky . . . young, blithe, buxom, and blooming . . . the eldest daughter of Virginia—not so young, however, as not to make a prudent match and sell her charms for their full value."[21]

Then, in what some historians call "the most offensive speech ever heard" in the US Senate, Randolph pretended to be the young foundling in the popular novel *Tom Jones*, declaring, "I was defeated, horse, foot, and dragoons—and clean broke down by the coalition of Blifil and Black George [two rogues in *Tom Jones*]—by the combination unheard of till then, of the Puritan [i.e., Adams] and blackleg [a card sharp—i.e., Clay]."[22]

Enraged by Randolph's gratuitous attack, Clay, being Clay, snatched up Randolph's gauntlet: "Sir," he wrote to the Virginian. "Your unprovoked attack of my character in the Senate of the United States, on yesterday, allows me no other alternative than that of demanding personal satisfaction."[23] Although his response to what many called the rant of a raving maniac drew derision, Clay held his ground.

"His [Randolph's] assaults were so gross, repeated, and unprovoked," Clay explained to Ohio lawyer/newspaperman Charles Hammond, "I could no longer bear them. . . . Submission, on my part, to the unmerited injury . . . would have made existence intolerable. . . . I regret that the religious and moral part of the community will feel themselves offended."[24]

Although Clay said he was aware "of the opinion . . . as to the state of Mr. Randolph's mind, I thought I ought not to be governed by that opinion, which was opposed by [Virginia's] recent act of electing him to the Senate."[25]

Randolph tried claiming immunity for having made his remarks in the Senate, but Clay refused to give ground, saying Senate immunity did not give Randolph the right to utter outright lies. "Malignant passions abound in him," George D. Prentice, editor of the *Louisville Journal* said of Randolph. "His tongue is little scrupulous in giving vent to them. They overflowed in epithets of even more than his usual venom and scurrility on Mr. Clay."[26]

Randolph yielded, and the two agreed to meet at 4:30 on Saturday afternoon, April 8, across the Potomac from Georgetown, in Virginia, the native state of each. Clay said nothing of the duel to Lucretia, who was still grieving over the loss of their daughters.

"Mr. Randolph, in defiance of established usage, went upon the field in a huge morning gown," journalist Prentice described the duel. "The unseemly garment constituted such a vast circumference that the locality of the thin and swarthy senator was . . . a matter of very vague conjecture. Mr. Clay might as well have fired into the outspread top of an oak in the hope of hitting a bird . . . snugly perched somewhere among the branches."[27]

Clay's second told the two duelists to stand about thirty paces apart and await the appointed second's shout to fire. They were to cease firing after the second called out, "One, two, three, stop!" If neither man succumbed or ceded, the duelists would prepare for a second round. Both men agreed and were about to shake hands before stepping away from each other when an explosive report sent everyone staggering backward. Randolph's gun had fired without warning.

CHAPTER 7

❧

A Mask of Smiles

The sudden discharge of Randolph's gun startled them all. The seconds looked at the duelists, expecting one to fall bathed in blood, but the shot had sunk harmlessly into the ground beneath a cloud of dust. Randolph's second had set the pistol on a hair trigger, and Clay quickly collected himself and feigned nonchalance at his opponent's obvious subterfuge. He and Randolph then turned their backs to one another and stepped off the required paces, came about, and faced each other.

"Fire!" barked Clay's second, and both men fired. Randolph's bullet missed its target, while Clay's penetrated Randolph's cloak, without touching flesh. Randolph's second appealed to both duelists to end the contest, but Clay refused and, on the second cry of "Fire!" again targeted his opponent. Again his bullet tore through Randolph's wide cloak without wounding the man.

"Mr. Randolph was saved by his gown," *Louisville Journal* editor Prentice concluded.

Randolph then fired into the air and stepped toward Clay, his hand outstretched. "I do not fire at you, Mr. Clay," Randolph called out. "Sir, I give you my hand."

Clay went to meet him, saying, "I trust to God, my dear sir, you are untouched."

"You owe me a new coat," Randolph smiled.

"I am glad the debt is no greater," Clay replied.[1]

The duel solved nothing, of course. Randolph left for Europe and proved as mad on shipboard crossing the Atlantic as in the US Senate.

"Drunk and bawdy every day and every night," according to Christopher Hughes, a US diplomat who had served with Clay at Ghent. Hughes reported Randolph asking a group of men at the dinner table in the presence of ladies, "I wonder if there was ever a young lady who did not long for the pains and perils of childbirth?"[2] Later Randolph brought up Clay's American System, ranting, "I hate improvements. Damn the steamboats! I wish they were all blown up. I wish there was not a single turnpike road to Virginia." As listeners blanched, Randolph changed topics and, according to Hughes, made this pronouncement:

> I would shoot my Negroes if everybody else would shoot theirs. It is the only way to get rid of two million Negroes. I could shoot all mine in two hours. I never call myself an American. I always say I am a Virginian, and so I am. The Yankees are the greatest scoundrels on the face of the earth.

"This sort of language very much resembles that of a mad man," a friend wrote to Clay, "and in future I hope you will treat him as such."[3]

Clay, however, had become a target of ridicule in the Jacksonian press for having challenged a lunatic and demeaned the office of secretary of state with a public encounter worthy of unruly schoolboys.

By then the Jacksonian Congress had paralyzed both the President and secretary of state, and their daily activities were devoid of consequence for the nation. President Adams described his day in his diary:

I rise generally before five—frequently before four. Write from one to two hours in this diary. Ride about twelve miles in two hours on horseback with my son John. Return home about nine; breakfast; and from that time till dinner, between five and six, in the afternoon, I am occupied incessantly with visitors, business, reading letters, dispatches, and newspapers. I spend an hour, sometimes before and sometimes after dinner, in the garden and nursery; an hour of drowsiness on a sofa; and two hours of writing in the evening. Retire usually between eleven and midnight.[4]

The President's political inactivity only intensified the barrage of criticism by Jacksonian newspapers. Press criticisms combined with influenza to leave Clay weak, distraught, and ready to take a leave of absence. Everything he and the President tried to do—even ceremonial appearances—worked against them. Invited to a July 4 groundbreaking for the heralded Chesapeake and Ohio Canal—a symbol of the very national improvements the President and Clay espoused—Adams addressed a friendly crowd of more than 2,000 spectators. He interrupted his talk to pick up a gilded spade and turn the first shovel of dirt—only to feel the tool rebound sharply with a clang and fly from his hands after hitting a hidden tree stump. As murmurs of disappointment spread among onlookers, the President picked up the shovel and tried again—and again—drawing laughter and ridicule.

Although Clay drew less ridicule perhaps, he was no more successful winning public approval than the President. Apart from the Panama fiasco, he tried and failed to interest Mexico into ceding Texas to the United States—at any price. He tried to help settle the border dispute between Maine and New Brunswick and left farmers there in a state of civil war. He tried—without success—to obtain US navigation rights to the St. Lawrence River, and his efforts to win free-trade rights for American merchants in the British West Indies met with British rejection. Instead of Union, Adams and Clay seemed to promote dissent and disunion.

"Poor Mr. Clay," lamented Margaret Smith. "The [*United States*] *Telegraph* gives him no rest. I think he must come out and defend himself. We have not seen Mrs. Clay since three weeks ago."[5]

Clay did indeed come out and defend himself.

"I defy my enemies," he challenged an audience in Lexington, Kentucky, "to point out any act or instances of my life in which I have sought the attainment of office by dishonorable or unworthy means.

> Did I display inordinate ambition when under the administration of Mr. Madison, I declined a foreign mission . . . and an executive department? Or when, under that of his successor Mr. Monroe, I was first importuned . . . to accept a secretaryship and was afterwards offered a carte blanche of all the foreign missions?[6]

President Adams was equally irate at the accusations. "Upon Mr. Clay," he raged, "the foulest slanders have been showered.

> The Department of State was a station which could confer neither profit nor honor upon him, but upon which he has shed unfading honor. Prejudice and passion have charged him with obtaining that office by bargain and corruption. Before you my fellow citizens, in the presence of our country and of Heaven, I pronounce the charge totally unfounded. This tribute of justice is due from me to him.[7]

Adams defied a group of citizens to "look around the nation . . . and name the man whom, by . . . his long experience in the affairs of the Union, foreign and domestic, a President intent only upon the honor and welfare of his country ought to have preferred to Henry Clay."[8]

Clay self-published a thirty-page pamphlet entitled, "An Address of Henry Clay to the Public . . . in Refutation of the Charges Against Him Made by Gen. Andrew Jackson." Reprinted in newspapers across the nation, Clay's pamphlet reviewed all the facts leading to his appointment as secretary of state and demonstrated "the falsity of every lie and innuendo" in the Jacksonian campaign "to crush me by steady and unprecedented calumny." He pledged to await "the enlightened judgment of the public . . . conscious of the zeal and uprightness with which I have executed every trust. . . . Whatever it may be, my anxious hopes will continue . . . that our union, our liberty, and our institutions may long survive."[9]

Clay's words provoked a group of supporters in Kentucky's legislature to call public hearings to look into charges of the "corrupt bargain," and although clearly proving Clay's innocence, the press coverage reprinted the charges so often that it left the public even more suspicious that Clay and John Quincy Adams had indeed made a corrupt bargain.

The controversy took its toll on both men and their families—left them puzzled, saddened, deeply wounded, not only at a loss to combat the contagion of lies but unable to promote programs they considered vital to the nation's future. Both John Quincy Adams and Henry Clay were dedicated patriots—visionaries with dramatic plans to promote national unity and advance the nation. Why, they asked, themselves, would so many Americans object to economic growth? They could not fathom popular objections to selective tariffs to protect and promote American manufacturing and agriculture. Why, they asked, did the public object to building a national network of modern roads and canals to tie the states to each other economically and end the threat of political disunion? What was the public's objection to harbor improvements to ensure expansion of foreign trade?

Adams and Clay did not seem to understand that objections to the American System lay not in the proposal itself but in the cession of state powers to the federal government it required. Only the federal government had the economic power to build interstate roads and canals and dredge the rivers and harbors of the American System. But the owners of baronial plantations who governed southern states—men like John Randolph of Roanoke—feared that federal incursions—even by road builders—would threaten their feudal control of their states. Federal highways and waterways, they feared, would open routes both for federal troops to march in and for slaves and poor whites to march out.

For Southern planters, slavery had generated wealth and power. Even the most unskilled slaves—children barely more than infants and crippled old men and women—could pick cotton. As long as they could crawl and pluck a cotton boll, they could work the cotton fields, and by endowing a few trusted slaves with basic skills—carpentry, brick laying, and the like—planters could hold down hourly and piecework wages of skilled white workers. By restricting the extent and ease of transportation, planters could keep blacks and poor whites in their thrall indefinitely. The American System threatened the future of slavery and the wealth of the southern oligarchy by opening the South to transportation, commerce, education, ideas, competition, and emancipation.

Ironically Clay's vision of emancipation did not include freeing slaves to live in America. From the first he and his American Colonization Society envisioned sending slaves back to Africa, shipload by shipload, over a decade or more, until they freed the American landscape of black people and slavery. Nearly 750,000 immigrants had arrived in the United States between 1820 and 1830; the American Colonization Society planned to use the ships that carried white immigrants to America to transport at least that many slaves back to Africa.

Among others, the young Illinois lawyer and rising political star Abraham Lincoln embraced Clay's vision:

"There is a moral fitness in the idea of returning to Africa her children, whose ancestors have been torn from her by the ruthless hand of fraud and violence," Lincoln asserted.

> Transplanted from a foreign land, they will carry back to their native soil the rich fruits of religion, civilization, law, and liberty. It will be a glorious consummation . . . if, as the friends of colonization hope, the present and coming generations of countrymen shall . . . succeed

in freeing our land from the dangerous presence of slavery and . . . restoring a captive people to their long-lost fatherland.[10]

Too many American slaveholders confused the American Colonization Society mission with abolition, thus adding to the growing torrent of criticism engulfing Clay. Inevitably, the attacks began to erode his usual optimism and cheer and, in turn, further depress his wife's sagging spirits. Already distraught over the loss of her daughters, Lucretia Clay found some comfort from her friend Margaret Smith, the newspaper publisher's wife.

"I spent a quiet and comfortable morning with Mrs. Clay, who is not well and talks of returning home," Mrs. Smith wrote to one of her sisters. "Mrs. Clay made us promise to go to church and spend the next day with her."[11]

Hoping to lift Lucretia's spirits, Clay moved her and the rest of the Clay family and household into a larger, more spacious house on the park facing the White House. It had been the home of naval hero Stephen Decatur, who had died in 1820. The Clays took turns with the Adamses holding weekly entertainments, but two months later Mrs. Smith wrote to another of her sisters that, far from cheering Lucretia, the entertainments had left her "overwhelmed with company."[12]

The entertainments did little to calm the rhetorical war between Jackson's supporters and the friends of the administration. Indeed, administration supporters were as vicious in their retaliation as Jacksonians in their attacks. After a Jacksonian newspaper charged the President's wife with malfeasance for spending public funds for her husband's billiard table, the pro-Adams editor of Cincinnati's *Gazette* retaliated. He charged Jackson with having maintained an adulterous relationship with his wife, Rachel, before she divorced her first husband.

Jackson blamed Clay for the newspaper story, calling him "the basest, meanest, scoundrel that ever disgraced the image of his god." Jackson pledged to effect Clay's "political, and perhaps, his actual destruction."[13]

In the end campaign rhetoric made little difference.

The hero of the Battle of New Orleans was simply too popular and the public too certain that their snobbish New England President from Harvard had ignored the will of the people and purchased his election by appointing Henry Clay secretary of state. To ensure popular mistrust of the President, Jackson formed a new and well-organized political party that operated at both the local and state levels and acquired consummate skills in obtaining newspaper publicity. Remaining stubbornly aloof, Adams insisted that the public was sensible enough to make the right choice without being badgered by candidate rhetoric.

As the 1828 election approached, New England textile manufacturers set up a drumbeat of demand for higher tariffs to protect them against imports. Other American industries quickly demanded similar tariff protection until the list of proposed tariffs before Congress grew so large and diverse that opponents labeled them collectively the "Tariff of Abomination." After the President signed it into law, Southern states, which depended heavily on imports for staples, reacted with outrage at the increased costs of imports, and they renewed their calls for secession. South Carolina's legislature called the tariff unconstitutional and blamed the President for not having vetoed it. Georgia, Mississippi, and Virginia followed suit, edging closer to disunion and costing President Adams the South in the 1828 election.

After votes were counted on December 3, 1828, Jackson had humiliated John Quincy Adams—with 647,276 voting for Jackson and 508,064 for Adams. In the Electoral College Jackson captured 178 votes, more than twice the 83 votes cast for the President.

"The sun of my political life sets in the deepest gloom," Adams sighed. To ease the pain of his loss, he took "a ride of an hour and a half on horseback."[14]

Henry Clay, however, fell ill from exhaustion. "I felt a shock," Mrs. Smith wrote after visiting Lucretia and finding Clay stretched out on the living room sofa "covered with a dark cloak that looked like a pall.

I had not seen him for three weeks and was much shocked at the alteration of his looks. He was much thinner, very pale, his eyes sunk in his head and his countenance sad and melancholy—that countenance generally illuminated with the fire of genius and animated by ardent feeling. . . . I do not think [he] has long to live.[15]

The President's wife, Louisa, tried cheering her husband by hosting a party in mid-February 1829 to celebrate his return to private life. Naturally, she invited her close friend Margaret Smith.

"The defeated party . . . are more smiling and gracious and agreeable than they ever were before," Mrs. Smith wrote to her sister. By then, she said, even Henry Clay had recovered from the election debacle.

Mr. Clay wears a mask of smiles. . . . I never liked Mr. Clay so well as I do this winter. The coldness and hauteur of his manner has vanished, and a softness and tenderness and sadness characterize his manner. . . . No bitterness mingles its gall in the cup of disappointment. He has a cause of domestic affliction in the situation of his son a thousand times more affecting than disappointed ambition.[16]

The "domestic affliction" of Clay's son—his oldest son, Theodore Wythe—included fits of uncontrollable rage that devoured his entire being with increasing frequency. Nor was Theodore Wythe his only troubled boy. His second son, Thomas Hart, had all but drowned himself in drink. Only seventeen-year-old Henry Clay Jr.—long his father's favorite—offered solace, having completed his secondary school studies and gained admission to the US Military Academy at West Point.

"You bear my name," his father wrote after the boy had enrolled. "You are my son, and the hopes of all of us are turned with anxiety upon you. . . . I have not much hope about my two older sons. Poor Thomas! He brought tears from me to behold him. He begins to show at his early age the effects of a dissipated life—swollen face, &c &c. He promises, but there I fear the matter will end. . . .

I was rejoiced to hear that you were contented and happy. My desire is . . . that you should continue at the Point and prosecute your studies there with assiduity and perseverance. When they are completed, the choice of professions will be before you. You may enter the army if you please or study the law. Whatever course you pursue, your studies will have been of the greatest advantage and . . . you will . . . never regret it. . . . We all send you our love and best wishes.[17]

At times, Mrs. Smith remarked, Henry Clay "looked gay and was so courteous and gracious and agreeable that everyone remarked it." Deeply touched by Clay's spirit in the face of defeat and personal troubles, she "took a seat in a corner by the fire, behind a solid mass of people, to conceal [her] tears."

"Why what ails your heart," Clay had seen her and approached to take her hand.

"Can I be otherwise than sad," Margaret Smith sobbed, "when I think what a good friend I am about to lose?"

Mrs. Smith said that Clay held her hand "without speaking. His eyes filled with tears and, with an effort, said, 'We must not think of this or talk of such things now,' and, relinquishing my hand, drew out his handkerchief, turned away his head and wiped his eyes, then pushed into the crowd and talked and smiled, as if his heart was light and easy."[18]

Shortly after the election results appeared in the newspapers, Rachel Jackson saw the story alleging her adulterous relationship with Andrew Jackson before she divorced her first husband. Shocked by what she read, she collapsed—a stroke, perhaps, or a heart attack. She died several days later and was buried on Christmas Eve without seeing her husband assume the presidency.

John Quincy Adams tried salvaging at least one triumph from his failed presidency by appointing Henry Clay to the US Supreme Court in the last hours of his administration. Adams's father had appointed his trusted Secretary of State John Marshall as Chief Justice of the Supreme Court early in 1801, after he had lost the election to Thomas Jefferson. Adams *père* called the appointment his greatest gift to the nation. When Adams *fils* tried to replicate his father's gift, however, Clay turned him down. Clay still envisioned creating an American System to unite the nation and knew he would never succeed from a courtroom bench. He needed to be in Congress or, better still, in the White House. Union remained his life's goal.

Unlike Clay, John Quincy Adams abandoned his dreams and planned to return to his father's farm in Quincy, Massachusetts, to practice law in nearby Boston the rest of his days.

On March 4, 1829, Andrew Jackson was inaugurated as seventh President of the United States. John Quincy Adams, as his father had done after Jefferson's election victory, refused to attend the inauguration or the new President's White House reception.

"I can yet scarcely realize my situation," Adams shuddered in disbelief, saying that "posterity will scarcely believe . . . the combination of parties and of public men against my character and reputation such as I believe never before was exhibited against any man since this Union existed.

> The combination against me has been formed and is now exulting in triumph over me, for the devotion of my life and of all the faculties of my soul to the Union and to the improvement, physical, moral and intellectual, of my country. The North assails me for my fidelity to the Union; the South for my ardent aspirations of improvement. Yet . . . the cause of Union and of improvement will remain, and I have duties to it and to my country yet to discharge.[19]

The words could well have been Clay's.

"The drama of the Adams administration is now closed," Mrs. Smith wrote to her daughter, "the curtain dropped, a kind of tragic comedy. . . .

> As soon as possible, they will take their departure. . . . Rank, honors, glory are such unsubstantial, empty things that they can never

satisfy the desires that they create. . . . Men have expended health of body and peace of mind, a large portion of their lives . . . watched and worked, toiled and struggled, sacrificed friends and fortune—and gained what? Nothing that I can perceive but mortification and disappointment. . . . Every one of the men who will retire from office . . . will return to private lives with blasted hopes, injured health, impaired or ruined fortunes . . . and probably a total inability to enjoy the remnant of their lives.[20]

"Not so Mr. Clay!" Mrs. Smith added with a flourish. "He is a very great man. . . . His late defeat—far from being disheartening—it has been positive in its effects."[21] The campaign had freed Clay from political encumbrances, she said—"like the lion breaking the net in which he had been entangled."[22]

Clay's friends and associates at the State Department staged an elaborate farewell dinner, where he assailed the new administration, saying President Jackson "had neither the temper, the experience nor the attainments requisite to discharge the complicated and arduous duties of Chief Magistrate.

A majority of my fellow citizens it would seem does not perceive the dangers I apprehended. . . . That majority . . . have chosen for chief executive a citizen who brings into that high trust no qualification other than military triumphs. But . . . he is the Chief Magistrate of my country. . . . Patriotism enjoins as a duty that . . . he should be treated with decorum. . . . Holding the principle that a citizen . . . is under an obligation to exert his utmost energies in the service of his country. . . . I shall stand erect, with a spirit unconquered, whilst life endures, ready in the cause of liberty, the Union, and the national prosperity.

He then raised his glass and toasted them all: "Let us never despair of the American Republic."[23] He still embraced Union, believed in it, and refused to countenance any alternative.

The next day the Clays left Washington on the long, arduous road to Lexington, Kentucky, and their beloved Ashland home. They had lost two daughters while in Washington and left the city with the realization that their oldest son, Theodore Wythe, was deranged and their second oldest son, Thomas Hart Clay, a chronic drunk. In the prescientific era, alcoholism was not uncommon. Water was often unsafe to drink once it left its source; milk equally so. Only "small beer" was a safe thirst quencher for most Americans, including children, and those with genetic proclivities toward alcoholism had few alternatives. Philadelphia police arrested Thomas Hart Clay for failure to pay his hotel bill, and a judge sentenced him to three months in jail. His father sent him a $250 check to pay the hotel keeper and return home to Ashland after serving his sentence.

Only their third son, West Point Cadet Henry Clay Jr., offered his parents solace. "You are one of my greatest comforts," Clay assured the boy, then wrote a check to cover expenses at school and a visit home to Ashland. Henry Clay Jr. replied immediately, saying he was "delighted at your kind desire to have me with you. . . . I shall most certainly avail myself of the opportunity to visit you at Ashland."[24]

Before leaving Washington, Clay and his wife realized more than $3,000 at auction for their unneeded household goods and furnishings—money he would soon invest in the house and grounds at Ashland. Although Clay had hired a superintendent to oversee his farm, he had also arranged for his oldest son's temporary release from the Lunatic Asylum and asked him to return home to keep an eye on things, hoping some responsibility would help the young man stave off insanity. Looking forward to reuniting his entire family at Ashland, he returned only to find Theodore blathering incoherently and Thomas drunk.

"Oh my son," Henry Clay sobbed as he wrote to Henry Clay Jr. "No language can describe to you the pain that I have suffered on account of these two boys. My hopes rest upon you and your two younger brothers."[25]

Theodore Wythe Clay was to inflict still more pain—on himself as well as his father. Slipping into a world of delusions, he fantasized marrying "the girl next door"—the daughter of John Brand, a founder of the Lexington and Ohio Railroad, the first railroad in the West, and owner of a large plantation next to the Clay property. Although she had rebuffed him several times, Theodore burst into the girl's home and threatened her, her father, and her brother at gunpoint. Although Brand and his son finally calmed and disarmed Clay, they filed a formal complaint before Judge Thomas Bodley, another Clay neighbor. A jury—all friends and supporters of Henry Clay—declared Theodore "a lunatic." Judge Bodley had no choice but to sentence him to an indefinite term in Lexington's Lunatic Asylum of Kentucky, where Theodore would spend most of the rest of his life.

Terrified when he awoke in his cell, Theodore wrote to his father, pleading for his release—without results. He wrote again and again:

"My dear Father: I believe I am at a loss to know how I am to be released from this place.

> I have no expectation that, in the press of business which must crowd upon you, time will be allowed you to answer my insipid and useless letters. . . . Nor have I much hope you will find it convenient or consistent with your views, or that an opportunity may occur in which you may aid me in my views of a place in some respectable commercial house in one of the large cities. . . . I have not the slightest mistrust about my habits or temperament. . . . I am young, my health is good, and I am buoyant with hope, and as yet untried in the world.[26]

Already devastated by Theodore's incarceration, Clay faced what seemed an endless procession of family tragedies as, one by one, his mother, stepfather, and brother died within a two-week period after his return to Ashland. Urged by Lucretia, he threw himself into farm work, helping workers repair, renovate, and improve lands and buildings. He added one hundred acres, bought fifty purebred merino sheep, built another conical ice house, and when Kentucky's summer heat grew intolerable, he took Lucretia and the younger children to nearby Olympian Springs, in Bath County, where Lucretia's father, Thomas Hart, had built a hotel and resort and promoted the health benefits of "taking the waters."

"I am getting so much attached to the pursuits on my farm," Clay wrote to his son at West Point, "that I have become more indifferent than I ever expected to be in regard to public life.

> My friends at Washington write to me in the best spirits and with great confidence as to our future success . . . [but] I consider life so uncertain and public affairs so full of vexation that I have become more indifferent. . . . You have another year . . . at West Point, and it will appear a very long one; but I hope you will command the fortitude necessary to carry you through it. Write me fully on that subject and consider me both as your friend and father.[27]

The boy did just that.

"My dear father," Henry Clay Jr. exulted following Independence Day ceremonies at the Academy. "I again appeared before an audience of between 400 & 500, and was once more eminently successful." At the dinner that followed, young Clay wrote, he gave a second address, prompting a prominent guest to raise his glass and toast: "The orator of the day. In the language of the turf, blood will show itself." A chorus of cheers followed for young Clay and, by proxy, his famous father.

In his letter home the boy wrote, "Do not accuse me, my father, of too broad an exhibition of vanity.

> I confess . . . I am subject to that besetting sin of the human race. But I have thought that to you a candid expression of my sentiments would be far more acceptable than any affected air of indifference. . . . By the way, I do not know that I have informed you that I

am 3d in general merit for this year. If . . . you still think I had better remain here another, there is not the smallest particle of doubt that I shall graduate 2d in general merit.[28]

The proud father wrote back, "My dear Son: I am truly rejoiced that you have concluded to pass the last year there [at West Point]. Your mama joins me in affectionate remembrance to you."[29]

Immersed in his farm work, Clay tried ignoring national politics and seemed determined to retire and devote himself to farm and family. His sole surviving daughter, Anne, and her husband, James Irwin, who lived in New Orleans, had come to Lexington and bought a plantation adjacent to Ashland as an escape from the blistering Louisiana summer heat and its associated illnesses. Within walking distance of her parents' home, the plantation allowed Anne and her mother to exchange daily visits and immerse themselves in the mysterious mother-daughter intimacy that fathers and sons seldom know. To Henry and Lucretia's delight, Anne gave birth to a girl while they were there and named her Lucretia after the baby's grandmother. Henry and Lucretia's two youngest boys also added to their parents' pride, with James Brown Clay, thirteen, doing well in nearby Transylvania College, and John Morrison Clay, nine, equally successful and happy in a Lexington preparatory school.

When their daughter Anne, their son-in-law, and their baby grandson returned to their home in New Orleans in late fall, the Clays decided to sail down the Ohio and Mississippi Rivers to vacation there. "Our voyage was quite agreeable," he wrote to Henry Clay Jr. "Your mother thinks her health has been benefited, and mine has been not bad. The time approaches when you will emerge from the Academy of West Point. I rejoice at it. My wish is that you should devote yourself to the profession of law. Such has always been my desire."[30]

While in New Orleans Clay and his wife seriously considered retirement there. Although they knew they faced future crises with their two oldest sons, they reveled in the love and successes of their other children. Even the two younger boys they had left back at Lexington delighted them with letters whose syntax and content provoked gales of laughter.

"I am doing very well with my studies," wrote thirteen-year-old James Brown,

> But I do not see why we should not be treated as well as the larger boys who are permitted to have fires and go to bed and get up when they please, whilst we smaller ones are kept studying until 9 o'clock and are obliged to get up by day break and study until 8. However, I will do my part as well as I can. . . . If you have no objections I should like to play on the flute. . . . I can play two or three tunes already.[31]

And their nine-year-old, John Morrison Clay, wrote a few days later that "I am at present studying Latin, French, geography, writing, and I believe I am going to study arithmetic. But tell Mama that I am studying French with a real Frenchman by the name of Mr. Du Ford [*sic*]. That she may not fear of my losing the pronunciation of the French."[32]

They had no sooner finished reading the delightful letters from their children when a more serious letter jolted Clay back to reality: The President and vice president had all but assaulted each other, and the cabinet had quit en masse.

"My dear Sir," Daniel Webster had written from Boston. "It is a long time since I wrote you. This omission has happened partly because what may as well be done tomorrow is often neglected today.

> You have seen all that has transpired at Washington and in the Country, in the last four months. Your opinion and mine are not likely to be different. . . . Undoubtedly the correspondence between the President and Vice President . . . shows feelings and objects so personal—so ambitious . . . that it creates no small degree of disgust. . . . I believe a majority would be glad of a change in men and manners.[33]

According to Webster, a bitter conflict had developed in the administration between Secretary of State Martin Van Buren of New York and Vice President Calhoun after the press regaled readers with a lurid exposé of forty-year-old Secretary of War John H. Eaton's "Petticoat Affair."

Both Calhoun and Van Buren, the latter a close personal friend of the President, had been vying to succeed Jackson as President when Calhoun's wife, Floride, initiated a collective snub by cabinet wives of Secretary Eaton's former mistress, the bold, brassy, beautiful Peggy O'Neal. A former Tennessee senator, Eaton was like an adopted son to the widowed President and an intimate of Van Buren, also an unmarried widower, who often escorted Eaton's bride both before and after her marriage to Eaton. A Washington tavern keeper's daughter, Peggy had gained notoriety for flaunting her figure in public flirtations—with the British bachelor minister Sir Edward Vaughan, for one, and Russian minister Baron Krudener, for another. Krudener was a married man.

"I had the attention of men, young and old, enough to turn a girl's head," she giggled.[34]

Incensed by Peggy Eaton's incursions into Washington society, Mrs. Calhoun and other cabinet wives refused even to look at Mrs. Eaton, let alone talk to her.

"After a thousand rumors and much tittle-tattle and gossip," Margaret Smith, Washington's gossip-in-chief, wrote of Peggy Eaton, "public opinion . . . doomed her to her lowly condition. On Inauguration Day, she was left alone and kept at a respectful distance from . . . distinguished women, with the sole exception of a seat at the supper table, where, notwithstanding her proximity, she was not spoken to by them."[35] A few days later Mrs. Smith reported, "Mrs. Eaton continues excluded from society except the houses of . . . the President and Mr. Van Buren. The Dutch Minister's family have openly declared against her admission into society. . . . And it is openly asserted that if Mr. Van Buren, our Secretary of State, persists in visiting her, our ladies will not go to his house."[36]

The chasm that the Petticoat Affair created between the President and Vice President Calhoun widened dramatically when the President discovered that Calhoun, as secretary of war under President Monroe, had urged censure, discipline, and even the arrest of then-general Jackson for invading Florida without government sanction. When Jackson demanded an explanation, the vice president refused.

"My course requires no apology," Calhoun responded, "and if it did, I have too much self-respect to make it to anyone in a case touching my official conduct."[37]

The response outraged the President, Webster told Clay.

"I had a right to believe that you were my sincere friend and until now never expected to say in the language of Caesar *et tu Brute*," the President told Calhoun. With that, the President ended all contact with his vice president, fixing on Van Buren as a vice presidential running mate in the next election. "Understanding you now," said Jackson to Calhoun, "no further communication with you on this subject is necessary."[38]

Both men's tempers continued to flare, and as cabinet members and congressmen took sides, the controversy reached a climax in the spring of 1832 when Jackson's entire cabinet resigned, save Eaton.

"We cannot fail to profit by the controversy," Clay exulted and declared it time for him and Lucretia to return to Washington and stage a political comeback with another run for the presidency. The Kentucky legislature obliged by electing him to the Senate, and once he arrived at the Capitol, Daniel Webster cooperated by ceding his position as Senate majority leader and allowing Clay to reprise the role he had played so effectively as House Speaker.

Hoping to lure Calhoun's support for his presidential aspirations, Clay urged political friends to side with Calhoun in the dispute with President Jackson and Van Buren. "As far as relates to his personal controversy with Jackson, I think he has been wronged, and justice as well as policy prompts that he should . . . be sustained."[39]

The President's split with his vice president, the mass resignation of the cabinet, and the Peggy Eaton Petticoat Affair seemed part of an endless series of presidential political blunders. Hoping to cement political ties to the South, President Jackson had rammed the Indian Removal Act of 1830 through Congress—only to provoke cries of protest from human rights advocates across the North and Europe. Henry Clay decried the act for inflicting "wrongs and sufferings on the Cherokee Nation."[40]

The genesis of the act was the discovery of gold on Cherokee territory in Georgia in the late 1820s. Infected with gold fever, Georgia speculators demanded that the state seize the gold fields and open them to white prospectors. Because Indian affairs lay within federal jurisdiction, Georgia's leaders asked President Jackson, a Democrat who had been an Indian fighter, to push Indian removal through the Democrat-controlled Congress. The act ended George Washington's successful, decades-old program to integrate southeastern Indians into American society.

After Congress ordained Indian removal, Georgia's state legislature dissolved the Cherokee Nation with the Cherokee Acts, which stripped Cherokees of citizenship, voided Cherokee laws, and divided 9 million acres of gold-flaked Indian properties into state counties. No longer citizens, the Cherokees were helpless to protect their lands, homes, and gold from seizure by the state and helpless to sue for protection in state courts.

Aware of Clay's empathy for blacks, Indian chief John Gunter pleaded with the Kentucky senator for help. Clay responded accordingly, declaring that US government policy toward the Cherokees "had been too long and too firmly established to be disturbed.

> According to those principles, the Cherokee nation has the right to establish its own form of government . . . to live under its own laws, to be exempt from the laws of the United States or of any individual state. . . . I consider the present administration of the government of the United States as having announced a policy in direct hostility with those principles and thereby encouraging Georgia to usurp powers of legislation over the Cherokee nation.[41]

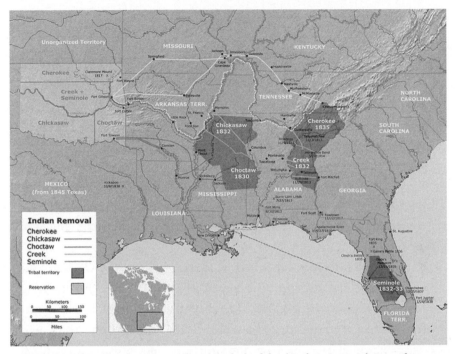

Map 3. Georgia's Cherokee Acts combined with the federal Indian Removal Act to force some 130,000 Cherokee, Chickasaw, Choctaw, Muskogee Creek, and Seminole Indians to flee their homes and travel the terrifying "Trail of Tears" across the Mississippi River to what is now Oklahoma. Some 60,000 men, women, and children died along the way from exposure, disease, and starvation.

Although outraged, Clay grew discouraged by the number of impossibly divisive issues threatening the Union that America expected him, as a champion of the Union, to solve. Clay reminded the Indian chief that his opinions were those of "a private individual, which can avail you nothing."[42]

In the end Georgia's government ignored Clay's protests and forced 130,000 Cherokee, Chickasaw, Choctaw, Muskogee, Creek, and Seminole Indians from their homes and properties onto a terrifying "Trail of Tears" across the Mississippi River to what is now Oklahoma. The trek condemned some 60,000 men, women, and children to slow, painful deaths from exposure and starvation—dwarfing the number of victims of the Spanish inquisition (fewer than 10,000) and the guillotines of the French Revolution (about 40,000) combined.[43]

In a desperate last effort to save themselves from exile, Cherokee leaders turned to the US Supreme Court and sued the state of Georgia. When *Cherokee Nation v. Georgia* came before the Court, however, Georgia's governor demonstrated his contempt for the federal courts and federal authority by refusing to send a representative to appear or respond.

"The Constitution, laws, and treaties of the United States are prostrate in the state of Georgia," former President John Quincy Adams lamented in his diary. "The Union is in the most imminent danger of dissolution."[44]

Asked to intervene on behalf of the Cherokees, the US Supreme Court could do nothing. On March 18, 1831, Chief Justice John Marshall expressed the Court's deep sympathy for the plight of the Indians but regretted that the court lacked jurisdiction. The Cherokees, he ruled, were in a unique situation—no longer a foreign nation nor citizens of the United States. The Court could have heard the case of either one, but Cherokee territories were now "part of the United States," and there was no Cherokee Nation. The case was moot; the Court had no authority to issue a ruling.

Although the Court had determined the status—or lack of status—of the Cherokee Nation under federal law, the case did not challenge Georgia's Cherokee Acts, which had evicted the Indians from the state. In a second suit, however, Samuel A. Worcester, a Congregationalist minister from Vermont, did just that.

An unpaid missionary among the Cherokees, Worcester had supported himself as a US postmaster. When he and another missionary refused to leave the state with the Cherokees, Georgia militiamen arrested them and sentenced them to prison and hard labor. They sued, and, given Worcester's status as a white citizen and federal official, Marshall and the Supreme Court agreed to rule on the laws under which he was arrested.

In a decision that left Georgians demanding secession, Marshall ruled the Cherokee Acts of the Georgia legislature "repugnant to the Constitution, laws and treaties of the United States.

> The forcible seizure and abduction of [Samuel A. Worcester], who was residing . . . by authority of the President of the United States [as postmaster], is also a violation of the acts which authorize the chief magistrate to exercise his authority.

With that, Marshall ordered Georgia's Cherokee Acts "reversed and annulled."[45]

All but ordering rebellion against the federal government, Georgia governor Wilson Lumpkin called Marshall's decision "usurpation" and said the state would respond with "the spirit of determined resistance."[46]

With no means of enforcing their decision, Marshall and the justices were helpless to prevent the collapse of the federal legal system. In Congress southerners voiced support for Georgia with shouts of defiance. Citing Jefferson's Kentucky Resolution, which stated that the Constitution was a compact between the states, South Carolina senator Robert Young Hayne called the Supreme Court decision "oppressive" and raised the banner of state sovereignty.

The eloquent Senator Daniel Webster of Massachusetts fired back:

> It is, sir, the people's constitution, the people's government; made for the people, by the people and answerable to the people. . . . The people . . . have declared that this Constitution shall be the supreme law. . . . Who is to judge between the people and the government? . . . Shall constitutional questions be left to four and twenty popular bodies,* each at liberty to decide for itself, and none bound to respect the decisions of others?[47]

---

* The number of states at the time.

25. *Massachusetts Senator Daniel Webster delivering his memorable speech assailing proponents of nullification and climaxing with the words every American could quote for generations thereafter: "Liberty and Union, now and forever, one and inseparable." (Library of Congress)*

Webster ended his defense of the Supreme Court and the Constitution with the stirring words that became a rallying cry across the North and parts of the West:

"Liberty and Union, now and forever, one and inseparable."[48]

As northern senators cheered, southern senators cried for armed resistance. Facing reelection in a matter of months, President Andrew Jackson declared allegiance to the South by telling New York journalist Horace Greeley, "John Marshall has made his decision. Now let him enforce it."[49]

The controversy set Henry Clay's political blood aboil, and he set out on a series of public appearances, assailing the Jackson administration for its "injustice" toward the Cherokees and the "deep wound" it inflicted on "the character of the American Republic." He used his attacks on the President to renew his advocacy of the American System, with higher tariffs to protect American-made products from imports and internal improvements to unite the nation with a modern transportation system.

With public opinion turning against the President in some parts of the country, Congress responded to Clay's appeals by passing an internal improvements bill designed to insult the President. It appropriated federal funds to extend the National Road from Maysville, on the Ohio border in northeastern Kentucky, to Nashville, Tennessee—the President's hometown—via Lexington, Kentucky—Clay's home town. The President vetoed it, insisting that the extension did not qualify for federal funds without a constitutional amendment.

The presidential veto so outraged Kentuckians that they pressured Clay to run again for the presidency. He agreed, convinced now that the Calhoun-Jackson feud and the defection of Jackson's cabinet and the vice president from the administration had undermined the President's political strength and created a perfect opportunity to topple him from power.

He tested the political atmosphere with a series of public appearances and speeches in Lexington, Louisville, Cincinnati, Columbus, and other communities near his home. The whoops of support and letters of encouragement convinced him he could win.

"My information from Washington from my friends evinces the most perfect confidence on their part in the success of our cause," Clay told a Kentucky Republican leader. "They believe that . . . I will be elected against any competitor."[50] Kentucky's legislature agreed, and to facilitate his climb to power, it reelected him to the US Senate in November 1831 and sent him back to the center of federal power in Washington. Adding to his elation over his state's support for his candidacy was the spectacle of his son Henry Clay Jr. graduating from the US Military Academy at West Point—second in his class.

When Clay returned to Washington, former President John Quincy Adams was there to greet him—much to Clay's surprise and delight. After his crushing defeat in the 1828 presidential election, Adams had left in a funk for his farm in Quincy, Massachusetts, resigned to a life of semiretirement. Friends and neighbors, however, implored him to return to Washington, insisting that, as a former President, he would "ennoble" the House of Representatives. Adams agreed but insisted on remaining independent of party affiliations. For the moment Senator Henry Clay believed Adams would be a firm ally in the other chamber of Congress. He had an even firmer, behind-the-scenes-ally in his wife.

"Mrs. Clay came and sat most of the morning with us and asked [my daughter] to go with her to choose a bonnet," cooed Margaret Smith, whose publisher-husband had just expanded the powerful *National Intelligencer* into the *Daily National Intelligencer*. "Wherever she went yesterday," Mrs. Smith said of Lucretia, "she was received with demonstrations of affection; tho' a very plain and unadmired woman . . . not as popular and admired as other women have been . . . she is so kind, good, and above all discreet that I do not think during the many years she lived here she made an enemy."[51]

Washington's warm reception spurred Clay's exuberance, and he confidently predicted Jackson's demise in the forthcoming election. "The old buck is mortally wounded," Clay said of Jackson. "He will run a while, make a show of vigor, and fall."[52]

CHAPTER 8

Ambition!

"There is no possibility of Mr. Clay's being chosen President," Margaret Smith predicted after Clay accepted the Republican Party nomination for President. "Yet the enthusiasm with which he was chosen as a candidate by the convention could not be but gratifying."[1]

For the first time in American history political parties held national conventions to write formal party platforms and nominate their candidates for President and vice president. The Republicans held their convention a year early in Baltimore, Maryland, on December 12, 1831, nominating Senator Henry Clay for President and Pennsylvania congressman John Sergeant for vice president. The early convention gave nominees more than the usual time to try to unseat the President.

The Democrats, of course, nominated President Jackson to run for a second term along with his former secretary of state Martin Van Buren of New York as vice presidential candidate to replace South Carolina's John C. Calhoun.

Confusing the 1832 presidential elections, however, was the emergence of a third political group, the Anti-Masonic Party. Led by the popular former Attorney General William Wirt of Maryland, the Anti-Masonic Party had adopted many of Clay's issues as its own, including a plan for internal improvements much like Clay's American System. Founded in 1828 with the backing of organized churches, the Anti-Masonic Party had sought to dislodge what they called a conspiracy of godless Freemasons from political power. Conveniently overlooking the Masonic membership of George Washington, Benjamin Franklin, and at least nine signers of the Declaration of Independence,* the Anti-Masonic Party tried to lure Henry Clay into its midst. Still a Mason, he refused, and the party nominated Wirt, who had served three terms as US attorney general—eight years under President Monroe (a Freemason) and four more under President John Quincy Adams.

Although the Senate would not create official majority and minority floor leaders until the 1920s, Henry Clay had entered as the all-but-acknowledged Senate leader. No other senators could claim his political credentials or stature as former House Speaker, peace commissioner at Ghent, and secretary of state. And few could match his gift for reconciling opposing factions or his speaking skills.

"His oratory was persuasive and spirit-stirring," wrote journalist Benjamin Perley Poore.

> The fire of his bright eyes and the sunny smile which lighted up his countenance . . . his unequaled voice . . . distinct and clear . . . rich, musical, captivating. . . . He gesticulated all over. The nodding of his head . . . arms, hands, fingers, feet, and even his spectacles, his snuff box, and his pocket handkerchief aided him in debate. He stepped forward and backward and from the right to the left. . . . The whole body had its story to tell.[2]

---

*Apart from Washington and Franklin, Masons in the revolutionary generation included John Hancock, Paul Revere, John Paul Jones, John Jay, James Monroe, John Marshall, Lafayette, and at least thirty-three of the seventy-four generals in the Continental Army.

Clay took full advantage of his de facto political authority to introduce and press enactment of his cherished American System, which included internal improvements paid for by the sale of public lands, higher tariffs, and extension of the charter of the Bank of the United States.

"Mr. Clay's manner," John Quincy Adams remarked, "with many courtesies of personal politeness was . . . super-presidential."[3]

Although the Senate passed his public lands bill, the House rejected it, preferring to leave proceeds from the sale of public lands to the discretion of each state rather than mandate their use for internal improvements as Clay had urged. Congress then passed a law raising tariffs on a handful of items, but the increases were so little and affected so few imports that Clay was "furious," according to Senator George Dallas of Pennsylvania. "His defeat and mortification were signal and manifest."[4]

He suffered another legislative defeat when a cholera epidemic threatened the nation, and he proposed calling on the President to proclaim a day of "fasting, humiliation, and prayer." His friend and political ally Massachusetts representative John Quincy Adams had to table the motion in the House when opponents mocked it as an election ploy.

Congress did respond favorably, however, to Clay's proposal to renew the charter of the Bank of the United States—only to have President Jackson veto the bill. Flouting a Supreme Court ruling that the government had a constitutional right to establish the bank, the President insisted the bank was unconstitutional. He called it an instrument designed to "make the rich richer and the potent more powerful" while leaving "the humble members of society—the farmers, mechanics, and laborers," subject to government injustice.[5]

Clay lashed out at the President, saying he had been guilty of "perversion of the veto power. . . . The veto is hardly reconcilable with the genius of representative government. . . . It is a feature of our government borrowed from a prerogative of the British king. . . . Ought the opinion of one man overrule that of a legislative body twice deliberately expressed?"[6]

Daniel Webster agreed: "According to the doctrines put forth by the President," Webster raged in the Senate, "although Congress may have passed a law, and although the Supreme Court may have pronounced it constitutional, yet it is, nevertheless, no law at all, if he, in his good pleasure, sees fit . . . to repeal or annul it."[7]

The nominal minority leader, Senator Thomas Hart Benton of Missouri, rose to chastise Clay and Webster for "wanting in courtesy, [and being] indecorous and disrespectful to the Chief Magistrate."[8]

Born in North Carolina, Benton moved to Nashville, Tennessee, as a young man, studied law, developed a prosperous plantation, and became Jackson's political ally. When the War of 1812 began, Jackson appointed Benton a colonel and his aide-de-camp, but the two had a bitter falling out, with both men issuing angry threats. Benton and Jackson finally came to blows in a Nashville barroom, and as they fell to the floor brawling, Benton's brother Jesse, a hot-headed junior officer, shot Jackson in the arm and shoulder and left him near death. As Jackson slipped into unconsciousness after the shooting, army doctors prepared to amputate his arm until Jackson muttered a direct order, "I'll keep my arm!" The doctors saved the arm, but the bullets that inflicted his wounds remained in his body for the rest of his life as painful reminders of the fight.

Faced with threats against his life from Jackson supporters, Benton—a brutish hulk of a man—fled Nashville and resettled in St. Louis, where he edited a newspaper and practiced frontier law, including shooting and killing one opposing attorney in a duel. When Missouri became a state, he won election to the US Senate where, in 1823, he and Jackson met again and, both of them being Democrats, put their differences aside to further Jackson's presidential ambitions in the 1824 election. As Democratic floor leader in the Senate, he staunchly defended the President.

Clay shot up from his seat to refute Benton: "I cannot allow the member from Missouri to instruct me," Clay raged. "I never had a personal rencontre with the President."[9]

Benton admitted he had fought with the President but that they had fought "like men. "When the contest was over, so was our enmity."[10]

As their voices blasted across the Senate Chamber, Benton and Clay drew closer and seemed poised to assault each other until the president of the Senate hammered the gavel on the sound block and demanded order. Both men calmed a bit and, their faces still beet red, offered apologies to the chair and the Senate:

"But not to the Senator from Kentucky!" Benton bellowed.

"To the Senate," Clay shouted back, "I also offer an apology; to the senator from Missouri, none."[11]

With order restored, the Senate voted down the bill to override the presidential veto, leaving Clay forced to return home to Kentucky without a single legislative victory and nothing with which to reward his supporters for their votes. Indeed, the widespread popularity of the President so surprised him that he began to doubt whether he could unseat Jackson.

A letter from his son Henry Clay Jr. offered some balm. The young man reported having completed his law studies and being admitted to the bar. In addition, he announced an "affaire du coeur":

"What would you say," he asked his father, "were I to present you with another daughter?

> Yesterday I was resolved upon a life of celibacy; today, I am almost equally resolved to propose a matrimonial union. Would it receive your sanction? . . . In all respects, the lady, Miss Julia Prather of Louisville, is worthy of being your daughter and my wife. But again, another question occurs: will she consent? I must confess that it is uncertain. But a few words will clear up that affair.[12]

Clay expressed delight: Julia Prather's father owned Louisville's first bank.

Less than a month before the presidential elections South Carolina's legislature threw the nation into political turmoil by passing an

Ordinance of Nullification, declaring the Tariff of 1828 "null, void, and no law, nor binding" upon South Carolina.* The Ordinance prohibited state officials from collecting federal duties and required all state officials to swear allegiance to the state. It committed the state to secession if the US government used force to ensure tariff collections.

Faced with violating his oath of office "to preserve, protect, and defend the Constitution" if he sided with nullifiers, the President risked his popularity in the South by declaring, "The laws of the United States must be executed." Then he stunned both North and South by signing a Proclamation Against Nullification—it remains one of the most important presidential acts in American history.

"My duty is emphatically pronounced in the Constitution," he stormed. "I have no discretionary power on the subject.

> I consider the power to annul a law of the United States assumed by one state, incompatible with the existence of the Union, contradicted expressly by the letter of the Constitution, unauthorized by its spirit, inconsistent with every principle on which it was founded, and destructive of the great object for which it was formed. . . . Those who told you that you might peaceably prevent the execution [of federal laws] have deceived you. . . . Their object is disunion. But be not deceived . . . disunion by armed force is treason. Are you really ready to incur its guilt?[13]

In the wake of the President's ultimatum Vice President Calhoun resigned and returned home to South Carolina, where the legislature immediately voted to send him back to Washington as the state's new senator.

---

*To protect cotton mills in the Northeast, Congress had imposed tariffs on foreign textiles. Southern cotton growers feared that England, the biggest manufacturer and exporter of finished cotton goods—and biggest buyer of raw cotton from the American South—would retaliate by cutting purchases of southern cotton.

Hailed for his courage in standing up to South Carolina's nulli-fiers, President Jackson crushed Henry Clay in the presidential elec-tion, capturing 688,242 popular votes and 210 votes in the Electoral College. Henry Clay won 473,462 popular votes and a mere 49 elec-toral votes—in Massachusetts, Rhode Island, Connecticut, Delaware, Maryland, and his home state of Kentucky. In New Salem, Illinois, a frontier village about fifteen miles from Springfield, Henry Clay won the vote of twenty-three-year-old shopkeeper Abraham Lincoln—his first vote ever in a presidential election.

The Anti-Masonic candidate William Wirt captured a surpris-ing 101,051 popular votes, but only 7 Electoral College votes—not enough to have altered the outcome. New York's Martin Van Buren won election as vice president, with 189 votes in the Electoral Col-lege, compared to 49 votes for Clay's running mate John Sergeant of Pennsylvania.

One Clay loyalist called the election a Waterloo, but Clay was less distraught over his defeat than he was over the possible consequences of Jackson's victory. Calling the President's triumph "menacing" and "alarming," he predicted, "Whether we shall ever see light and law and liberty again is very questionable."

"Still," he added, "we must go onto the last . . . to discharge our duty."[14]

All the news at the Clay household was not bad, however. Henry Clay's son Henry Clay Jr. married Julia Prather, the daughter of Louisville's principal banker. "My son Henry," a jubilant Henry Clay Sr., wrote to his brother-in-law, "has recently married Miss Prather, a young lady of good fortune and, what is better, of amiable disposition and cultivated mind. I went to the city to be present at the ceremony."[15]

Confident of retaining power for four more years, the President ordered the Treasury Department's fleet of cutters—later called the Coast Guard—into Charleston Bay to enforce the tariff law. South Carolina's legislature struck back by authorizing the governor to call out the militia and, if necessary, draft able-bodied men between the ages of eighteen and forty-five. It appropriated $200,000 for military preparations for civil war.

The President, in turn, called on Congress for a Force Bill, authorizing him to use federal troops and ships to crush South Carolina's rebellion. Former vice president Calhoun, now senator from South Carolina and bitter political enemy of the President, stood to assail Jackson as a despot. He called the Force Bill a "war bill" and warned, "Our union stands on the brink of civil war."[16]

When Daniel Webster defended the President's action, Virginia's John Randolph reposted irrationally—as he always did: "I want to see Webster die, muscle by muscle."[17]

The President's flirtation with civil war appalled Clay, and in a bold act of statesmanship, he reached out to Calhoun. Although he called South Carolina's actions "rash, intemperate, and greatly in the wrong," he told the Senate, "I do not want to disgrace her nor any other member of this Union.

> Has not the state of South Carolina been one of the members of this Union in days that tried men's souls? Have not her ancestors fought alongside our ancestors? . . . I hope our posterity will mingle with hers for ages and centuries to come, in the united defense of liberty, and for the honor and glory of our Union. I do not wish to see her degraded or defaced as a member of this confederacy.[18]

Clay then left the Senate and absented himself when it voted to enact the Force Bill. Outside the Senate Chamber, however, he and Calhoun huddled together, longtime allies and friends, determined to find a formula for tariffs that would satisfy both North and South as well as retain and strengthen ties that bound the Union. Until Congress enacted the Tariff of 1828, British textile manufacturers had used cheap cotton picked by slaves in the American South to undersell textiles made in New England. The Tariff of 1828 raised costs of British textiles high enough to protect New England textile producers, but it also raised costs of other British imports so high that the agricultural South could no longer afford to buy many British manufactured goods on which they depended.

Clay and Calhoun sought a formula for tariffs that would protect American industry in the North without penalizing the South. It seemed an impossible task—until Clay suggested a different approach—to buy time for both northerners and southerners to adjust gradually to market changes. They agreed to reduce tariffs on a handful of imports deemed essential to the southern economy and gradually reduce all other tariffs over a decade, until 1842, when they would drop to 20 percent. At 20 percent, the reduced tariffs would remain high enough to give American manufacturers some protection while reducing the price of imports to levels most Americans could afford. The compromise offered a little to everyone without giving everything to anyone.

After Calhoun agreed to the plan, Clay spent the ensuing weeks trying to convince northern and southern congressmen along with manufacturers' representatives of the commercial and economic advantages of the compromise tariff over the horrors of civil war. Then, before the Senate and a packed gallery of spectators, he pleaded,

> Let us save the country from the most dreadful of all calamities, and
> let us save its industry, too, from threatened destruction. . . . We
> are for peace . . . union, and liberty. We want no war, above all, no
> civil war, no family strife. . . . no sacked cities, no desolate fields,
> no smoking ruins, no streams of American blood shed by American
> arms.[19]

Shocked by the call for tariff reductions by the longtime champion of high tariffs, some Clay supporters—unable or unwilling to embrace true statesmanship—called him a turncoat for knocking down the very tariff wall he had helped build to protect American manufacturers.

"The American System is dead," Representative Francis Granger of New York concluded, adding that Clay's allies were walking Capitol hallways "in a rage. They curse and damn him."[20] Some Clay critics accused him of caving in to southern interests to win support from that region for his presidential ambitions—another "corrupt bargain" akin to his giving his presidential votes to John Quincy Adams to win appointment as secretary of state.

"I have been accused of ambition in presenting this measure," he struck back at critics. "Ambition!" he shouted at the senators. "Ambition! Inordinate ambition!

> I have no desire for office, not even the highest. . . . Pass this bill! Tranquilize the nation! Restore confidence to and affection in the Union, and I am willing to return home to Ashland to renounce public services forever. . . . Yes, I have ambition, but it is the ambition of being the humble instrument in the hands of Providence to reconcile a divided people; once more to revive concord and harmony in a distracted land—the pleasing ambition of contemplating the glorious spectacle of a free, united, prosperous, and fraternal people.[21]

The applause and cheers were deafening. Even John Randolph, now sickly and approaching death, staggered to his feet to acclaim his longtime opponent. Clay saw him "looking as if he were not long for this world, and being myself engaged in a work of peace . . . I shook hands with him. The salutation was cordial on both sides." Randolph died three months later.

On March 1, 1833, Congress ended the threat of secession—for a while at least—by passing Clay's Compromise Tariff. Clay was elated, calling it the proudest day of his life. Clay's statesmanship scored a final victory when, at Calhoun's behest, South Carolina repealed its Ordinance of Nullification.

"I never was in favor of what I regarded as a high tariff," Clay later explained. "We believe . . . such discriminations ought to be made as will afford moderate and reasonable protection for American interests against the rival and prohibitory policy of foreign powers."[22]

President Jackson signed Clay's Compromise Tariff bill the moment it reached his desk, but Senator Thomas Hart Benton fueled the Jacksonian press into insinuating that Clay had made another "corrupt bargain" in obtaining its passage.

Nothing Benton or the press could say or write, however, could detract from Clay's joy over having held the Union together with the compromise that he and Calhoun had worked out. Adding to his joy was news from Louisville that Henry Jr.'s wife, Julia, had given birth to their first child, whom they named Henry Clay III—to the boundless delight of his grandfather, who wrote his son,

> We most cordially felicitate you and our dear Julia on her safe delivery and . . . if we are to credit your account of him, so 'noble a boy.' Tell Julia to make haste and get able to bring her prize here that we, as well as her Louisville friends, may have the satisfaction of seeing and caressing him. . . . Give the love of your mother and myself to Julia and kiss the little stranger for us.[23]

After an initial effort at practicing law, Henry Clay Jr. decided against it, and his father agreed to finance his son's purchase of a farm near Louisville. Not long after, Clay's second oldest son, Thomas, returned home, having shaken his dependence on alcohol and he too turned to farming. Delighted over his son's recovery, Henry Clay bought a second farm at auction adjacent to Ashland and turned it over to Thomas to run. Although Theodore Wythe returned home for occasional visits, he showed no improvement and continued living at the Kentucky Lunatic Asylum.

As his sons ventured into an uncertain future in farming, Clay embarked on an equally uncertain political campaign to succeed President Jackson in 1836. Although Clay's Republicans were a majority in the Senate, Jackson's Democrats controlled the House, and despite his opposition, Clay was helpless to prevent the President from withdrawing federal funds from the Bank of the United States (BUS) and redistributing them to state banks. Even worse, the President

parceled some federal funds to so-called pet banks owned by his supporters, many without specie (gold, silver) in their vaults to back the
paper they issued.

Until then BUS had been the foundation of the American financial system, providing the nation with a sound, uniform, and univer-
sally accepted national currency backed by gold and silver. It had all
but replaced unstable state banknotes in populated areas of the nation. Without government deposits, however, BUS could no longer
ensure a flow of funds for loans to businesses and farms. Wildcat
banks with printing presses as their primary assets sprouted across the
nation, producing their own money to fill the vacuum. By late 1833
the flood of worthless paper was drowning farmers in debt, and as
bankers, merchants, and farmers alike plunged into bankruptcy, the
nation faced economic collapse.

Attorney William Sullivan sent Clay a description of the economic disaster in Boston:

> Here, in the midst of plenty and prosperity, we are suddenly plunged
> into an artificial distress . . . business is completely at a standstill and
> the attention of mercantile debtors is entirely absorbed in saving
> themselves from being bankrupt. . . . In the last thirty-five years, I
> never saw the intelligent men of our city so utterly despondent.[24]

Henry Clay began to worry about the stability of the bank that
held his own financial assets and wrote to his son Henry Jr., "I should
like to know how my account stands at the bank. What premium is
paid in Lexington on Eastern checks?"[25]

Merchants and farmers alike castigated the President. Criticism
came from all political directions, splitting Jackson's own Democrats
and sending many into the arms of Republican critics and members of
the Anti-Masonic Party. Clay, Webster, and Calhoun bonded politically to form what many called the "Great Triumvirate" and attracted
enough supporters to form a new, loosely knit political alliance that

called itself Whigs, the name of an eighteenth-century British political group that opposed the absolute monarchy of the Stuarts.

Acting in concert, the Great Triumvirate took control of the Senate: "We carried the appointment of every chairman of the committees as we wished, and . . . every member of several committees," Clay boasted to his longtime friend in Richmond, Francis T. Brooke. "There is a fair prospect of our having in the Senate a majority of 26 or 27."[26]

Clay cautioned that "whether it will be practicable to rescue the government and public liberty from the dangers which Jacksonism has created depends . . . mainly on the South, and . . . the South will be guided mainly by Virginia." Knowing Brooke to be among the most popular figures in Virginia, he urged his friend to run for governor.

> I know the sacrifices you must make if you accept that station, but cannot you make them? What is a public man worth who is not ready to sacrifice himself for his country? Everything for which you fought or which you and I hold valuable . . . is in imminent hazard . . . the public Treasure . . . the very existence of liberty and the government is, in my judgment in peril. I mean myself to open and push a vigorous campaign. It is the campaign of 1777. I want aid. . . . Can you not assist us?[27]

With the Republican press assailing President Jackson as "King Andrew," Clay took the Senate floor and accused the President and his Treasury Secretary-designate Roger B. Taney with having provoked the economic disaster. The President, he said, had assumed "authority and power not conferred by the Constitution and laws, but in derogation of both." He said Jackson had acted unconstitutionally by firing Taney's two predecessors for refusing to obey orders to withdraw Treasury deposits from BUS.

Taney, a Maryland slaveholder who had served as Jackson's secretary of war and attorney general, stood firmly with the President in opposing recharter of BUS and had withdrawn all government deposits from the Bank prematurely. Although the President had appointed him secretary of the Treasury, the Senate had not yet voted on the appointment when he began exercising the powers of the office.

As Christmas approached in 1833, Clay continued his relentless attack for three days, using specious arguments so laced with patriotic fervor that he convinced a majority of senators that the President and Treasury Secretary Taney had violated their oaths of office and the Constitution by exercising their legitimate authority—the one as chief executive, the other as the nation's chief banker. Although the Senate lacked powers to impeach the President or his Treasury secretary, Clay urged the Senate to censure them both.

"We are in the midst of a revolution," Clay argued, "a total change of the pure republican character of the government and to the concentration of power in the hands of one man."[28]

Clay's accusations echoed across the land, with Whigs and many Jacksonians blaming the President and Secretary Taney for every imagined economic setback—even the lack of street lights in Pittsburgh.

"Everything is falling . . . going down, down," Clay warned the Senate, "and will be still lower unless some remedy should be found." Senators had a choice, he said, between "the will of one man and that of twelve millions of people. It is a question between power—ruthless, inexorable power—on the one hand and the strong, deep-felt sufferings of a vast community, on the other."[29]

His speech roused the nation. A flood of letters inundated the White House—some pleading, others demanding, others threatening:

"Damn your old soul," one writer from Cincinnati assailed the President. "Remove them deposits back again and recharter the bank or you will certainly be shot in less than two weeks and that by myself."[30]

Although Webster and Calhoun stood by Clay, months passed with no collective response by the Senate, and Clay, exasperated, decided on a last, desperate effort, putting into play his finest acting skills. In one of his greatest political gambles, he stood in the Senate on March 7, 1834, and instead of addressing the senators who would vote yea or nay, he turned to Vice President Van Buren, the presiding officer of the Senate who had no vote except to break ties. Van Buren was the all-but-certain Democratic presidential candidate in the next election and the sitting President's closest political ally.

"You!" Clay pointed at the vice president. "You can, if you will, induce him to change his course," Clay displayed his most practiced histrionic tones. "Go to him and tell him . . . the actual condition of his bleeding country.

> Tell him it is nearly ruined and undone by the measures which he has . . . put in operation. . . . Tell him that in a single city, more than sixty bankruptcies involving a loss of upward of fifteen millions of dollars have occurred. Tell him of the alarming decline in the value of property, of the depreciation of all the products of industry, of the stagnation of every branch of business, and of the close of numerous manufacturing establishments. . . . Depict to him . . . the heart-rending wretchedness of thousands of the working classes cast out of employment . . . the tears of helpless widows . . . of unclad and unfed orphans.[31]

As ladies in the gallery sobbed, Clay paused to let his words have full effect.

"Tell him how much true glory," Clay spoke softly, "is to be won by retracing false steps than by blindly rushing on until his country is overwhelmed by bankruptcy and ruin."[32]

Although the Republican Senate responded to Clay's appeal by censuring the President—the only such censure in American history—the Democratic House voted it down along with Clay's motion to restore government deposits in BUS.

The President sent the Senate a formal protest, saying it had charged him with an impeachable offense without the opportunity to defend

26. After John C. Calhoun resigned as vice president in a split with President Jackson, the President named his former secretary of state, Martin Van Buren, as his running mate. Bitter over his split with Jackson, Calhoun called Van Buren "one of the meanest . . . beasts of the forest." (Library of Congress)

himself, but the Senate rejected the President's protest and went a step farther by refusing to approve Jackson's nomination of Taney as the new secretary of Treasury.

Although Senator Thomas Hart Benton made periodic attempts to expunge the censure from the official record, he failed until 1837, when a Democratic majority ordered the secretary of the Senate to recover the official Senate records for the 1834 censure and draw black lines through the words,

> Resolved that the President in the late executive proceedings in relation to the public revenue, has assumed upon himself authority and power not conferred by the Constitution and laws, but in derogation of both.

In bold lettering across the passage he then wrote, "Expunged by order of the Senate, this 16th day of January, in the year of our Lord, 1837."

Daniel Webster denounced Benton, calling defacement of Senate records unconstitutional, and Clay called the action nothing short of presidential tyranny. "What object of his ambition is unsatisfied?" Clay demanded to know of Benton. "What more does he want?

> Can you make that not to be which has been? Can you eradicate from memory and from history that . . . a majority of the Senate . . . passed the resolution which excites your enmity? Is it your vain and wicked object to arrogate to yourselves that power of annihilating the past? . . . Black lines! Black lines! Sir, I hope the Secretary of the Senate will preserve the pen with which he may inscribe them and present it . . . to some future American monarch . . . in gratitude to those . . . he has enabled to erect a throne upon the ruins of civil liberty.

Clay urged creation of "a new order of knighthood . . . the Knight of the Black Lines."[33]

Although Clay, Webster, and Calhoun continued opposing Jackson, theirs was a losing war. "Old Hickory" was as indomitable in political battle as he had been in military conflict. The BUS charter expired in March 1836. As a consequence, Congress passed the Deposit Act of 1836, requiring the Treasury to designate at least one bank in each state and territory as a repository for federal government funds. Although the Bank of the United States ceased doing business as a national bank, it reopened under a state charter as the Bank of the United States of Pennsylvania and became the public repository for federal funds in that state.

Clay nonetheless tried to rally those who supported the Clay-Calhoun-Webster alliance against the President. "Do not despair . . . my countrymen," he called out on the Senate floor. "You are a young, brave, intelligent, and, as yet, a free people. A complete remedy for all that you suffer . . . is in your own hands." Clay urged them to solidify their new Whig political alliance. The term *Whigs*, he said, had originated "among our British ancestors. . . .

> The Tories were the supporters of executive powers. . . . The Whigs were champions of liberty. . . . During our Revolutionary War, the Tories took sides . . . with the king, against liberty and independence. And the Whigs . . . contended . . . for freedom and independence. . . . Let us perform our duty in a manner worthy of our ancestors; worthy of American senators. Let us pledge our lives, our fortunes, and our sacred honor to rescue our beloved country from impending dangers . . . in the cause of the people, of the Constitution, and of civil liberty.[34]

Clay's appeal succeeded in uniting five disparate groups into the new Whig political coalition: the remnants of the Anti-Masonic Party, Democrats opposed to Jackson's bank policy, northern and southern industrialists who favored tariff protection, supporters of state sovereignty alienated by Jackson's stand on nullification, and Republican Party members who had supported John Quincy Adams and Clay's American System.

With the demise of the Bank of the United States, a shortage of sound currency set loose a wave of economic woes across the nation. On January 30, 1835, a crazed English-born house painter attempted to assassinate President Jackson as Jackson emerged from the Capitol. His pistol misfired; the President and nearby onlookers leaped at the thirty-five-year-old assailant, with Jackson beating him to the ground and Tennessee congressman Davy Crocket helping. The President called the assault part of a plot engineered by Senator Calhoun, but a jury declared the would-be assassin Richard Lawrence a raving lunatic—and not guilty by reason of insanity. The court sentenced him to a lunatic asylum, where he remained until his death in 1861 at the age of sixty-one.

Although Henry Clay had urged supporters not to despair after his election defeat, by mid-winter of 1835 it was he who began to despair.

"I am truly sick of Congress," he confided to his son Henry Clay Jr. after losing almost all his legislative battles. He and Lucretia looked forward to returning home to tend their farm at Ashland. He arranged a loan of about $15,000 from fur-baron John Jacob Astor to buy another farm in partnership with his son Henry Clay Jr., whose wife had just given birth to their second child, a daughter.

"I congratulate you on the event," wrote the proud grandfather. "It is a great addition to your previous ample means of happiness and I sincerely pray that Julia and you both may justly appreciate it."[35]

As always, there was some bad news to balance good news. Their youngest boy, fourteen-year-old John Morrison Clay, had narrowly avoided dismissal from his Princeton, New Jersey, boarding school. Openly unhappy at being far from home and family, the boy had insulted a teacher—perhaps hoping to provoke his dismissal. Instead, the headmaster made the boy make a personal apology and an inauspicious debut in public speaking: "a public confession of his error, in the presence of the whole school."[36]

Reluctantly Henry Clay returned to Congress in late autumn 1835—this time without Lucretia. Not only had she tired of Washington, but the deaths of so many of her children and their spouses had left her with too many grandchildren to raise to consider leaving home. Although the Clays sent some of the more mature boys to boarding schools, Lucretia often had four, five, six, or even seven orphaned grandchildren to care for at one time. In addition, Ashland had become an enormous agricultural enterprise that required hands-on management by its owners. From her first days at Ashland she had enjoyed dairy operations—especially butter and cheese making—and had gradually taken charge of what began as a hobby and turned it into a thriving business. She now assumed responsibility for the entire Ashland enterprise and would never again return to Washington.

Henry Clay, meanwhile, made a detour on his way to Washington, stopping at John Morrison's school to see his son. Two of his grandsons had enrolled there by then, and Clay wrote home to Lucretia that all three were "contented with their situations" but that he was deeply concerned about having left her at home.

Of equal concern, he wrote, was the condition of their last surviving daughter, Anne, who had not recovered fully from the birth of her last child two weeks earlier. "I feel very uneasy about our dear daughter," he wrote to Lucretia. "I sincerely hope she may get well and that all my apprehensions may prove groundless."[37]

They did not.

CHAPTER 9

Blackguards, Bankrupts, and Scoundrels

"My home," Anne's husband wrote to his father-in-law, "lately the happiest, which I have shared for years with a beloved wife . . . that home is now to me insupportable. Every object . . . every tree and flower, once so dear when objects of her care—now serve only to make known to me my loss and my misery. The beloved object who gave life and animation to all has left us."[1]

Anne was dead.

Henry Clay was as distraught as his son-in-law. "She was my favorite; so frank, gay, and warm-hearted," he told Margaret Smith, who related the news to her sister. "Their plantation adjoined Mr. Clay's and afforded a daily intercourse. Of five daughters, she was the last . . . and poor Mrs. Clay in her declining age is left alone and bereaved of the support and comfort which daughters and only daughters can afford."[2]

Almost never at a loss for words, Henry Clay struggled to express thoughts he never imagined his mind would ever entertain: "I would have cheerfully submitted to a thousand deaths to have saved this dear child," he wrote to his wife, Lucretia, wiping away his tears with his free hand.

> She was so good, so beloving, and so beloved, so happy, and so deserving to be happy. My dear, I ought to endeavor to comfort you, and I am showing my weakness. I cannot help it. This dear child was so entwined around my heart . . . that I shall never, never be able to forget her. My tears . . . have flowed almost in a continuous stream. . . . I pray my dear Wife that you may have been able to bear, and may continue to bear, this great affliction better that I have or shall . . . kiss my dear grandchildren for your affectionate and afflicted husband.[3]

It took weeks for Clay to recover. Although he appeared in the Senate, he broke into tears and walked off the floor almost every time he tried to speak. For the first time in his life the once-brash, hard-drinking card sharp with the quick tongue, biting wit, and exaggerated smile was at a loss to understand—let alone control—his emotions or the events in his life, unaware how the selfless love of his wife and children had changed him into a deeply caring husband and father.

"The sympathy of no friend that I have could have more soothing effect than yours," he wrote to Francis T. Brooke in Richmond, Virginia.

> Alas, there are some wounds which nothing can heal, and I feel that such a one has been inflicted on me. . . . Never was [a] father blessed with one more affectionate or who was more beloved. . . . She was my nicest neighbor . . . with a husband devotedly attached to her . . . with four sweet children besides the infant recently born, with a circle of the most warm hearted friends, such is the daughter I have lost. . . . I feel, my dear friend, as if nothing remained for me in this world but the performance of duties.[4]

In response to a Kentucky political supporter who urged him to run for governor, he wrote, "I am considering quitting public life altogether. . . . There is no conceivable state of things in which I would concur to serve as governor of Kentucky. I am tired of . . . public life. I most unaffectedly desire repose."[5]

Three weeks later he remained as morose as ever, writing his wife that "I confine myself almost exclusively to my room except when I go to the Capitol. I see nobody except my mess mates . . . and I desire to see no one."[6]

In the first address he could bring himself to make to the Senate after Anne's death, he acknowledged being "borne down by the severest affliction with which Providence has ever been pleased to visit me" and concluded by announcing his intention to retire from public life.[7]

Dramatic events, however, would force him to reconsider.

Although he tried to ignore it, what had been a rivulet of inflammatory abolitionist propaganda in 1831 swelled into a flood by 1835, flowing beyond Washington into and across the South, outraging and terrifying plantation owners. Most southerners remembered the decade-long slave rebellion in Santo Domingo (Haiti) that culminated with the massacre of more than 10,000 French troops and 3,000 civilians in 1803.

The specter of similar massacres in the United States haunted every white southerner. Even as the slaughter in Haiti raged, an enslaved blacksmith named Gabriel had organized a slave rebellion on a plantation near Richmond in August 1800. Then-governor James Monroe sent militiamen to raid slave quarters on a dozen plantations, uncovering large caches of weapons and gunpowder and capturing and hanging twenty slaves, including Gabriel.

Slave uprisings had continued across the South with increasing regularity. In 1811 some 200 slaves burned five plantations on the east bank of the Mississippi near New Orleans. Militia companies hunted and killed most of the rebels, whom they executed by hanging or decapitation, sticking heads on pikes along the river bank to warn other slaves.

In August 1831 Nat Turner and a group of slaves had killed 55 whites in Southampton County, on Virginia's southeast border with North Carolina. Infuriated white mobs retaliated by killing 200 blacks, while authorities hung 56 more, including Turner. Virginia and other southern states punished the black population with laws banning education of blacks, restricting rights of assembly, and requiring a white minister at every black church service. Protests by northern abolitionists only provoked harsher laws. Georgia imposed the death penalty for printing materials that incited black defiance, and all southern states seized printed abolitionist materials and expelled editors of abolitionist publications and agents of abolitionist organizations.

The expulsions provoked more petitions to Congress, which responded with three resolutions. One asserted its lack of constitutional powers to interfere with slavery in any state or territory in which it already existed. A second resolution said it "ought not" to abolish slavery in the District of Columbia. And the third resolution went beyond the abolition issue and the Constitution by abridging free speech in Congress and the rights of citizens to petition:

> All petitions, memorials, propositions, or papers, relating in any way,
> or to any extent whatsoever, to the subject of slavery or the abolition
> of slavery shall without being either printed or referred, be laid on
> the table, and that no further action whatever shall be had thereon.[8]

When former President John Quincy Adams demanded recognition to object to the resolution, Speaker James K. Polk, a Tennessee slaveholder, ignored him and recognized only southern congressmen. Adams repeatedly shouted "Mr. Speaker! Mr. Speaker!" but Polk—using tactics Clay had introduced when he was Speaker—looked in every direction but that of Adams. After southerners had finished arguing for the first two resolutions, Polk put the third resolution to a vote. While Adams continued barking protests, the House passed it, 95 to 82, and the Speaker ended all further debate, preventing Adams from contributing a word.

27. *Speaker James K. Polk tried to silence Representative John Quincy Adams with a "Gag Rule" that banned mention of the word "slavery" in the House of Representatives, along with presentation of citizen petitions to abolish slavery. (Library of Congress)*

"Am I gagged?" Adams called out in disbelief, inadvertently giving Polk's new rule its historic name—the "Gag Rule." Southerners tried shouting Adams down with cries of "Order! . . . Order!!"

The Speaker called out over the din, "The motion is not debatable," and when Adams appealed to the House to overrule the Speaker, it sustained the Speaker, 109 to 89.

Adams tried shouting above the roar: "I hold the resolution . . . to be in direct violation of the Constitution of the United States, of the rules of this House, and of the rights of my constituents."[9] But before Adams could make his point, Polk adjourned the session and members streamed out the door.

The Gag Rule infuriated Americans across the North and parts of the West as much as it did John Quincy Adams. Thousands of petitioners rallied to his side, arguing that if the House could gag the reading of petitions against slavery, it could gag reading petitions against or for anything.

"Will you put the right of petitioning, of craving for help and mercy and protection on the footing of political privileges?" John Quincy Adams asked the House later. "No despot of any age or clime has ever denied this humble privilege to the poorest or meanest of human creatures. . . . That would be a sad day, Sir . . . when a vote should pass this House that would not receive a petition from slaves. . . . When the principle is once begun of limiting the right of petition, where would it stop?"

South Carolina senator John C. Calhoun sought to introduce the Gag Rule into the Upper House, but Henry Clay, still ready to stand beside his former chief, protested. Echoing John Quincy Adams's words, Clay called it unconstitutional to limit a senator's right of free speech and the rights of citizens to petition. Clay charged that "southern ultras"—and, by implication, Calhoun himself—"are quite as mischievous as the abolitionist ultras have been."[10] A majority of senators agreed and rebuffed Calhoun's motion.

Calhoun countered, however, with six sweeping resolutions. The first revived Thomas Jefferson's discredited assertion in his Kentucky Resolution that the Union was a "compact" between states, each of which retained control over internal affairs, including slavery, and was immune to federal "meddling." Calhoun urged the Senate to ban federal interference with slavery, disavow intent to end slavery in the District of Columbia, and, as an afterthought, annex Texas (and all other territories) without deference to abolition, thus linking a number of explosive issues, each of which alone threatened to divide the Union.

Taken aback by the scope of Calhoun's resolutions, Clay tried to make light of Calhoun's concern with the District of Columbia. "The actual abolition of slavery in the District," Clay sneered, "is about as likely to occur as the abolition of the Christian religion."[11]

Clay, however, believed that Calhoun's all-encompassing resolutions had less to do with the individual issues than the South Carolinian's presidential ambitions. Annexation of Texas, where slavery was legal, would give slave states control of Congress and enough Electoral College votes to put Calhoun in the White House.

Mexico had declared independence from Spain in 1824, incorporated Texas as a Mexican state, and opened its borders to further colonization. Thousands of Americans streamed in, soon outnumbering Mexicans. In 1830 the Mexican government banned slavery and further immigration by US citizens, but it was too late. By 1834 an estimated 30,000 Americans, mostly from the South, had settled in Texas with 5,000 slaves, compared to only 7,800 Mexicans. In 1836 former Tennessee governor Sam Houston, who had married a Cherokee and moved to Texas, organized a militia and declared Texas independent.

On February 23, 1836, Mexican President General Santa Anna led 3,000 troops into San Antonio and laid siege to the Roman Catholic Alamo Mission, where 188 armed, pro-independence settlers had taken refuge, including former Tennessee congressman Davy Crockett. Like Houston, Crockett had married a Cherokee, broken with President Jackson over the Indian Removal Act, and resettled in Texas. After four days Santa Anna's troops massacred Alamo rebels and swept eastward through every American settlement before reaching Galveston Bay.

On April 21, however, Sam Houston's militiamen counterattacked. Crazed with anger and shouting "Remember the Alamo," the outnumbered Americans overwhelmed a force of 3,000 Mexicans and captured Santa Anna. Although the Mexican leader signed a peace treaty and pledged to secure Mexican recognition of Texan independence, the Mexican Congress repudiated both actions. Interim Texas "President" David G. Burnet wrote to Henry Clay, announcing his state's "final separation from the miserable . . . government of Mexico." He asked Clay, as chairman of the Senate Committee on Foreign Relations, to support Texas independence and annexation by the United States.

Burnet explained "this momentous act" as a consequence of "the utter dissimilarity of character between the two people." The New Jersey–born Burnet had moved to Cincinnati, Ohio, and studied law before marrying a Comanche and moving to Texas. He described Texans as "Anglo-Americans" and Mexicans as "a mongrel race of degenerate Spaniards and Indians more degenerate than they." Citing the determination of Texans to be "independent of the unprincipled, priest-ridden, faithless Mexicans," he admitted that "we are few in comparison to our enemies, and we need all the external aid that can be had.

"To you, Sir," he pleaded with Clay, "we look with confidence for an advocate and a friend. . . . The voice of Henry Clay has never been raised in a more righteous cause than this."[12]

To Clay, however, Texas was a cauldron boiling with racial conflicts that would spill across the United States and bring simmering conflicts there to a boil. With slaveholders a majority in Texas, Clay feared annexation would prove even more divisive than admission of Missouri had been in 1820.

"My desire [is] to calm every part of the Union," he told the Senate in response to Calhoun's support for annexation. "We allow ourselves to speak too frequently and with too much levity of a separation of the Union.

> It is a terrible word to which our ears should not be familiarized. I desire to see in continued safety and prosperity this Union and no other Union. I go for this Union as it is, one and indivisible, without diminution. I will neither voluntarily leave it nor be driven out of it by force.[13]

Adding to Clay's political troubles was the illness of his youngest child, fourteen-year-old John, who had contracted typhoid fever after reaching Washington from his Princeton, New Jersey, boarding school to visit his father. Racked by fears of another death in his ill-fated family, Clay stood vigil each night, passing time by writing to his wife and sons.

"I wish his mother was present with us to assist in nursing him," Clay wrote to his son Thomas Hart, "but he does not suffer from nurses, and many offer to sit up with him at night on whom I have not called."[14]

Margaret Smith was first to volunteer. "Dr. Hunt thinks John better this morning," Clay replied to Mrs. Smith. "Many thanks for the jelly and for your friendly offer of service. He rests well, and Charles [Clay's servant] and I sleep in the same room with him without much disturbance to any party. . . . Should a different and unfortunate state of things arise, I will avail myself of your goodness."[15]

To Clay's immense relief, a different state of things did not arise. John Clay recovered a few weeks later and returned home to Ashland with his father. Late that summer he enrolled at Transylvania University in Lexington to continue his education.

The return to Ashland permitted Clay to try to resolve in his mind issues he had long dodged in the Senate. To hold the Union together, he would need to work out policies that appealed to all regions of the country—an all-but-impossible task for any leader in any era and even more difficult in 1830s America. Although he owned slaves, Clay claimed he had always despised slavery and regularly "gave slaves their freedom in recognition of their faithful service."[16] His grandson Thomas Hart Clay Jr. insisted that his grandfather "sincerely abominated the system of bondage . . . and wished the country in all its parts rid of the evil."[17] Clay himself told the Colonization Society of Kentucky, "If I could be instrumental in eradicating this deepest stain from the character of our country . . . this foul blot . . . I would not exchange the proud satisfaction which I should enjoy for the honor of all the triumphs ever decreed to the most successful conqueror."[18]

Nonetheless, Clay knew that any overt opposition to Calhoun's resolution to ban federal interference with slavery and annex Texas would further embed the wedge that Calhoun had driven between North and South.

When Clay returned to the Senate, he assailed Calhoun for reviving the Jeffersonian concept of the Constitution as a compact between states. "The historical fact is that it was framed by a convention of delegates appointed by state legislatures and then ratified by conventions of delegates chosen by the people." Calhoun's resolutions, Clay charged, "can only increase and exasperate . . . particularly at the North."[19] Clay pledged, nonetheless, to defend the rights of states as specified in the Constitution. "I shall contend for all the rights of the state which has sent me here," he declared. "If . . . the rights and the security of the slaveholding states shall be assailed by any authoritative act emanating from the Capitol, a state . . . of forcible resistance will then occur. It will be time enough then to act."[20]

Clay countered Calhoun's provocative resolutions with moderate resolutions of his own—another classic Clay compromise that offered a sop to every constituency to prevent disunion and, by then, a likely civil war. Seventeen years earlier, when Clay proposed the Missouri Compromise, the nation had also faced a threat of secession by southern states, but the chances of civil war had been all but nil. Abolitionism was still in its infancy in 1820; John Brown was only twenty years old, about to get married, and thinking only about starting a family. Had any southern states seceded, few in the North would have objected strongly enough to fight and die to free any slaves. Only New England had freed slaves at the time. New York would not emancipate its slaves until 1827, and mobs there rioted against abolition as late as 1834. Pennsylvania and New Jersey had ended the slave trade but continued to tolerate slavery and opposed depriving property owners of their rights by liberating any slaves.

By 1836, however, a new, younger generation of northern abolitionists had emerged, raised without slaves and schooled by preachers to detest slavery as sinful and sacrilegious. As the number of abolitionists grew and the volume of their voices intensified, many called for a war of emancipation. Clay tried quieting them with a lesson in constitutional law. "Domestic slavery is subject to the exclusive control of the slaveholding states," Clay reminded them. He then assailed them for stirring hatreds that would leave the Union in ruins, "and beneath the ruins of the United States would be buried . . . the liberty of both races."[21]

Although Clay agreed that Congress had jurisdiction over the District of Columbia, he said it could not abolish slavery without violating agreements with Virginia and Maryland, both of them slave states that had ceded the land to the federal government on condition that no district citizens be deprived of their property—and slaves, under the law, remained property.

Clay had strong words for southerners as well. By then they had imposed the Gag Rule in the House, and Calhoun had tried to introduce it in the Senate.

"The Constitution," he lectured his colleagues, "requires the Senate to accept petitions," and "the constitutional right of petition to abolish slavery clearly exists. . . . Will not the Senator," Clay stared at his grim-faced friend Calhoun, "comprehend the difference between the act of receiving the petition and the grant of the thing petitioned for?"[22]

As for the Texas question, Clay said he believed "those gentlemen at the South have been unwise who have expressed a wish for the incorporation of Texas in order to strengthen the slave interest."[23] Clay urged the Senate "to keep these two unhappy causes—abolition and annexation—separate and distinct."

To soothe the ruffled feelings of Calhoun and his Senate allies, Clay agreed to recognize Texas independence from Mexico and said he would join with Calhoun in protecting the "just rights" of slave states. Their only difference, he argued, was that Calhoun "goes for strong language, menacing tones, and irritating measures; I, for temperate, but firm language, conciliation, and for obeying the injunction of the Constitution in respect to the right of petition.

> I cannot believe that it is prudent or wise to be so often alluding to the separation of the Union. . . . We are too much in the habit of speaking of divorces, separation, disunion. In private life, if a

wife pouts and frets and scolds, what would be thought of the good sense . . . of the husband who should threaten her with separation, divorce, disunion? No man who has a heart or right feelings would employ such . . . terrible menaces upon every petty disagreement in domestic life. . . . He would approach the lady with kind and conciliatory language and apply those natural and more agreeable remedies which never fail to restore domestic harmony.[24]

With that, according to Senate records, senators erupted in "a general burst of laughter, which continued for some time."[25] Clay had bridged the fissures in the Capitol again: the Senate agreed to a compromise that left many southerners and northerners—if not Calhoun—ready to walk down Capitol corridors arm in arm and, most importantly, talk to each other in civil tones. They helped Calhoun save face by passing four of his resolutions, but not before incorporating Clay's conciliatory modifications.

Unfortunately the thin-skinned Calhoun left the Senate floor feeling humiliated by the compromise and all but unwilling to talk to Clay or even look at Daniel Webster, the fierce Massachusetts abolitionist. Although Clay's compromise restored ties between his other Senate colleagues, it cut the bonds between the heralded Great Triumvirate.*

Henry Clay's success with another great political compromise did not assuage his melancholy over the loss of his daughter Anne, however. As a result, he left the Senate abruptly, returned home to Kentucky, and announced his retirement from politics. His withdrawal left the Whigs so fragmented that they were unable to hold a national convention. Regressing to earlier forms of candidate selection,

---

*Despite their breakup, the members of the Great Triumvirate were named three of the five greatest senators in American history by a select committee headed by Senator John F. Kennedy in May 1957. Besides Clay, Calhoun, and Webster, the committee named Robert La Follette Sr. (1855–1925) of Wisconsin and Robert Taft (1889–1953) of Ohio.

28. *Like Andrew Jackson, the sixty-four-year-old General William Henry Harrison was a war hero. Governor of Ohio when he ran for President, he was born in Virginia and, before moving to Ohio, he had been governor of the Indiana Territory and advocated slavery to stimulate the farm economy. (Library of Congress)*

Massachusetts nominated Senator Daniel Webster, while the remnants of the Anti-Masonic Party nominated General William Henry Harrison.

Like Jackson, Harrison was a frontier hero. He had crushed the Shawnee Indians at the Battle of Tippecanoe in 1811, ending years of Shawnee attacks on American settlers. Then, in the War of 1812, he led American troops to victory over a coalition of Indian nations in the West, killing the fabled Chief Tecumseh and earning enough acclaim to win election to Congress as an Ohio representative and then as senator.

In contrast to the Whigs, Jackson's Democrats united behind Jackson's chosen heir, Vice President Martin Van Buren of New York.

Jubilant over their unanimity, they held a national presidential nominating convention that was more a celebration of the Jackson years than a political selection process.

Although Clay portrayed Van Buren as a Jackson puppet—a surrogate whom Jackson would manipulate while retaining power behind the scenes—he did not convince enough voters. Jackson remained the most popular figure in America, and if he trusted Van Buren, that was good enough for most voters. The vice president pledged to "tread generally in the footsteps of President Jackson," and that too was good enough for most voters.[26]

Clay despaired "with the existing prospect of public affairs. It can hardly be worse," he wrote to Francis T. Brooke. "Blackguards, bankrupts, and scoundrels, profligacy and corruption are the order of the day, and no one can see the time when it will be changed.

> But the history of the nation records long periods of misrule and abuse and subsequent regeneration. . . . The time approaches when I must decide whether to return to the Senate. I have a strong disinclination to go back. If indeed our election should so terminate as to make the election of a Jackson man probable, I feel bound to hold on.[27]

Although Van Buren collected only 50.9 percent of the popular vote—764,198—the distribution allowed him to win fifteen states with 170 electoral votes. Harrison won six states, with 73 electoral votes and a popular vote of 548,966.

As Van Buren was winning election to the presidency of the United States, Henry Clay won election to the presidency of the American Colonization Society, succeeding James Madison, who had died in June 1836. "No man is more sensitive to the evils of slavery than I am," Clay insisted and called ACS "the only practical scheme . . . for separating advantageously . . . the European descendants upon this continent from the free people of color . . . and of ultimately effecting a more extensive separation of the two races."[28]

Shortly after Clay became ACS president Kentucky's legislature reelected him to the US Senate—a position he had not sought.

> It is upwards of thirty years since I was first honored by an election to the Senate. . . . I have thought that my long public service gave me some title to repose, of which I feel most sensibly great need. . . . But when I reflect upon the great and numerous obligations which I am under to the people of Kentucky . . . I feel there is no sacrifice which I ought not make.[29]

Van Buren's popularity at the polls did not follow him into the White House. Before he could cross its threshold a financial panic sent thousands of frantic Americans racing to shuttered banks to try to salvage what funds they could. Without the Bank of the United States to hold and protect the government's financial resources, the US government itself faced bankruptcy as banks closed by the hundreds—many of them former President Jackson's pet banks.

President Van Buren called a special session of Congress to deal with the panic and proposed establishing an "independent Treasury," with complete control of government funds. The Treasury would keep all government monies in federal depositories instead of state banks, with one man—a presidential appointee—as treasurer to oversee the public purse without congressional oversight.

Henry Clay and Daniel Webster bounded from their Senate seats in tandem to lead the Whig attack against the scheme, while South Carolina's John C. Calhoun, still smarting from humiliation in the Clay compromise debate, sided with the President.

Clay was appalled, reminding Calhoun that he had recently called the President "the most crafty, most skulking, and one of the meanest . . . beasts of the forest." Clay then added with a smile,

> I do not altogether share with the senator from South Carolina this opinion of the President of the United States. I have always found him, in his manners and deportment, civil, courteous, and

gentlemanly. . . . An acquaintance with him of more than twenty years' duration has inspired me with respect for the man, although I regret to be compelled to say, I detest the magistrate.[30]

Clay recalled how he and Calhoun had united for many years "to restrain the enormous expansion of executive power . . . arrest the progress of corruption . . . rebuke usurpation . . . and drive the Goths and the Vandals from the Capital. I thought we had been contending together for our common country . . . her threatened liberties, her prostrate Constitution. Never did I suppose that personal or party considerations entered into our views."[31]

Clay's assault infuriated Calhoun and provoked one of the most bitter exchanges in Senate history.

"Whatever the senator charges on me," Calhoun responded, "he has actually done! He went over on a memorable occasion." Calhoun's reference to Clay's "corrupt bargain" was unmistakable, and Clay shot to his feet to interrupt.

"If the senator means to allude to the stale and refuted calumny . . . I assure him I can hear it without the slightest emotion, and if he can find any fragment of that rent banner to cover his own aberrations, he is perfectly at liberty to enjoy all the shelter which it affords."

As it happened, former President John Quincy Adams had come from the House to hear Clay speak and had taken a seat beside his former secretary of state. After reminding the Senate that Calhoun had served as vice president for four years under Adams, Clay asserted, "Nor have I, for a single moment regretted the vote I then gave for the eminent gentleman who sits beside me."

Clay paused, apparently holding back tears before turning to address Calhoun personally. "We began our public careers together," he sighed. "We remained together through the war [of 1812] and down to the peace. . . . We concur now in nothing. We separate forever."[32]

Not to be ignored, Daniel Webster interrupted, charging to Clay's defense and asking in disbelief, "Where am I? In the Senate of the United States? . . . Is that John C. Calhoun of South Carolina?"[33]

Webster reminded the Senate—and Calhoun—of the South Carolinian's influence in creating the Bank of the United States in 1816. He then condemned Calhoun for his unseemly public quarrel with Clay.

Calhoun did not let up, however, claiming, "Mr. Clay's American system . . . was the source of all our oppression, disorder, and corruption."[34]

The breakup of the Great Triumvirate was complete, and that of the nation they loved seemed near. After the three men ended their mutual recriminations, Congress voted in favor of the Independent Treasury Act, to take full effect in June 1843.

"Mr. Calhoun," Clay lashed out at his old friend, "will die a traitor or a mad man. His whole aim . . . is to sow the seeds of dissension between the different parts of the Union and . . . prepare the way for its dissolution."[35]

For perhaps the only time in their lives, Henry Clay and Andrew Jackson were in total accord. Asked what act in his administration posterity would "condemn with the greatest severity," the former President replied, "Posterity will condemn me more because I was persuaded not to hang John C. Calhoun as a traitor than for any other act in my life."[36]

The ill will generated by the breakup of the Great Triumvirate poisoned the Capitol atmosphere, provoking angry outbursts by adversaries in both houses. In the House Maine congressman Jonathan Cilley, an ardent Democrat and Van Buren loyalist, assailed James Watson Webb, the Whig editor of the *New York Courier and Enquirer*. Unable to breach the House floor to respond, Webb asked his friend Kentucky congressman William Graves to deliver his written reply to Cilley. When Cilley spurned him, Graves took it as a personal insult and challenged Cilley to a duel and asked his friend Henry Clay to draw up the formal challenge in writing.

Although Clay tried to prevent the encounter, the two representatives, armed with rifles, met on the dueling field across the Anacosta Bridge in Maryland on February 24, 1838, with Graves—a crack shot—killing Cilley.

Clay's enemies—and the widely read *New York Tribune*—charged him with having provoked the duel, and like all such accusations in the press, it took days, often weeks, before a denial appeared in print—if at all. Worse, such charges never disappeared entirely from the public mind. A weary Henry Clay could only protest, saying he had wanted to call the police to prevent the duel, but "I did not know the time and place of the meeting of the two parties."[37]

By mid-winter 1838 the endless barrage of unmerited attacks and the burdens of office were again exacting a heavy toll on Clay, now sixty-one years old. The death of a grandchild, Henry Clay Jr.'s infant daughter, added to his misery.

But Clay remained obsessed with strengthening ties that bound the Union, and he knew he needed enormous authority to do so. So when Kentucky's legislature nominated him for the presidency in the spring of 1838, his hopes and spirits began to revive.

"In regard to my being a candidate for the presidency, if I am to judge from information which daily, almost hourly, reached me," he exulted, "there is everywhere an irresistible current setting in towards me. I believe that if the election were to come on in sixty days, I should be elected by acclamation."[38]

Maryland and Rhode Island soon followed Kentucky's lead, and after Daniel Webster announced he would withdraw from the presidential race in favor of Henry Clay, Clay recovered the high spirits of his earlier days in politics. America seemed ready to seat its greatest statesman in its highest office.

CHAPTER 10

Double Dealing

After Daniel Webster withdrew from presidential contention in early 1839, Boston's influential daily newspaper *Atlas* shocked Henry Clay and other Whigs by declaring for General William Henry Harrison, the unsuccessful candidate against Martin Van Buren in the previous presidential election. New York State's Whig leaders then added to Clay's distress by citing political compromises as having turned him into a political liability as a presidential candidate. Although they agreed he had saved the Union, the benefits of every compromise have political costs, and voters often tend to remember the costs more than the benefits. Few Americans treasured Union as much as he.

"We are divided," proclaimed South Carolina's venerable Judge Henry William de Saussure, who had mentored John C. Calhoun. "The separation of the Union will inevitably follow."[1] And in the North, Massachusetts senator Timothy Pickering, a trusted aide to Washington during the Revolutionary War, had long embraced separation. "In the North, I will rather anticipate a new confederacy," he declared. "The white and black population will mark the boundary."[2]

Even those who favored Union did not necessarily embrace Clay's American System. He won praise, even cheers and financial backing from the nation's wealthiest bankers, merchants, manufacturers, and business leaders, including John Jacob Astor, the multimillionaire fur baron and real estate tycoon. Astor had willingly loaned Henry Clay tens of thousands of dollars for Clay's own land investments.

But the American System was anathema to owners of small banks and businesses as well as southern planters. They saw Clay as the pawn of moneyed interests and feared that a network of interstate roads, canals, and railroads would open their isolated bailiwicks to big, out-of-state competition that would drive them out of business and ease the flight of runaway slaves to freedom. Neither southern slaveholders nor northern abolitionists, therefore, saw preservation of the Union as a reason to modify their political positions; indeed, many saw considerable advantages to North-South separation.

Southerners decried Clay's attack on Calhoun, while northerners were equally vocal in condemning Clay's ownership of slaves and his hope that "our posterity will mingle" with that of South Carolinians "for ages and centuries."[3]

But the darkest political cloud hovering over Henry Clay's road to the presidency had darkened his way since President John Quincy Adams had appointed him US secretary of state. "You cannot escape the malignant attacks of an infatuated enemy," warned a New York supporter. "There are many here in our city . . . who are ever ready to apply the harsh epithets of bribery, corruption, etc., whenever the name of . . . Henry Clay is mentioned."[4]

On February 7, 1839, Clay fixed on a bold move in the Senate. In one of the most dramatic speeches of his career, he stunned all "ultras"—northern and southern—by presenting, of all things, a petition from "several hundred residents of the District of Columbia . . . among them the highly esteemed mayor of the city. They state that they do not desire the abolition of slavery within the district."

In presenting the petition, Clay purposely violated the Gag Rule that banned all petitions that mentioned the word "slavery"— ironically, even those *for* slavery as well as those against.

Insisting he was "no friend of slavery," Clay went on to assail the Gag Rule as an instrument of southern ultras. "It would have been wisest," he argued, "to receive [petitions] and refer them to committee without opposition and report against their object in a calm and dispassionate [way]." The failure of Congress to do so, he charged, had opened the way for abolitionist extremists "to acquire a considerable force" by blending abolition "with a collateral and totally different question . . . that of the right of petition."[5]

Clay then switched his attack by assailing "ultra-abolitionists who are resolved to persevere . . . without regards to any consequences, calamitous as they may be.

> With them, the rights of property are nothing; the deficiency of the powers of the general government is nothing; the acknowledged and incontestable powers of the states are nothing; civil war, a dissolution of the Union, and the overthrow of a government, in which are concentrated the fondest hopes of the civilized world, are nothing. A single idea has taken possession of their minds . . . to manumit forthwith . . . without moral preparation, three million negro slaves. . . . All their leading prints and publications . . . stimulate the rage of the people in the free states against the people in the slave states.[6]

Clay scoffed at abolitionist arguments that Congress had the power to halt the slave trade under the commerce clause.* He called the constitutional power of the commerce clause one of regulation, not prohibition. "It is [a] conservative not destructive . . . regulation

---

*Article I, Section 8, paragraph 2: "The Congress shall have the power . . . To regulate commerce with foreign nations, and among the several states, and with the Indian tribes."

designed to facilitate and accommodate, not to obstruct and incommode the commerce to be regulated.

> No power whatever was granted to the General Government in respect to domestic slavery. All . . . power in regard to the institution of slavery was retained exclusively for the states. . . . Why not leave it to us, as the Constitution of our country has left it, to be dealt with under the guidance of Providence as best we may or can?[7]

Clay called it rash to think of "throwing loose on the community . . . ignorant . . . unprepared . . . untutored slaves." Abolition, he said, raised the danger of "a civil contest which might terminate in the extinction of one race or the other." Rather than abolition and instant manumission, he called for careful deliberation. "What is best to be done for their happiness? . . . how are they to be best governed?

> The slaves are here! No practical scheme for their removal or separation from us has been yet devised, and the true inquiry is what is best to be done with them. . . . In the slave states, the alternative is that the white man must govern the black or the black govern the white. In several of those states, the number of the slaves is greater than the white population. Immediate abolition, as ultra-abolitionists propose . . . would be followed by instantaneous collisions between the two races, which would break out into a civil war that would . . . deluge our country in blood.[8]

Clay asserted his belief in civil liberty but insisted that liberty of slaves was incompatible with the safety and liberty of whites. He called slavery "an exception . . . to the general liberty in the United States" but declared, "We did not originate it nor are we responsible."[9]

Silence engulfed the Senate when Clay ended—almost two hours after he had begun. John C. Calhoun damned Clay with praise for recognizing, at long last, the threat that abolitionists posed to the Union. "His speech is far from being sound," Calhoun commented

29. *Whig presidential candidate Henry Clay seemed on his way to a landslide victory in 1844. "Get out da way," his supporters sang to the tune of* Old Dan Tucker. *(Library of Congress)*

scornfully, "but he has said enough to offend mortally the abolitionists, which will do much to divide the North and consolidate us."[10]

Abolitionists immediately accused Clay of having switched sides on the slavery issue and having made another "corrupt bargain"—this time with Calhoun. "Is it to be inferred from these expressions," Massachusetts governor Edward Everett asked Daniel Webster, "that there is a political understanding between Messrs. Calhoun and Clay and that the South is to be consolidated in favor of the latter as a presidential candidate?"[11]

When South Carolina senator William Preston warned Clay that the speech would offend both North and South and hurt his chances

in the presidential election, Clay responded with one of the most pre-
scient replies of his life—indeed, in the history of presidential politics:

"I had rather be right than be President."[12]

To try to prove he could be both, sixty-two-year-old Henry Clay
set out on a grueling campaign tour across the Northeast, preaching
moderation and compromise and describing his vision of a united,
prosperous nation. It turned into one of the most triumphant political tours in American history, as cheering crowds hailed the "Great
Pacificator" for saving the Union.

"The farmer and the mechanic, the merchant and the manufacturer acknowledge their indebtedness to your wise and fostering coun-
sels for the prosperity of their pursuits," wrote the chairman of the
Young Whig Men of New York, who promised "spontaneous accla-
mations . . . wherever you go."[13]

Accompanied by his twenty-one-year-old son James Brown, he
traveled through Ohio to Cleveland and across Lake Erie to Buffalo
and Niagara Falls. From western New York he traveled eastward
across the state to Rochester and Syracuse, then on the Erie Canal
to the Hudson Valley. "Enthusiastic demonstrations" and "vast con-
courses of people" greeted and embraced him at every stop and even
along the roads as he passed.

"I escaped to the [Canadian] Provinces," he wrote to a friend to
describe a brief vacation in Montreal and Quebec.[14]

Resuming his campaign in Vermont, he encountered his first de-
tractors, largely New England church-goers who disdained Clay's
worldliness and his reputation for gambling and easy ways with
women. "There is something of the Puritan spirit left in us," Vermont's representative Isaac Fletcher grumbled to his fellow Democrat, Tennessee governor James Polk. "We revere Christianity and
hold in high respect the moral values. . . . The bearing of the man is
reckless, his moral influence is bad. His manners and conversations
are those of a man who neither fears God or regards man."[15]

Others, however, saw him in a different light and listened in awe:
"What an orator he was," wrote Lewis Garrard Clarke, an escaped

Kentucky slave who became a leader of the Liberty Party and, later, some believe, the model for the character George Harris, Eliza's husband in Harriet Beecher Stowe's *Uncle Tom's Cabin*.[16]

"He commenced amidst the most breathless silence," Clarke effused about Clay, "looked around as if he were in an assembly of personal friends . . . tall, erect as a statue. . . . Such a voice I never heard . . . there was not a look of his eye, not a movement of his long, graceful right arm, not a swaying of his body that was not full of grace and effect."[17] According to New York governor William H. Seward, even avowed abolitionists "came to him confessing their preference for and devotion to him."[18]

Clay kept his speeches to about thirty minutes each, apparently tiring of repeating the same points so often. He asked one crowd whether they really wanted him to repeat his well-known political views. When they shouted a collective "No," he regaled them with humorous stories that left them embracing him as they laughed through their tears.

In one speech he recalled having returned to America after signing the Treaty of Ghent and meeting "an odd old fellow" in Kentucky reading the treaty aloud to neighbors. One of them asked the meaning of the phrase "sine qua non." Knowing no Latin, the stubborn old man plowed ahead without missing a beat: "Why, Sine Qua Non is three islands in Passamaquoddy Bay . . . And Henry Clay is the last man to give them up! 'No Sine, Qua, Non, no treaty!' Clay told them, and he'll stick to it!"

As crowds roared at his humor, Clay turned to a question-and-answer format in which his quick-witted responses drew a combination of laughter, applause, and love, which only grew as he continued south, first to Saratoga, New York, then to Troy and across the Hudson River to Albany. Ladies crowded onto balconies of private homes and public buildings to wave, threw flowers on his carriage—and swooned.[19] One historian called it "a conqueror's voyage of triumph."[20]

And it was. Henry Clay was the clear choice of the American people for President of the United States. The press called Clay America's most popular political figure by far. The "Great Pacificator, whose

30. *Whig campaign badge worn by supporters of Henry Clay's candidacy for the presidency. Uncontestably the most popular of the candidates, he nonetheless lost three runs for the presidency. Seen in the lower portrait of the badge is Clay's running mate New Jersey Senator Theodore Frelinghuysen. (Library of Congress)*

praise is now on the lips of every American of every party," was the only political leader capable of uniting the nation.[21]

When Clay set sail south on the Hudson River from Albany, crowds stood cheering on river banks and on the docks at Kingston, Poughkeepsie, Newburgh, and, finally, New York City. New York gave him the grandest reception since Lafayette's visit in 1824, with thousands showering him with flower petals from every window as he rode up Broadway.

And after New York it was more of the same in Baltimore and Washington. A trip through Virginia followed, with a stop at his boyhood home in Hanover County.

"Everything has changed," he told his wife later.

> If I had been put there without information, I should not have been able to recognize it. The spot in which my father and maternal grandmother and grandfather were buried were marked by no stone, and a crop of wheat was growing over their remains. . . . The old dwelling house was still standing, but much altered, and [I recognized] the room in which I was born.[22]

He drew "the most marked and approbatory responses," according to one newspaper, with a "playful allusion" emphasizing his need for rest in the "dominion of the virgin queen . . . as a means of temporary relief."[23]

While ordinary citizens rocked with laughter at Clay's witticisms, some political leaders were less amused, and Clay sensed it. In a letter to his friend, Whig senator Oliver H. Smith of Indiana, he asked, "I am desirous to obtain as accurate information as may be practicable in respect to the probable course . . . in the approaching presidential election." Clay assured his friend, "I can hear accounts unfavorable to myself with as much composure, if not with as much pleasure, as those of an opposite character."[24]

A flow of obsequious letters from Whig Party leaders had actually unnerved him. "Your election would to no man in the Union be more gratifying than to me," New York governor William H. Seward assured him. And General Harrison, the Whig candidate for President four years earlier, all but damned him with praise. "I can only say that my present position as it regards yourself is distressing and embarrassing," the old general wrote to Clay.

A few years ago I could not have believed in the possibility of my being placed in a position of apparent rivalry to you. Particularly in relation to the presidency, an office which I never dreamed of attaining and which I had ardently desired to see you occupy. I confess that I did covet the second [that of vice president] but never the first office. . . . Fate, as Bonaparte would say, has placed me where I am and I wait the result which time will determine with as little anxiety as anyone ever felt.[25]

But it was a letter from Virginia senator John Tyler that most confused him. A former governor of Virginia, Tyler owned a 1,200-acre plantation worked by hundreds of slaves. A staunch southern Democrat, he had broken with Jackson over Jackson's nullification proclamation and joined the Whigs to censure Jackson over closure of the Bank of the United States. Hardly a Whig at heart, Tyler was well aware of Clay's open scorn for the Jeffersonian "compact" theory of government. He nonetheless sent Clay what appeared to be an ultimatum: "I have never heard you do other than declare that the [federal] government was the creature of the States," Tyler wrote, and that the Constitution was "a compact among equals."

Tyler expressed "great solicitude . . . for your elevation to the Presidency" but pulled up short of openly endorsing Clay with a curiously mixed message: "I have but just returned from the North," he warned, "where I was sorry to find so many opposite opinions prevailing. . . . I should regard your election as certain if in accepting the nomination you would emphatically declare your determination to serve but a single term."[26]

Although Clay did not know it, both Tyler and Seward had met with Thurlow Weed, a Rochester, New York, newspaper publisher who had helped found the Anti-Masonic Party a decade earlier. Pledged to stripping Freemasons of their grip on national political affairs, Weed assailed secret Masonic rituals as a danger to American democracy, and his *Rochester Telegraph* championed Jacksonian populism and egalitarianism. He founded the Anti-Masonic *Inquirer* to support the Anti-Masonic Party in the 1828 elections and helped elect fifteen anti-Masonic candidates to the New York Assembly.

By 1832 Weed's Anti-Masonic Party claimed forty-six members of the New York Assembly and fifty-five in the Pennsylvania Assembly. After it failed to influence the 1836 presidential elections, it established ties to the Whigs. Weed emerged as Whig party boss in New York State and propelled Seward to the gubernatorial election victory of 1838. Weed not only despised Clay for his Masonic affiliation but also feared Clay's independent political stance and recognized that as a political boss, he would have little influence in a Clay White House.

Far from seeking national reconciliation and unity, Weed, Seward, and Tyler saw disunion and separation of North and South as a peaceful solution to the national conflict over slavery and state sovereignty. All three considered Clay a political liability, given his efforts to reconcile the two regions. Even as Weed plotted Clay's defeat, he nonetheless deluged Clay with smiles when they met and proclaimed his "warm" support. He called Clay his "personal preference" over all other Whig candidates.

Besides Weed, Seward, and Tyler, Pennsylvania senator Thaddeus Stevens was also plotting Clay's defeat. A lawyer and successful business leader, the sour-faced Stevens had also been a fierce Anti-Masonic Party leader and quite open about his dislike of Clay. So when the nation's Whigs convened in Harrisburg to nominate their candidate for the presidency, Stevens called anti-Clay forces together—Weed and Seward from New York, Tyler from Virginia, and so forth—and developed a scheme to block Clay's nomination. With most Americans blaming Van Buren for the economic collapse, the Whigs believed victory a certainty, and the Stevens-Weed bloc wanted a man in the White House whom they could control—they knew no one could "control" Clay but Clay. Sixty-four-year-old General William Henry Harrison, however, was less set in his political views and had come close to defeating Van Buren in the previous election.

Although Harrison was governor of Ohio, he had been born in Virginia and, before moving to Ohio, had served as governor of the Indiana Territory, where he had advocated the introduction of slavery to stimulate the farm economy. His embrace of slavery would appeal to southern voters, while his heroism slaying the legendary Shawnee chief Tecumseh in the Battle of Tippecanoe made him a hero to Americans in the North and West. He was a perfect presidential candidate.

Before the convention began balloting, Stevens implemented a parliamentary subterfuge that Clay himself had used nearly four decades earlier as Speaker to gain control of the House of Representatives. While overconfident Clay supporters spent evenings prematurely toasting their man's expected victory, Stevens filled seats of key committees with political allies who rewrote convention rules. They gave each state only one vote, based on the majority's choice in each delegation. Later called the "unit rule," it changed voting procedures and caught Clay supporters unaware. Missouri senator Thomas Hart Benton called the rule "a model contrivance of the few to govern the many"—a combination of "algebra and alchemy . . . and the quotient was political death to Mr. Clay."[27]

Angry but helpless to reverse it, Clay's men could only watch as balloting got under way. Before they realized what had happened, Clay's certain victory began to slip away. After the first ballot Clay had captured twelve states—a majority, but not a large enough majority to win the nomination. Harrison had six states, and General Winfield Scott, a hero of the War of 1812, won three. In fact, Stevens and Weed had rigged the voting, directing three state delegations they controlled to vote for Scott on the first ballot and give the proceedings the appearance of an open convention. As the comedy continued, the Scott delegates switched to Harrison, giving Harrison the lead on the second ballot and victory on the third. To win Virginia and other southern states in the general election, Weed and Stevens chose the slaveholder Tyler as their vice presidential candidate to run with Harrison—the same Tyler who had previously expressed "great solicitude" for Clay's election as President.

"Double dealing and treachery accomplished the result the intriguers had been for months laying the plans to effect," Senator Benton bristled.[28]

Right or wrong, Clay's speech advocating a middle-ground compromise on abolition had cost him dearly. As South Carolina senator Preston had warned, both North and South had misunderstood his words, with abolitionists convinced he embraced slavery and slaveholders just as convinced he embraced emancipation. Clay's political enemies bent the meanings of his phrases to sustain arguments against him. As a result, they blocked the nomination and all-but-certain election to the presidency of the one man in the nation who could preserve the Union and avoid civil war.

Fearing he might run as an independent candidate, Clay's political enemies continued attacking him after the convention, charging him with having reacted to defeat with insane tantrums. In fact, he accepted defeat with grace.

"You will have heard of the event in Harrisburg," he wrote to his son Henry Clay Jr. after returning to Washington. "It fell upon us all here with great surprise," he admitted, but "acquiescence . . . was the only course of honor, good faith, and duty. I have accordingly both publicly and privately expressed my determination to abide by and support the nomination. I shall be glad if you and my other connections shall come to the same conclusion."[29]

At a dinner for delegates later Clay rose to speak, praising them for having "traveled the length and breadth of the land in the public service" and calling, as always, for them to support the Union:

> If I have friends connected with me by ties of blood, by my regards of friendship—if I have anyone that loves me—I assure them that they cannot do me a better service than to follow my example and vote heartily, as I shall, for the nomination which has been made.

The audience interrupted him, rose to its feet as one, and exploded in thunderous applause and cheers.

"Talk not of sacrifice," he called out above the roar. "What is a public man worth to the country . . . if he is not always ready to sacrifice for his country?

> There has been no sacrifice. We have not been contending for Henry Clay, for William Henry Harrison . . . for Winfield Scott. . . . No, we have been contending for principles. . . . Look not then to Harrisburg but to the White House—not to the nomination but to the mountain of corruption which it is designed to overcome. . . . Go home then, gentlemen of the convention . . . tell your constituents . . . to put forth all the energies they possess to relieve the land from the curse which rests upon it.[30]

Although Clay returned to the Senate, the campaign had left him discouraged. "No veteran soldier covered with scars and wounds inflicted in many battles and hard campaigns ever received his discharge with more pleasure than I should mine," he confessed. "But I think that, like him, without presumption, I am entitled to an honorable discharge."[31]

In addition to his undeserved defeat at the Whig convention, Clay faced painful personal setbacks. Princeton had dismissed his youngest son, John Morrison. The boy had left campus without permission and gone on excursions to New York and elsewhere and had all but abandoned his studies. Meanwhile Clay's next youngest son, James Brown, who had abandoned his studies, had failed in a commercial enterprise in Missouri and returned home to Lexington. And then Henry and Lucretia Clay suffered another crushing blow: Henry Clay Jr.'s wife, Julia, died of a massive hemorrhage after giving birth to their second son, Thomas Julian Clay. In disclosing his loss, Clay's son frightened his father by implying that he, Henry Clay Jr., might choose, by his own hand, to follow his wife and dead sister Anne to the grave.

"My dear son," Clay wrote hurriedly to his disconsolate son. "The death of your dear wife, my poor daughter Julia . . . overwhelmed me with sorrow and grief. . . .

> I do condole and sympathize with you from the bottom of my soul. But I hope you will not forget that she has left you tender and responsible duties to perform towards the children of your mutual love and affection. These will require all your care. . . . During the short remnant of my life, I too shall need your kindness and affectionate attention. I beg therefore, on my account, as well as that of my dear Grandchildren you will take care of yourself.[32]

Clay then wrote to his wife, telling her of his fears for their son and of his reply: "Henry writes in terms of the greatest grief and seems to be overwhelmed. Poor fellow. His life has not been long, but he has had his full share of misfortune. I have told him of the duties and responsibilities to the sweet little children Julia has left him. I have not failed, my dear Wife, to think of the addition to your cares and responsibilities which this sad event may occasion."[33]

Within a few weeks Clay's personal and political disappointments combined with a series of winter illnesses to overwhelm him.

"I am not well," he wrote to his wife. "I am sincerely and unaffectedly tired of remaining here and wish to God that I was with you at home." He still hoped to save the Union, however, and added, "I should be glad to be spared a few years longer until I see the country through its difficulties and get over my own. But that depends on the will and goodness of Providence."[34]

The warm Washington spring helped Clay recover his health, and the ever-present, albeit aging showman in him accepted a series of invitations to stump for the Harrison-Tyler Whig ticket. Already thinking of the 1844 elections, he realized that only by showing himself a loyal party supporter would he win the party's loyal support in the years ahead. "Clay is truly a noble fellow," conceded Thurlow Weed, who had engineered Clay's defeat at the Whig convention. And William Henry Harrison wrote Clay a warm letter of "gratitude . . . for the magnanimity of your conduct towards me. . . . I must beg you to believe that I shall highly appreciate any advice or suggestions you may think proper to give."[35]

As the election campaign got under way, a Democratic newspaper mocked Harrison with a cartoon depicting him as a log-cabin yokel swilling hard cider from a barrel. Clever Whig managers converted the negative caricature into a positive portrait, with a slogan of a common man's success. Already hailed as the hero of the Battle of Tippecanoe, Harrison now became America's "Log Cabin–Hard Cider" candidate. *New York Tribune* editor Horace Greeley designed and edited a campaign newspaper—*The Log Cabin*—that reached 90,000 subscribers, and the *Baltimore Republican* ennobled Harrison's humble origins in poetry that mocked President Martin (Mat) Van Buren, as eating off gilded plates in the White House:

> Old Tip he wears a homespun suit,
> He has no ruffled shirt,
> But Mat he has a golden plate
> And he's a little squirt.[36]

Whigs everywhere chanted the euphonious slogan "Tippecanoe and Tyler Too"; Clay and Daniel Webster and other Whig leaders patched up differences and appeared together, extolling the nation's future under the new Whig government: an end to the "independent treasury," restoration of the Bank of the United States, implementation of the American System, and other Whig programs to enrich Americans and America.

"Tippecanoe and Tyler Too" won nineteen of twenty-six states in the general election, accumulating 234 electoral votes to Van Buren's 60. The Whigs won control of both houses of Congress. And after the results were in, Harrison made a pilgrimage to Ashland. Despite his humiliation at Harrisburg, Clay had campaigned hard for

Harrison, and the Whigs and restored his national leadership role. Harrison sought to reward Clay by traveling to Lexington and asking him to be secretary of state in the new administration. Clay was not foolish—or egotistical—enough to make the same mistake twice in a lifetime, and he refused, allowing Harrison to name Daniel Webster to the post and leave Clay free to transform the Whig program into legislation as de facto majority leader in the Senate.

On March 4 William Henry Harrison took his oath as ninth President of the United States. He named his cabinet the following day, appointing Clay loyalists to four of its six posts. Only Secretary of State Daniel Webster and Attorney General Francis Granger were independent of Clay's influence.

The President all but barred Vice President Tyler, the former Democrat, from the White House. With no one in government interested in a word he had to say, Tyler quit the capital and returned to his Virginia plantation to oversee his slaves and sulk.

On March 15 Congress recessed, and three weeks later, on April 4, 1840—a month after he had assumed the presidency—William Henry Harrison died of pneumonia.

For the first time in American history a man who had not been elected President seized the reins of national power. Even more threatening to Union, the man who now held those reins was a southern slaveholder and avowed nullifier.

In an effort to restrict Tyler's powers, the cabinet urged him to govern by committee with the cabinet, retaining his title of vice president and adding the subtitle "acting President." Infuriated by their presumption, Tyler rejected the plea and invited the cabinet to resign or try to stage a palace revolt if they dared.

CHAPTER 11

Get Out Da Way!

In the absence of Daniel Webster, Henry Clay returned to the Senate as de facto majority leader in May 1841 and immediately dictated the legislative program he expected Whigs in both houses to enact: among other bills, repeal of the Independent Treasury Act, reestablishment of a Bank of the United States, tariff increases from 20 to 30 percent to restore government revenues and reserves, and, after restoring fiscal order, some spending on internal improvements.

By mid-August Congress had repealed the Independent Treasury Act and restored the Bank of the United States under a new name—the Fiscal Bank of the United States.

In his first message to Congress President Tyler proclaimed his wholehearted respect for the wishes of Congress as representatives of "We the People" but returned to the White House and immediately contradicted himself by vetoing the bank bill. All but scoffing at a twenty-year-old Supreme Court decision to the contrary, he called the bank unconstitutional, knowing that Clay's Whigs lacked the two-thirds majority needed to override his veto.

31. President John Tyler, the first American President not elected to office, was a Virginia plantation owner who owned slaves and defended slavery as a perfectly proper American institution. (Library of Congress)

Clay went to the White House to confront the President. To Clay's amazement, the usually courtly Tyler grew angry and ordered Clay out: "Go you now, Mr. Clay, to your end of the avenue, where stands the Capitol, and there perform your duty to the country as you shall think proper. So help me God, I shall do mine at this end of it as I shall think proper."[1]

Clay did as he was told and returned to the Capitol to help write a new, revised bill, clearing every clause with the President and incorporating his suggested changes.

Again Tyler astonished Congress—and, indeed, the nation—by vetoing the bill that he had helped write.

Infuriated by his betrayal of the Whigs, every member of his cabinet, save Webster, resigned in September, with all but Webster issuing statements describing the President's duplicity.

"That the second [bank bill] charter was prepared according to his wishes and that he pledged to approve cannot be now controverted," Clay raged. "How is he to be justified for his breach of good faith?"

Webster was as astonished as the rest of the cabinet by the President's actions, but he was uncertain whether he could win back his Senate seat, given his association with a President who had blocked restoration of a central bank devoted to national economic recovery.

"Where am I to go, Mr. President?" Webster is said to have asked Tyler after the rest of the cabinet had quit. Told to decide for himself, Webster replied, "If you leave it to me, Mr. President, I will stay where I am."

"Give me your hand on that," the President told Webster, "and I will now say to you that Henry Clay is a doomed man from this hour."[2]

Clay called Tyler's rejection of the Whig program tantamount to treason, and as Tyler's cabinet members had done, he decided to quit government and leave the Senate at the end of his term. "An army which believes itself betrayed by its commander in chief," he explained to Francis T. Brooke, "will never fight well under him or whilst he remains in authority."[3]

Clay nonetheless attempted to push as many remnants of the Whig program through Congress as he could—and scored a few successes. Congress passed a bankruptcy bill that allowed debtors to make voluntary declarations of bankruptcy, and it passed a remarkable land bill that gave squatters living on federal government land the right to purchase up to 160 acres for $1.25 an acre. The buyer had to be a citizen over twenty-one, head of a household or a widower, and have lived on the land for at least fourteen months and be working to improve it. In Clay's mind the Union gained strength as each citizen obtained economic stability by acquiring property—and the voting rights that came with it. To Clay's surprise and delight, the President signed both bills—perhaps to silence so-called bank ruffians who paraded outside the White House night and day shouting "Bank!" "Bank!" "Bank!"

Tyler's rejection of the two bank bills doomed passage of Clay's broad economic program. Indeed, Tyler announced his intention to veto almost any bill the "Clay Congress" passed as long as he remained President. He called his veto the only way to preserve "the independence of the executive" and "good of the country."

"I am abused in Congress and out, as man never was before," the President railed in defense of his views, "assailed as a traitor and threatened with impeachment. But let it pass. Other attempts are to be made to head me, and we shall see how they will succeed."[4]

A mysterious illness felled Clay at the end of 1841 and confined him to bed for a week with a painful, undiagnosed facial swelling. As usual, he unburdened himself to his favorite son: "The [government] Treasury is empty, with very little prospect of being speedily filled," he lamented to Henry Clay Jr. "I have never witnessed such a state of affairs."[5]

And to retired New York congressman Peter B. Porter, Clay fretted, "All is confusion, chaos and disorder here. No system! No concert of action! No prospect of union and harmony!

> This discouraging state of things I believe attributable to the President, who yet shows no disposition to change his fatal course. . . . Our bleeding country is the sufferer. I sometimes think that an awful crisis is nigh at hand. Most certainly the existing state of things anywhere but in the United States would lead to civil commotion.[6]

Clay condemned Tyler's use of the "miserable despotic veto power," and when he recovered enough to return to the Senate, he moved—unsuccessfully—for a constitutional amendment to limit it. He believed his only hope for saving his economic program—and the Union—lay in rallying Whigs across the nation behind his own candidacy and wresting the presidency from Tyler in 1844.

"There does not exist the remotest prospects of any reconciliation between Mr. Tyler and the Whigs," Clay concluded.[7] He said the President's aim was now "the formation of a third party, with a view to his own aggrandizement." Clay accused Secretary of State Daniel Webster of having "exerted much pernicious influence with him . . . plied him with flattery and held out to him vain hopes of another election. He must soon see the error of his course if he be not blind to madness."[8]

The midterm congressional elections saw voters—apparently bent on disunion—reject Clay and the Whigs in favor of the President. The Whigs lost control of the Senate—and Clay his role as majority leader. In February 1842, with his sixty-fifth birthday a few weeks away, Henry Clay resigned from the Senate to begin another presidential campaign. In his farewell speech to the Senate he repeated "a declaration I made thirty years ago . . . that I have been actuated by no personal motives . . . have sought no personal aggrandizement. I have had an eye, a single eye, a heart, a single heart, ever devoted to what appeared to be the best interests of the country.

> But I have not been unsustained during this long course of public service. . . . If I have difficulty in giving utterance to . . . the feelings of gratitude which fill my heart towards my friends, dispersed throughout this continent, what shall I say, what can I say at all commensurate with my feelings of gratitude towards that state whose humble servitor I am?[9]

With that, according to witnesses, "Mr. Clay's feelings overwhelmed him, and he proceeded with . . . difficult utterances."[10]

After composing himself, Clay thanked the "warm-hearted and enthusiastic and devoted friends who knew me and appreciated justly the motives by which I have been actuated."

"But the ingenuity of my assailants is never exhausted," he smiled broadly. "It seems I have subjected myself to a new epithet, which I do not know whether to take in honor or derogations. I am held up to the country as a dictator.

"Dictator!" he cried out.

If I have been a dictator, I think those who apply the epithet must at least admit two things . . . my dictatorship has been distinguished by no cruel executions . . . no deeds of blood . . . and that I have at least voluntarily surrendered the post within a shorter period than was assigned by the Roman laws for its continuance.[11]

Clay admitted that his nature was "warm" and "ardent" but said that those who saw his conduct as being dictatorial had mistaken ardor "for what I supposed to be patriotic exertions" on behalf of those who elected him to his seat. Clay then introduced his successor, former Kentucky congressman John J. Crittenden, who had been William Henry Harrison's attorney general but had resigned rather than serve under Tyler.

Clay concluded his Senate farewell with "fervent wishes that all the great and patriotic objects for which it [the Senate] was instituted may be accomplished—that the destiny designed for it by the framers of the Constitution may be fulfilled.

May the blessing of Heaven rest upon the heads of the whole Senate and every member of it; and may every member of it advance still more in fame, and when they shall retire to the bosom of their constituencies, may they all meet there that most joyous and grateful of all human rewards, the exclamation of their countrymen: 'Well done, thou good and faithful servants.' Mr. President and Messieurs Senators, I bid you one and all a long, a last, a friendly farewell.[12]

Few in the chamber could control their tears. Senators of every political color took their turns embracing him in the stillness that followed his valedictory. Only John Calhoun of South Carolina stood apart and aloof, and Clay approached him. They had known each other for more than three decades, and without a word, they set aside their differences and embraced. "It was something like the soul quitting the body," said John Crittenden.[13]

Clay spent the next month in Washington organizing his papers, then set out on a cross-country tour aimed at locking up the Whig nomination for the presidency in advance of any convention. Town after town welcomed him with banquets, festivals, and other opportunities to speak on the American System, on tariff protection for American goods, and on broader distribution of lands. "Clay Clubs" in every town sought his presence, including one in Springfield, Illinois, whose executive committee included thirty-three-year-old attorney Abraham Lincoln, now a member of the state legislature.

At the time Lincoln was wooing Mary Todd, a Lexington, Kentucky, beauty whose parents were close friends of the Clays. Mary had known the Clays when she was a child. At thirteen she had galloped to Ashland to show the Clays the white pony her father had bought her. When Henry Clay emerged from the house, Mary "touched the pony with a whip and up he went gracefully on his hind legs." After explaining that her father had bought the animal from strolling players, the delighted statesman lifted Mary off her pony and announced, "You're just in time for dinner."[14]

After Mary's older sister married a man from Springfield, Illinois, and went there to live, Mary went for an extended visit, during which she met and fell in love with the young lawyer Abraham Lincoln. He became an active Whig and devoted member of the local Clay Club.

"Dear Sir," Lincoln wrote to his wife's friend Henry Clay,

> Although we cannot but believe you would be highly gratified with . . . a visit to the prairie-land, the pleasure it would give us and thousands such as we is beyond question. You have never visited Illinois . . . and should you now yield to our request, we promise you such a reception as shall be worthy of the man on whom are turned the fondest hopes of a great and suffering nation.[15]

Henry Clay spent the summer of 1842 working his farm and reopening his law office in Lexington. Although he planned to tour

Ohio and Indiana in the fall, he turned down Lincoln's invitation to cross into Illinois.

Clay had no sooner returned to Ashland when Mexican troops invaded Texas, and in Clay's absence President Tyler talked triumphantly of annexing Texas to the United States. Mexico, however, warned that annexation would mean war, and the White house retreated, realizing that the abolitionist North would refuse to support such a war.

When Clay embarked on his campaign in the fall of 1842, abolitionists confronted him at every stop. A Quaker millwright and abolitionist Hiram Mendenhall presented him with a petition in Richmond, Indiana, a largely Quaker community midway up the state along the Ohio border. Citing the Declaration of Independence, Mendenhall's petition asked Clay, as a "patriot, philanthropist, and Christian to . . . let the oppressed under your control, who call you 'master,' go free."[16]

If Mendenhall's petition caught Clay by surprise, Clay didn't show it. Few things ever caught Henry Clay by surprise except death.

"I assure my fellow citizens," he replied with grace, "the petition has not excited one disagreeable emotion. I prefer that it should be done in the face of this vast assemblage." In one of the most important speeches of his life, Henry Clay offered a defining examination of American slavery and proposed a compromise between continued subjugation of blacks and summary abolition—a compromise he believed essential to the Union's survival.

First, however, he scolded Mendenhall for his rudeness in "presenting a petition to me . . . like yourself a private citizen . . . a total stranger passing through your state . . . advanced in years. Neither myself nor my place of residence is unknown to the world. You might at any time during these last twenty-five or thirty years have presented your petition to me at Ashland."

Clay paused, then shot a friendly smile at Mendenhall and added, "If you had, you should have been received and treated . . . with liberal hospitality."

After the laughter subsided, Clay asked, "Now, Mr. Mendenhall. Let us reverse conditions." As the crowd listened in silence, Clay asked how Mendenhall would feel if he, Clay, showed up with a petition "to you to relinquish your farm or other property. Would you have thought it courteous?" Clay acknowledged that opponents of slavery denied the status of slaves as property, "but the law of my state and other states has otherwise ordained . . . and unless you can show some authority to nullify our laws, we must continue to respect them."

Clay then recognized the basis of Mendenhall's appeal as the pronouncement in the Declaration of Independence "that all men are created equal," but he called it an abstract principle and argued that "there had never been nor would there ever be a society in which all men are equal." He cited "women, minors, the insane, transient sojourners and others who remained subject to the government of another portion of the community." Few of the Founders, he added, would have signed the Declaration of Independence if they thought that the new government seriously intended promulgating a doctrine of equality of man.

"Never!" he called out. "Never!

> I know the predominant sentiment in the free states is adverse to slavery. . . . I look upon it as a great evil and deeply lament that we have derived it . . . from our ancestors. I wish every slave in the United States were in the country of his ancestors. But here they are and the question is how they can best be dealt with. . . . In my opinion, the evils of slavery are . . . nothing in comparison with the far greater evils . . . from a sudden . . . indiscriminate emancipation. . . . Does any man suppose that they would become blended into one homogeneous mass? Does any man recommend amalgamation? . . . No human law could enforce a union between the two races.[17]

He predicted that immediate, universal emancipation or abolition would produce slaughter. A struggle for political ascendency would follow emancipation, with blacks seeking to acquire power and whites seeking to retain it. "A contest would inevitably ensue between the two races—civil war, carnage, conflagration, devastation. . . . Nothing is more certain.

"I believe that gradual emancipation [is] the only method of liberation that has ever been thought safe or wise."[18]

Clay then turned to the question of his own slaves. Clay told Mendenhall he owned about fifty slaves, together worth $15,000. "But," he cautioned, "some half dozen of them, from age, decrepitude, or infirmity, are wholly unable to gain a livelihood, and are a heavy charge upon me.

"Do you think," he mocked Mendenhall's petition, "that I should conform to the dictates of humanity by ridding myself of that charge and sending them forth into the world with the boon of liberty to end a wretched existence in starvation?

"Another class," Clay went on, "is composed of helpless infants, with or without improvident mothers. Do you believe as a Christian, that I should perform my duty toward them by abandoning them to their fate?

"Mr. Mendenhall!" Clay called out, staring his Quaker questioner in the eyes,

> Go home and mind your own business and leave other people to take care of theirs! Limit your benevolent exertions to your own neighborhood. Within that circle you will find enough scope for the exercise of all your charities. Dry up the tears of the afflicted widows . . . console and comfort the helpless orphan, clothe the naked, and feed and help the poor, black and white, who need succor, and you will be a better and wiser man than you have this day shown yourself.[19]

It was a dangerous speech in the heart of abolitionist country, but Clay hoped to expose emancipation as far more complex than most of his audience had imagined, and many—those who listened carefully—applauded his thoughtful response and his willingness to share his thinking with them. Ultra-abolitionists misunderstood, however, all but ignoring his assertion that he saw slavery "as a great evil" and that "if a state of nature existed and we were about to lay the foundations of society, no man would be more strongly opposed than I should be to incorporating the institution of slavery among its elements."[20]

Years later, when campaigning in Illinois for the Senate seat held by Senator Stephen Douglas, Abraham Lincoln denied favoring abrupt emancipation where it existed but, citing Henry Clay, instead demanded that it be barred in lands where it did not exist.

> When Mr. Clay says that in laying the foundation of societies in our territories where it [slavery] does not exist, he would be opposed to the introduction of slavery. . . . I insist that we have . . . his license for insisting upon the exclusion of that element, which he declared in such strong and emphatic language was most hateful to him.[21]

Incorporating parts of his reply to Mendenhall in his other speeches, Henry Clay continued touring Indiana and Ohio until the onset of winter.

In Indianapolis he clarified the legislation he would seek if elected President, listing these key elements: federal government spending cuts to balance the budget; reestablishment of the Bank of the United States; creation of a single, uniform currency across the nation; selective tariff protection for American industry; distribution of proceeds from the sale of public lands to state governments; federal government projects to build and improve harbors and national roads; restricted presidential veto powers; and a single-term limit for the President.[22]

Clay spent the winter of 1842–1843 in New Orleans, far from Kentucky's debilitating cold. He had taken the boat from Louisville down the Ohio and Mississippi Rivers, with stops at Vicksburg and Natchez. "At all the principal places of stopping, crowds assembled around the boat and the wharves to greet and welcome my arrival," he wrote to Lucretia, who had stayed in Ashland to care for their grandchildren. He said he found the economic depression evident in every area of business life "and reduction of prices of everything greater than I anticipated."

Although Clay spent most of his time in New Orleans relaxing, he did try to win contracts for the family's expanding enterprises. He had bankrolled the purchase near Ashland of a hemp farm and rope-production facility for his son Thomas Hart Clay, by then a recovering alcoholic. "Owing to the low prices of cotton, the low price of bagging and rope and the uncertainty of the future," Clay explained with regret, "I shall not be able to make any contracts."

He was more successful selling his wife's prized hams, which, at twelve and a half cents a pound, commanded a premium of about two cents above the average price of ham but nonetheless found great acceptance because of their exceptional flavor. As with so many of his letters to her, he signed it, "God bless you, my dear Wife. Give my love to all our children and grandchildren."[23]

Clay maintained a steady correspondence with his Senate replacement John J. Crittenden, a loyal, longtime supporter. "How do you find the Whig senators?" he asked in one letter. "Is there any want of fidelity among them?"[24]

As winter's end approached, Clay began the long journey home, stopping to campaign before cheering crowds in Baton Rouge, Mobile, and Memphis. "The papers have not exaggerated the enthusiasm of my reception everywhere," he wrote Crittenden, "and I find a good and confident feeling prevailing with the Whigs."[25]

Clay evidently misinterpreted the good will of his audiences, however. He lived in an era when speeches were the main form of mass entertainment—for many the only form. Americans packed churches to hear Sunday sermons—believers and nonbelievers alike—and they thronged to hear Fourth of July orations on village and town squares across the nation. Election campaigns, more than any other events, provided a carnival-like atmosphere, as candidate after candidate marched through town, often with bands playing, sometimes with a fireworks display, and always with a supporting claque to whoop and holler, stir crowd emotions, and quench listener thirst with free drinks. The practice dated back to the colonial era, when Colonel George Washington campaigned for a seat in Virginia's House of Burgesses by drenching election-day voters with forty gallons of rum, twenty-six gallons of rum punch, and forty-three gallons of beer—an average of a half-gallon of spirits per voter.

Campaign speeches were enormously popular, and Clay's more so. He was the consummate actor/entertainer, his voice rising and falling and his arms flailing, waving, pointing, and gesturing. His oratorical gifts matched Patrick Henry's, singling out "that intelligent looking man over there," "that lovely lady here," and "those beautiful children over there—like my own" as he dabbed a tear. Gales of laughter inevitably followed when he began a tale, "You know, this reminds me of the time . . . " To hear Henry Clay speak was a once-in-a-lifetime experience that Americans related to their children and grandchildren.

But it did not mean they would vote for him.

After he returned to Lexington he resumed practicing law there—until a $40,000 loan from John Jacob Astor put his finances in order and allowed his return to the presidential campaign.

Clay set off on a tour of the Southeast to complement his tour of the Southwest. As he had hoped, thousands hailed his arrival; bands played, and high officials praised him in every town and village. Alabama, Georgia, and South Carolina adored Henry Clay, called him their next President. Into North Carolina he ventured, stopping in Raleigh for one of the most rousing welcomes any town in America had ever given a celebrity visitor. The governor greeted him and ignited a spectacular shower of fireworks that illuminated every corner of town. He then led Clay on a night-time march through the city in a carriage overflowing with flowers. Bands and militiamen in dress uniforms led their honored guest to the banquet hall for the most sumptuous feast the city had ever held.

The next day the governor took Clay to the Capitol to speak to state legislators, after which he took his guest to one of the biggest public barbecues ever seen in America—with food and drink for 7,000!

Again and again, however—and particularly in Raleigh—locals peppered Clay with questions on Texas annexation. President Tyler had just named Clay's old friend John C. Calhoun of South Carolina as secretary of state, and when Clay arrived in Raleigh, he learned that Calhoun had in fact signed a treaty annexing Texas as the nation's twenty-seventh state—subject to Senate approval. Clay would now have to deal squarely with the issue; the Senate, the Whigs, and the nation awaited his dictum. Was he for or against it?

As always, he talked of union! Always union and, necessarily, compromise.

Annexation of Texas had already divided the Union, with northern abolitionists opposed to admitting another slave state, while southerners were eager to welcome it and gain a political advantage over free states in Congress. On a national level Clay knew annexation meant assuming the new state's debt of $13 million at a time when an economic depression had curtailed federal government revenues and plunged the nation into debt. Still worse, annexation would almost certainly provoke Mexico to declare war on the United States and, even worse, call on its European allies for support.

Personally Clay, like most Americans, embraced the concept of manifest destiny, with the nation eventually annexing Texas and all the lands "from sea to shining sea," from the Great Lakes and St. Lawrence River to the Gulf of Mexico and Rio Grande River, from the Atlantic to the Pacific Oceans. With the Senate—and the nation—awaiting his pronouncement, Clay sent his recommendation to Kentucky senator Crittenden.

Clay urged the Senate to vote against annexation because the nation "already had quite as much, if not more, territory than [it] could govern well." It was "more important to the happiness of the people of the United States that they should enjoy in peace, contentment, and harmony what they have than to attempt further acquisition of territory.

"Texas," Clay asserted, "is destined to be settled by our race, who will carry . . . our laws, our language, and our institutions, and that view of her destiny reconciles me much more to her independence. . . .

We can live as good neighbors, cultivating peace, commerce, and friendship."[26]

With his pronouncement in Raleigh, Clay ended his swing through the Southeast, and on April 26 he arrived in Washington, where the *National Intelligencer*—on Clay's instruction—published his opinion on Texas. Whigs across the nation hailed it as a masterpiece of statesmanship. In Springfield, Illinois, Abraham Lincoln addressed the State House and won approval of his motion sustaining Henry Clay's opposition to annexation.

Four days after Clay arrived in Washington, Whig delegates gathered in Baltimore for their national convention and nominated him as their presidential candidate. In Illinois Abraham Lincoln was euphoric, winning passage of a resolution at the Whig Convention in Peoria "that the Whigs of Illinois respond to the nomination of Henry Clay as the Whig candidate for the Presidency . . . with an enthusiasm only equaled by . . . our respect and gratitude for . . . his patriotic services to our country."[27]

A month later the Senate rejected the treaty of annexation, with all but one of the twenty-nine-member Whig majority voting against and enough Democrats—seven of twenty-two—supporting Clay's position to deny Texas statehood. Until then former President Van Buren had been the front-runner for the Democratic nomination, but after he, like Clay, voiced his opposition to annexation, Democrats summarily rejected him and nominated House Speaker James K. Polk of Tennessee, who had championed Texas annexation and imposed the Gag Rule that silenced John Quincy Adams and other abolitionist voices in the House.

As Whigs mocked the little-known Democratic candidate with the rhetorical question, "Who is James K. Polk?" the Clay election train gained what seemed like unstoppable momentum as Daniel Webster jumped on board, then William Seward, and political bosses across the North.

In Illinois, State Assemblyman Abraham Lincoln, "thinking I might aid some to carry the state of Indiana for Mr. Clay," went to

*32. Springfield, Illinois, lawyer Abraham Lincoln cam-
paigned hard for Henry Clay, winning passage of a resolution at the Whig Convention "that the Whigs of Illinois
respond to the nomination of Henry Clay as the Whig
candidate for the Presidency . . . with an enthusiasm only
equaled by . . . our respect and gratitude for . . . his patriotic services to our country." (Library of Congress)*

campaign in "the neighborhood in that state in which I was raised,
where my mother and only sister were buried."[28] In Washington
the essayist and prolific author Calvin Colton proposed writing the
story of Clay's life and became Clay's official biographer. He eventually combined the story of Clay's life with a compilation of Clay's
speeches and correspondence in a massive, eight-volume work, *The
Works of Henry Clay* (See Bibliography).

"Get out da way," Whigs across the nation sang for Clay to the
then-popular minstrel tune *Old Dan Tucker*:

Get out da way, you're all unlucky;
Close da track for old Kentucky.[29]

In mid-summer, however, a new, third party—the Liberty Party—appeared, and by autumn it had complicated the campaign. With but one issue—abolition—it named as its candidate James G. Birney, an Alabama lawyer who had been born and bred in Kentucky. He had attended Transylvania University in Lexington, near Clay's home, before going to Princeton University in New Jersey. He moved to Alabama, bought a plantation that he later sold at a huge profit before practicing law and emerging as a fire-breathing abolitionist. Although Clay and Polk had both sought to keep slavery out of the campaign, Birney's entry drew support from ultra-abolitionists in all parts of the nation and changed the campaign complexion.

Also coloring the campaign were whispers, rumors, and printed innuendoes reminding America of Clay's so-called corrupt bargain with John Quincy Adams. Retired President Andrew Jackson, still seething with hatred for Clay, reinforced the attack. Democrats distributed pamphlets everywhere, some accusing Clay of responsibility for the Cilley-Graves duel, others reminding voters of his gambling and drinking, his failure to observe the Sabbath, his membership in the Masons . . .

The list of Henry Clay's sins seemed endless, but his stand—or lack thereof—on abolition hurt him most. "If anyone desires to know the leading and paramount object of my public life," he cried out in vain to both North and South, "the preservation of the Union will furnish him the key."[30] His words would define the thinking of the young Illinois Whig Abraham Lincoln and a generation of Lincoln's followers.

Although Clay insisted that "truth and justice . . . abide in the middle ground," too many Americans abided elsewhere. Henry Clay failed to see how deeply northern voters embraced abolition and how deeply southern voters embraced extending the slavery economy with the Texas annexation. Both rejected compromise, cared little for the Union, and, too often, thirsted for blood to punish those who disagreed. And in the end they punished Henry Clay.

About 79 percent of eligible voters turned out to vote in the 1844 presidential elections. Polk won 1,339,494 votes, enough to win 170 electoral votes and fifteen states; Clay won 1,300,004 popular votes and 105 Electoral College votes in eleven states.[31] Birney, the single-issue candidate, received no electoral votes but captured 62,054 popular votes—almost entirely ultra-abolitionists—who cost Clay victories in New York and Pennsylvania, key states that would have earned him the presidency.

"If the Whig abolitionists in New York had voted with us," Abraham Lincoln lamented, "Mr. Clay would now be President."[32]

Clay was with Lincoln's parents-in-law, the Todds, in Lexington when he received the news of his defeat. "He opened the paper . . . and stood for a moment as if frozen," Lincoln's mother-in-law, Elizabeth Todd, wrote to her step-daughter Mary, who had married Lincoln two years earlier. Mrs. Todd and her husband, business leader Robert S. Todd, were attending a wedding reception with the Clays.

> He laid down the paper and filled a glass with wine, and raising it to his lip with a pleasant smile, said, 'I drink to the health and happiness of all assembled here.' Setting down the glass, he resumed his conversation as if nothing had occurred and was, as usual, the life and light of the company. The contents of the paper were soon known to everyone in the room and a wet blanket fell on our gaiety. We left the wedding party with heavy hearts.[33]

The Clays contained their emotions until they returned home and had shut the door behind them. They then embraced and wept in each other's arms.[34]

The results stunned former President John Quincy Adams, still seething under Polk's Gag Rule in the House. "The people have elected a mere Tom Tit,"* he grumbled in disbelief.[35] But former President Andrew Jackson rejoiced over Clay's defeat, saying, "I thank my God that the Republic is safe."[36]

But the Republic was far from safe. On March 1 the Senate voted to annex Texas and defy Mexico's threat of war. By then Henry Clay had retired from politics and turned his full attention to his wife, his farm, and his growing family. The untimely deaths of so many of their children and their children's spouses had left the Clays—both of them aging and increasingly subject to illnesses—to care for an ever-increasing flock of grandchildren. Altogether the Clays' sons and daughters gave their parents thirty-one grandchildren, of whom at least twenty-two survived infancy and at least eight came to live with the Clays at Ashland at one time or another during their childhoods.

In the months after the presidential election Clay freed eight of his slaves, offering them the option to return to Africa under the sponsorship of the American Colonization Society, which he still headed. Although he offered to free his personal servant, the man refused. He declared himself too old to start life afresh, having no skills and no family other than the Clays.

In the spring following the election Clay's youngest son, twenty-four-year-old John Morrison, suffered a nervous breakdown, and Clay committed him to the Lunatic Asylum of Kentucky, which housed his oldest son, Theodore Wythe. The widowed Henry Clay Jr., meanwhile, left some of his children, including Henry Clay III, at Ashland while he moved to Louisville to enter politics.

"Your children are very well," Clay assured his son, adding, "It would afford me very good pleasure if you could be elected to Congress. I hope that your connection with me . . . may not injure you."[37] Although Henry Clay Jr. lost the election in Kentucky, Abraham

---

*Perhaps a reference to the small, white-breasted or black-breasted robin-like bird found in New Zealand.

Lincoln, a self-described disciple of the Henry Clay Sr., won election to Congress as representative from Springfield, Illinois. In the four years that followed, Lincoln was an outspoken advocate of Clay's American System—with considerable success implementing it in his home state. He pushed through creation of the State Bank of Illinois, improvement of state roads, construction of the Illinois Central Railroad, and creation of a statewide network of navigable waterways.

Over the next two years retired Senator Clay helped his sons Thomas and James build homes on lands he had bought them adjacent to Ashland, and he helped Lucretia manage Ashland, which became a model farm. Beyond the magnificently landscaped grounds near the mansion, its fields produced profitable crops of corn, wheat, rye, and hemp. Clay's herds of livestock brought top prices at auction, while Lucretia's dairy remained a profitable producer of butter and cheese in the Lexington market.

The rest of America did not forget the Clays. Gifts for both Henry and Lucretia—and their grandchildren—flowed in from all parts of the nation. Friends in New York inquired at the bank in Lexington about Clay's financial condition and, learning that his presidential campaign had left him more than $25,000 in debt, paid it off—anonymously.

As in the past, however, death continued to stalk the Clay family.

Depressed over his election loss and with no career goals in sight, Henry Clay Jr. answered a call by the Kentucky Volunteer Infantry to fight in the Mexican War. After the United States annexed Texas, President Polk ordered General Zachary Taylor to deploy troops along the Rio Grande River. When the Mexicans fired on an advance party, President Polk asked Congress to declare war, and American troops invaded Mexico. By the end of summer Taylor had seized Monterrey and, with American ships blockading both Mexican coasts, other troops pressed westward through New Mexico and southern California to the Pacific Ocean.

The American government declared California a US territory in July 1846 and sent troops deeper into Mexico. The following winter Henry Clay Jr. and his men joined Taylor's forces at Monterrey.

33. Second in his class at the US Military Academy at West Point, Henry Clay's son Henry Clay Jr. was killed leading his men into enemy fire at the Battle of Buena Vista in the Mexican War. His son, Henry Clay III, would also attend West Point and died in the Civil War. (Library of Congress)

Promoted to lieutenant colonel by then, he led his men into enemy fire at the Battle of Buena Vista in February 1847 and was killed.

A month later General Winfield Scott and his force took Vera Cruz and joined other American forces in a push along a broad front toward the Mexican capital. Mexico City fell to the Americans on September 14, and the two nations signed a treaty of peace the following February.

Henry Clay Jr.'s death shattered his father, driving him into the arms of the church. On June 22, 1847, an Episcopalian churchman baptized Henry Clay and four of his grandchildren at Ashland. Even then his critics gave him no respite, calling his baptism "farcical" and his new house of worship "an aristocratic church."[38]

Clay called the loss of his namesake son "one of the greatest afflictions which has ever befallen me." The only consolation "from the fall of my beloved son on the bloody field of Buena Vista . . . would

Map 4. Territory acquired by the United States in the Mexican War included present-day California, Arizona, Nevada, and Utah, and parts of New Mexico. As an adjunct to the war, the United States annexed Texas and extended the nation's boundary to the Rio Grande River. (Kballen/Wikipedia)

be . . . I know he preferred to meet death . . . in the service of his country. The consolation would be greater if I did not believe that the Mexican War was unnecessary and of an aggressive character."[39]

Henry Clay III was twelve when his father, Henry Clay Jr., went to war. The boy pleaded with his grandfather to enroll him in the Franklin Military Academy, near the Kentucky state capital at Frankfort. Two years later, when he learned of his father's death, he was determined to follow in his father's footsteps and attend West Point. His grandfather wrote to their congressman for the necessary sponsorship "for my grandson Henry Clay III, the eldest son of Lt. Col. Henry Clay.

"He is now fourteen years of age, has been eighteen months at the Franklin Military Institute and is a boy of much promise," Clay wrote with a mixture of pride, trepidation, and sorrow. "He has lost, as you know, both of his parents. If you have any difficulty . . . I flatter myself that if you would mention my wishes to the President [James K. Polk], he would direct it to issue."[40] Two years later Henry Clay III enrolled as a cadet in the US Military Academy at West Point.

"General [Winfield] Scott has written to me about you and spoken in favorable terms," Clay wrote to his grandson, whom he and Lucretia had showered with love and attention since the death of the boy's father.

"You will find the life of a cadet a little hard at first," Clay wrote, "but you will come to like it after a while."

Three months later, however, the boy was not doing well.

"I am sorry that you find your confinement disagreeable," Clay consoled his grandson, "but my dear child it is impossible that you should ever become distinguished and worthy of your lamented father and worthy of me without study and some sacrifices of ease and comfort. These I hope you will cheerfully make. The longer you remain the more will your studies become light and agreeable. Such was your father's experience."[41]

The boy's performance at West Point did not improve, and his distraught grandfather pleaded with him. It was not easy for the old man to assume the role of someone half his age.

"I am afraid, my dear child," Henry Clay implored his grandson, "that you do not sufficiently appreciate your position at the Academy, nor the disgrace that you would have attached to your name if you should be compelled to leave. . . . I pray you to redouble your efforts and act a part worthy of your poor father's name and mine. Imagine him to be looking down on you! How would his spirit be mortified if you dishonored him or me. . . . Your grandma joins me in love to you."[42]

The boy did not dishonor either his father or grandfather, however. After he completed his first year successfully, his grandfather sent him a letter of congratulations, adding, "Your grandmama laid her hands on the enclosed letter from your father to her, which I send to you, as I thought you might like to read and preserve it."[43]

Secure that his grandson was on the right track at West Point, Clay turned his attention back to politics. Despite his advancing age and three failed efforts to be President, he remained the favorite candidate of many Whig leaders for the 1848 contest.

"There are conditions on which I would . . . consent to being placed before the country as a candidate," he replied to a plea from Delaware's Whig senator John C. Clayton. "First, the continued possession of my health . . . and, secondly, a perfect persuasion that my services were demanded by an unquestionable majority of the country. The latter condition, I apprehend, is not likely to exist."[44]

For once Clay sensed the nation's mood correctly. Although the Battle of Buena Vista had cost him his son, it had raised Army commander Zachary Taylor to heroic status—in the tradition of George Washington and Andrew Jackson.

"People everywhere begin to talk of converting you into a political leader when the war is done," Kentucky senator Crittenden wrote to Taylor. Although Crittenden had been Clay's successor in the Senate and ostensibly Clay's staunchest supporter, he decided to abandon Clay and support Taylor for the Whig nomination in 1848. Taylor was a Louisiana planter and slaveholder who appealed to traditional southern Whigs more than Clay and, because of his battlefield heroics, to northern Democrats.

Unable to make up his mind about running in 1848, Clay traveled to Washington to get a better sense of the national political picture. Greeted enthusiastically by old political friends, he fell victim to the seductive arguments of *New York Tribune* editor Horace Greeley and, on April 10, 1848, announced he would make a fourth bid for the presidency. "I left my residence . . . under a determination to announce to the public . . . my desire not to be thought of as a candidate," he wrote in a letter to the *Lexington Observer & Kentucky Reporter* on April 12, 1846, and addressed "To the Public."

"Since my return home, I have anxiously deliberated upon my duty to myself, to my principles, to my friends, and, above all, to my country," he continued. "I have, therefore, finally decided to leave to the National Convention . . . the consideration of my name . . . for President of the United States."

The Whigs had never been a cohesive political "party" in the traditional sense. From the beginning they were a loose-knit coalition of anti-Masons, northern abolitionists, southern Federalists, and anti-Jackson Democrats, among others. All voted as one against Andrew Jackson but as often as not went their separate ways on other issues. Although Henry Clay had been able to unite them *against* Jackson, Van Buren, and Tyler, he had never been able to unite enough of them *for* Henry Clay.

Just after Clay's return to Washington, John Quincy Adams collapsed while trying to address the House of Representatives. Members found a couch to bring onto the House floor and helped their stricken colleague stretch out. The House, Senate, and Supreme Court adjourned immediately. A group of congressmen carried the sofa into the Speaker's office, where they barred everyone but physicians, family, and close friends. Adams revived enough to thank those around him and ask for Henry Clay, who arrived weeping. He clasped his old President's hand, unable to say a word before he finally left, inconsolable.

Eighty-year-old John Quincy Adams lay in a coma for the next two days, and at 7:20 p.m. on February 23, 1848, he died in the Capitol.

Although Clay left for the Whig convention in Philadelphia, he was too distressed by Adams's death to make a formal address. "A great patriot has died," he told the assemblage. "A bright light has gone out." He said he had been closely connected to Adams "for many years, both in private and public life," and would always remember him with "feelings and emotions of friendship, admiration, and affection."[45]

Clay proved no more successful uniting Whigs behind his candidacy at the 1848 National Whig Convention in Philadelphia than he had been in three previous presidential elections.

On the first ballot General Zachary Taylor—"Old Rough and Ready"—won 111 delegate votes, Clay 97, Scott 43, and Webster 22.

34. *The death of Congressman John Quincy Adams, the former President, in the House Chamber, with his former Secretary of State Henry Clay holding his right hand. (From 1852 Nathaniel Currier lithograph in the Library of Congress.)*

As other delegates gasped with surprise, even Kentucky's delegation preferred Taylor to Clay, giving Taylor 7 votes and Clay only 5.

Taylor won the nomination on the fourth ballot, garnering 171 votes—including all the Kentucky votes—to Clay's 32. As a sop to Clay and his disappointed supporters, the Convention named former New York congressman Millard Fillmore, an outspoken Clay admirer, as its candidate for vice president.

Taylor's victory stunned Clay supporters. Taylor's "qualifications for civil service," wrote one angry Whig to Clay, "consist in sleeping forty years in the woods and cultivating moss in the calves of his legs."[46]

Clay agreed, calling Taylor "totally incompetent to the office. I lament to say that he is . . . vacillating and unstable. . . . I fear that the Whig Party is dissolved. . . . I am compelled . . . to believe that the Whig party has been succeeded by a mere personal party, as much a Taylor party as was the Jackson party."[47]

35. *The Battle of Buena Vista, which cost Henry Clay his son, raised Major General Zachary Taylor to heroic status—and to the presidency of the United States. (Library of Congress)*

Although fervent supporters urged Henry Clay to run for the presidency as an independent candidate in 1848, he refused. "I think my friends ought to leave me quiet and undisturbed in my retirement. I have served my country faithfully and to the utmost of my ability. . . . My race is run. [In] the short time which remains to me in this world, I intend abstaining . . . from all active participation in public affairs and occupying myself with my private and more solemn duties."[48]

Clay kept his word, even abstaining from voting in the presidential election. After his experience with Andrew Jackson, Clay could not bring himself to vote another military man into office, and the election gave him no choice. General Zachary Taylor's Democratic opponent, Lewis Cass, had been a brigadier general in the War of

1812 and secretary of war under Andrew Jackson. Clay wanted no part of Cass either.

After President Taylor's inauguration Kentucky senator John Crittenden decided to run for the governorship of his state, and the state assembly sent Clay back to the Senate. Like other southern states, Kentucky had plunged into the national debate over extending slavery into territories seized during the Mexican War. The discovery of gold in California turned what had been a regional problem into a national dilemma as thousands of "forty-niners" rushed to California mountainsides from all parts of the nation—some with slaves, others not.

To discourage the flight of slaves into the new western territories, southerners demanded that Congress strengthen the 1793 Fugitive Slave Law to require local authorities across the nation to catch runaway slaves and return them to their owners and to increase fines and even imprison those who helped escaped slaves in any way.

The US Supreme Court, however, ruled that state and local authorities had no constitutional obligation to enforce federal laws. Massachusetts, Vermont, Pennsylvania, and Rhode Island immediately passed laws forbidding state officials from enforcing the federal Fugitive Slave Act, and other state legislatures in the North and in "border" states like Kentucky debated passing similar laws.

Kentucky's legislature called for a convention to revise the state constitution, and its members besieged Henry Clay with pleas to propose a solution to the controversy. As usual the "sage of Ashland," as Kentuckians now called him, worked out a compromise he hoped would unite slaveholders and abolitionists.

"The question," he explained, "is whether African slavery in Kentucky shall be . . . perpetual or [whether] some provision shall be made in the new constitution for its gradual and ultimate extinction.

> A vast majority of the people of the United States . . . regret the introduction of slavery into the colonies under the authority of our British ancestors . . . [They] regard the institution as a great evil to

both races, and would rejoice in the adoption of any . . . plan for the removal of all slaves from among us.[49]

Clay said that when Kentucky had written its constitution, those who called for emancipation had encountered "a great obstacle"— the lack of a land to which they might transport and liberate them. "Now by the successful establishment of flourishing colonies on the western coast of Africa, that difficulty has been obviated." Still president of the American Colonization Society, Clay said it would right the wrongs that Africa had suffered if American slaves returned "to their original home, civilized and imbued with the benign spirit of Christianity and prepared to redeem that great continent from barbarism and idolatry."[50]

Clay proposed a system of gradual emancipation, "slow in its operation, cautious and gradual, so as to occasion no convulsion." He proposed fixing a specific date—1855 or 1860—to begin the process, transporting about 5,000 selected slaves a year to Africa. All slaves in Kentucky born before that date would remain slaves for life; all slaves born afterward would be freed at age twenty-five, then "hired out under the authority of the state for a term not exceeding three years . . . to raise a sum sufficient to pay expenses of their transportation [to Africa] and to provide them with an outfit for six months after their arrival there.

> Kentucky enjoys high respect . . . throughout the Union and throughout the civilized world. But in my humble opinion, no deeds of her former glory would equal . . . establishing the descendants of Africa . . . in the native land of their forefathers.[51]

Recognizing the interests of the South, he insisted that gradual abolition in Kentucky would have no bearing on her relations with states unwilling to abolish slavery. "The power of each slave state within its limits is absolute, supreme and exclusive . . . of Congress and any other state," he declared. He said that slave labor was less profitable in farm states like Kentucky, where semiskilled white workers paid by the piece were more productive than unpaid slaves. In contrast, slave labor was more profitable in states that needed only unskilled field hands to plant and harvest cotton, rice, and sugar cane.

"Just as slave states cannot . . . control the judgment of Kentucky," he insisted, "if Kentucky abolishes slavery, I trust she would be as ready . . . to defend the slave states in the enjoyment of all their lawful and constitutional rights."

Clay acknowledged that abolition would require "some sacrifices on the part of slaveholders," but he said their losses would have "some compensation" with the increased productivity of paid white labor and the consequent increase in the value of their lands. Then, in phrases he chose carefully to mean what both slaveholders and abolitionists wanted them to mean, he listed what he called "the general benefits accruing to the whole state from the extinction of slavery:

> We shall remove . . . the contamination of a servile and degraded race of different color; we shall enjoy placing that race where they can enjoy . . . liberty and civil and political equality; we shall acquire the advantage . . . of free labor [freemen], instead of the carelessness, infidelity, and unsteadiness of slave labor; we shall . . . elevate the social condition of the white laborer, augment the value of our lands, improve the agriculture of the state, attract capital [for] commerce, manufactures, and agriculture. . . . Kentucky would [be] the Pioneer State in removing from her soil every trace of human slavery and in establishing the descendants of Africa . . . in the native land of their forefathers.[52]

Reactions to his proposal astonished him. Far from appealing to both sides of the slavery issue, his plan infuriated them. Clay, they said, was old and out of touch with the times, and they rejected his compromise.

36. A daguerreotype of Henry and Lucretia Clay at the time of their fiftieth wedding anniversary. (From the original at the Henry Clay Memorial Foundation Papers, University of Kentucky)

"I regret to hear it is not popular," Clay wrote to his son James two weeks later. He conceded it would "bring on me some odium. I nevertheless wish it published. I owe that to the cause and myself and posterity."[53]

Despite his disappointment, Henry and Lucretia Clay celebrated their fiftieth wedding anniversary on April 11, 1849, and marked the occasion by posing for a then-new photographic process called the daguerreotype.

Before returning to the Senate, Clay went to Newport, Rhode Island, at the end of summer for a seaside holiday—only to have his personal servant "carried or enticed away by abolitionists."

"I supposed that I had lost him," Clay wrote to Lucretia, "but he voluntarily returned to me . . . a few hours before I left Newport, and is now with me. He says that they offered and paid him $3000 and that he intended to get all the money out of them that he could and to have returned to me. They became distrustful of him and he of them in Boston, and he restored their money and came back to me."[54]

In December 1849 the Great Pacificator reclaimed his seat in the US Senate and found the Capitol in chaos again. House membership consisted of 112 Democrats, 103 Whigs, and 13 members of the Free Soil Party, a single-issue group that opposed the spread of slavery in the West and now held the balance of power in the House. Of 59 senators, there were 32 Democrats and 2 Free Soilers. Clay and his Whigs counted 25 members—split between southerners and northerners. Clay took his Senate seat without his accustomed powers as majority leader and, for once, seemed helpless to prevent the Congress—and the nation—from dividing into feuding factions.

"The feeling for disunion among some intemperate southern politicians," Clay lamented, "is stronger than I hoped or supposed it could be."[55] Henry Clay knew it would be pointless to continue struggling for passage of the American System to strengthen commercial ties and bind the Union more firmly. Those ties had frayed, and his task now lay in preventing their rupture.

CHAPTER 12

On Board Our Omnibus

America's victory in the war with Mexico seemed as much a defeat for the United States at first as it did for Mexico, though not in the military sense. Although military victory had added endless thousands of square miles to the United States, the new territory came with equally endless political problems.

The discovery of gold in California had lured thousands of Americans to ore-laden western mountainsides—many with slaves. As a preliminary to statehood, California drew up a constitution that prohibited slavery. Fearing that free states would then have a big enough majority to ban slavery nationally, southern congressmen called for a convention of southern leaders in Nashville the following June to consider secession.

With New Mexico and Utah yet to become states, northern senators pressed for passage of the so-called Wilmot Proviso, which Pennsylvania congressman David Wilmot had proposed in 1846, prohibiting slavery in territories acquired in the Mexican War. Although the House had approved the measure, southerners in the Senate defeated it. It suffered the same fate two years later but remained one of the issues senators continued to debate when Clay arrived in December 1849.

There were many other issues: where to fix the Texas–New Mexico border; whether to admit California and New Mexico as territories, preliminary to their admission as states, or skip territorial status and admit them as states immediately; whether to admit New Mexico as a free state or slave state; whether to permit slavery in the rest of the territory seized from Mexico; whether to abolish slavery in the District of Columbia; whether to tighten the Fugitive Slave Act to discourage slaves from running away and increase recapture rates; whether to regulate the interstate slave trade.

As they had when they faced intractable problems in the past, congressional eyes automatically turned toward Henry Clay.

"I am staying at the National Hotel," he wrote to Lucretia, "where I have a good parlor and bedroom for which I pay thirty dollars per week. The British minister occupies rooms near mine, and I yesterday dined with him. He has his wife with him, a niece of the Duke of Wellington, a plain but sensible person."[1]

A few days later, on January 2, 1850, he wrote to Lucretia again, saying he had attended President Taylor's New Year's Day reception. "I shook hands with hundreds and found myself an object of as much attraction as the President himself. . . . Colds still annoy me. I do not go out at night and decline invitations to dinner. I have been only to one formal one and that was at the President's." No longer the gambling, hard-drinking roué, Clay confessed, "I go to bed regularly at 10 o'clock."[2]

Racked by a persistent cough, Clay lacked bounce in his step as he walked up the Capitol steps on January 29, 1850. He carried with him a mammoth, all-encompassing compromise to present to the Senate as five resolutions. Each contained "equal concessions and forbearance on both sides," although he had "asked from the free states of the North a more liberal and extensive concession:

> You are numerically more powerful than the slave states . . . there is
> a vast and incalculable amount of property to be sacrificed [in the
> South], and to be sacrificed not by your sharing in the common

burden but exclusive of you. . . . The social intercourse, habit, safety, property, life, everything is at hazard . . . in the slave states.[3]

Clay's five-part solution later became what was called the Omnibus Bill: (1) California would enter the Union as a free state; (2) Utah and New Mexico would enter as territories, with settlers to determine whether or not to prohibit slavery; (3) to placate the North, Congress would abolish the slave trade in the District of Columbia; (4) to placate the South, Congress would tighten the Fugitive Slave Act; and (5) Texas would abandon claims to territory in New Mexico in exchange for $10 million.

Holding up a sliver of wood he said was a fragment of George Washington's coffin,* Clay called it a symbol of "a warning voice" from the grave to members of Congress "to beware, to pause, to reflect before they lend themselves to any purposes which shall destroy that Union which was cemented by his exertions and example."[4]

South Carolina's John C. Calhoun countered with a speech assailing Clay's compromise, but he was too old and frail to rise and deliver his speech himself. He let a colleague from Virginia intone the words. Daniel Webster followed with his famous—some called it *infamous*—"Seventh of March Oration" seconding Clay's plea for moderation, but he shocked his northern supporters by advocating a strengthening of the Fugitive Slave Act. The proposed changes to the act would double the fine to $1,000 and mandate six months'

---

*In 1847 John A. Washington, George Washington's great nephew, had been unable to maintain the Washington home at Mount Vernon, Virginia, and offered to sell it to Congress for $100,000. A petitioner who had favored the purchase and obtained a sliver of wood from Washington's coffin at Mount Vernon had presented it to Clay, who proposed that Congress purchase the property. Congress rejected the acquisition, and in 1860 a group of wealthy southern ladies, incorporated as the Mount Vernon Ladies Association, bought the mansion and 200 acres of surrounding property for $200,000. They began restoring the mansion and its surrounding structures and lands to its condition when Washington lived there—a task their successors continue today without government subsidies.

imprisonment for helping a slave flee captivity. Captured blacks were to be denied trial and barred from protesting their capture or defending themselves—all but ensuring capture and enslavement of many freedmen.

Webster's speech stunned abolitionists. Massachusetts congressman Horace Mann, the pioneer of universal free public education who was elected to fill John Quincy Adams's seat, assailed Webster as "a fallen star—Lucifer descending from heaven. He has disappointed us all."[5]

John C. Calhoun died on March 31, 1850, but the interminable debate over Clay's resolutions continued into the spring, with so many motions added that few if any knew exactly what the original proposals had been. Senators sounded every note on the gamut of opinions from ultra-abolitionism to the benefits of slavery as a reflection of God's will. The legendary names of the nineteenth-century Senate all spoke—to each other, to the American people, to posterity, and to their God: Salmon Chase, William Seward, Stephen Douglas, Lewis Cass, Jefferson Davis, and others.

On April 13 the Senate elected a committee of thirteen to simplify matters. With Clay as chairman, it finally produced the Omnibus Bill.

While southern congressional leaders debated the compromise, minor figures from a southern secessionist groups met as planned in Nashville on June 3 but adjourned after nine days, unable to agree on just how to secede but pledging to meet again.

President Zachary Taylor died on July 9, 1850. A slaveholder himself, he had favored rejecting Clay's compromise and letting westerners decide the issues for themselves. The last President to own slaves while in the White House,* President Taylor was the second President to die in office and the second and last Whig ever elected to the presidency. The accession to the presidency of Vice President

---

*Andrew Johnson owned slaves before becoming President but not while President, and Ulysses S. Grant may have had control over relatives' slaves but, again, not while in office.

Millard Fillmore, a fervent Clay supporter from New York, helped sway opinion in Congress in favor of Clay's Compromise.

On July 22 Henry Clay made what would be his last great speech to the Senate, urging passage of his compromise and, evoking Patrick Henry's impassioned words that called for war,* Clay called for peace.

"Shall a being so small, so petty, so fleeting . . . oppose itself to the onward march of a great nation?" Clay asked.

"Forbid it, God!

"What are we? What is any man worth who is not ready and willing to sacrifice himself for the benefit of his country when it is necessary?"

Recalling the Missouri Compromise thirty years earlier, he reminded the Senate that "then, as now . . . it was said, 'It will not quell the storm nor give peace to the country,' but when it was approved, bells rang, cannons fired, and every demonstration of joy was made.

"The nation wants repose!" Clay declared. "Acceptance of this measure . . . will lead to a joy and exultation almost unexampled in our history." He called the compromise "the reunion of the Union . . . the dove of peace, which taking its flight from the dome of the Capitol carries the glad tidings of assured peace and restored harmony to all the remotest extremities of this distracted land."

Turning to senators with ties to the Revolution, he asked Senator James Murray Mason, who carried "the revolutionary blood of George Mason in his veins—the blood of his own grandfather—the obligation of your noble ancestry," whether he would "put at hazard this noble Union? If we go home doing nothing to satisfy and tranquilize the country, what will be the judgment of mankind? Will not all the monarchs of the Old World pronounce our republic a disgraceful failure?"

Clay lashed out at a critic who accused him of having conspired with Senators Webster, Cass, and others to compromise the nation.

---

* "Is life so dear or peace so sweet as to be purchased at the price of chains and slavery? Forbid it Almighty God." Patrick Henry, March 23, 1775, St. John's Church, Richmond, Virginia.

States and Territories of the United States of America
March 3, 1849 to September 9, 1850

Map 5a. *The United States before Henry Clay engineered the Compromise of 1850. Texas claimed sovereignty over much of New Mexico. (Golbez/Wikipedia)*

States and Territories of the United States of America
September 9, 1850 to March 2, 1853

Map 5b. *Under the Compromise of 1850, California was admitted to the Union as a free state, and Utah and Nevada became territories, with settlers to determine whether or not to ban slavery. In exchange for $10 million, Texas agreed to abandon claims to territory in New Mexico. (Golbez/Wikipedia)*

Reanimating the biting humor that had characterized his greatest House and Senate oratory, he asked, "May I ask to what keyhole he applied his ear or his eye—in what curtain he was ensconced—to hear and perceive these astonishing circumstances which he narrated with so much apparent self-satisfaction?"

It was vintage Clay and drew a sustained roar of laughter.

Far from politics, he said, "the subject of pacifying, if possible, the distracted parts of this country . . . absorbed all our thoughts.

> And so . . . did the consultations relate to the dignity, honor, and safety of the Union, and the Constitution of our country. When calm prevails, there is no incongruity in the freight nor in the passengers on board our Omnibus. . . . We have no Africans or abolitionists in our Omnibus—no disunionists or Free Soilers, no Jew or Gentile. Our passengers consist of Democrats and Whigs who . . . have met together, forgetting political differences to take up this great measure of reconciliation and harmony.[6]

He then leaned forward, his eyes focusing one by one on each senator, like a hawk eyeing his prey, transfixing each and all:

> Discard all resentments, all passions, all petty jealousies, all personal desires, all love of place, all yearning for the gilded crumbs which fall from the table of power. . . . Let us go to the limpid fountain of unadulterated patriotism . . . and think alone of our God, our country, our consciences, and our glorious Union.[7]

With those words Henry Clay ended his last great address to Congress and the American people and scored his last great legislative victory. In quick succession Congress passed all the elements of Clay's Compromise of 1850: the Admission of California Act, the Texas and New Mexico Act, the Utah Act, the Fugitive Slave Act, and An Act Abolishing the Slave Trade in the District of Columbia (See Appendix, page 265). Although ultra-abolitionists howled at the

37. A symbolic group portrait of those responsible for the Missouri Compromise and the Compromise of 1850, which preserved the Union: Front row, left to right, Winfield Scott, Lewis Cass (holding document), Henry Clay, John Calhoun, Daniel Webster, and (holding shield) Millard Fillmore.[8] (Original engraving at Ashland)

Fugitive Slave Act, the vast majority of congressmen in both houses—southerners and northerners alike—hailed Clay's Compromise of 1850 as the final, permanent solution to the nation's sectional problems and a welcome alternative to secession and civil war. Indeed, the 1851 off-year elections across the South confirmed widespread public support for Clay's Compromise with the defeat of almost all secessionist candidates for Congress. Clay—and the nation—believed he had fulfilled his dream of saving the Union without civil war.

Clay left the Senate convulsed by tubercular coughing, and after resting in his hotel for a few weeks, took a short seaside vacation in Newport, Rhode Island, before returning home to Lexington in late September.

38. A daguerreotype of Henry Clay at the time of his last speech in the US Senate. (Library of Congress)

A large crowd greeted his arrival on the evening of October 2, 1850, with thunderous applause, to which he responded with words of appreciation that are said to have ended, "I must ask you to excuse me, for, strange as it may seem, there is an old lady at Ashland whom I would rather see than all of you."[9]

Two weeks later Clay attended an enormous "free Barbecue given by Democrats and Whigs alike" to express their "feelings of admiration and gratitude for his service in preserving the Union and the Constitution."

"I cherish the hope and . . . belief," he responded to the crowd, "that the system of measures passed by Congress will finally . . . lead to quiet and tranquility. Malcontents at the North and in the South may seek to continue or revive agitation, but rebuked and discountenanced by the masses they will ultimately be silenced and induced to keep the peace."[10]

Clay returned to Washington in December, but a severe cold combined with his cough to weaken him dramatically. All but confined to his bed, he ventured out only occasionally—once with Secretary of State Daniel Webster to attend the once-in-a-lifetime performance of the fabled Jenny Lynn, the "Swedish Nightingale." The two senators arrived late, but after someone noticed their presence, the audience began to applaud, then cheer and stand, interrupting the concert. Already in the audience and standing to applaud was President Millard Fillmore.

Clay returned to Ashland after the Senate session in the spring of 1851, and apparently sensing his approaching end, he inquired about purchasing space in the Lexington Cemetery—only to have one of its founders present him with a gift of four lots.

"My health is not good," he admitted to his son James. "A troublesome and inconvenient cough has hung by me for six months past and enfeebled me very much. . . . I must get rid of the cough or it will dispose of me."[11] Six weeks later the summer heat and his cough—now evident as tuberculosis—sapped much of his strength, and he made out his will.

The trip back to Washington across the Appalachian Mountains left him still weaker. He attended the opening session of the Senate in March 1852, but it was his last appearance. Staggered by coughing fits, he slipped in and out of unconsciousness. Although he said he wanted to die in his Kentucky home, the doctor rejected the idea and telegraphed his son Thomas Hart Clay to come to Washington.

On May 7 the Senate chaplain, the Reverend Clement M. Butler, came to Clay's suite at the National Hotel and administered the sacrament, then sat at Clay's bedside for an hour. "I heard him in the slight wanderings of his mind . . . murmuring . . . 'My dear wife!' as if she were present."[12]

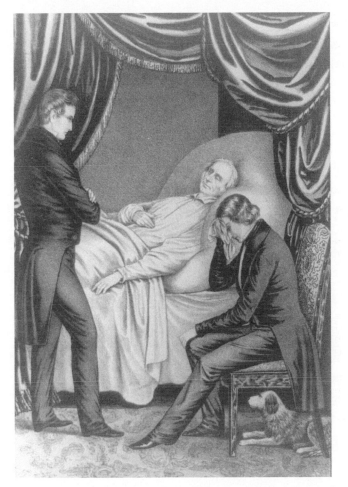

39. *As his son Thomas Hart Clay held his hand, Henry Clay died of tuberculosis in his hotel suite in Washington, DC, on June 28, 1852, at 11:17 a.m. (Original engraving at Ashland)*

As darkness fell on June 28, 1852, Thomas Clay Hart arrived at his father's bedside. The next morning the old man gained consciousness long enough to insist that his servant shave him. Then he grasped his son's hand, and at 11:17 seventy-five-year-old Henry Clay died, believing he had saved the Union.

Epilogue

The first church bells began tolling the news of Clay's death at sunrise on July 29, 1852. By noon every church tower had joined the chorus. President Fillmore issued an executive order, closing all federal offices for the day; Congress adjourned. Thomas telegraphed Lucretia and others in Lexington; the entire city shut down as church bells pealed in mourning.

On June 30 the nation's most powerful men—its generals, Supreme Court justices, congressmen, and President—trooped into the Senate Chamber with foreign ambassadors to pay homage to Henry Clay. Pall bearers carried his casket into the chamber for viewing by government officials, then to the Capitol Rotunda the next day for public viewing—the first American ever to be so honored. A removable face plate allowed mourners to see the Great Compromiser's visage for the last time.

Church bells pealed in Washington and across the land as Americans all—North, South, East, and West; Whigs, Democrats, and Republicans—mourned the man who had held them together in Union over most of the first half of the century. His death sent tremors of fear through those who sensed that the end of Henry Clay might presage the end of the Union.

"Alas!" Abraham Lincoln all but sobbed. "Who can realize that Henry Clay is dead! Who can realize, that the workings of that mighty mind have ceased . . . that freedom's champion—the champion of a civilized world . . . has indeed fallen."[1]

"He knew no North; he knew no South," wrote the editor of Washington's *National Intelligencer*. "He knew nothing but his country."[2]

On July 2, 1852, a week-long funeral procession got under way—like none ever seen before in America. Although born in Virginia and elected in Kentucky, Henry Clay had represented every American—and every American, it seemed, turned out to say good-bye. Traveling along a transportation network spawned by Clay's own American System, his coffin left Washington by train for Baltimore, then to Philadelphia's Independence Hall, and on to New York's City Hall. During the July 4 weekend 100,000 New Yorkers shuffled past his coffin. A steamboat took him up the Hudson River to Albany. Thousands lined both shores as guns and cannons boomed farewell salvos in every town and village. From Albany a train carried him to Schenectady, Utica, Rome, Syracuse, Rochester, and, finally, Buffalo, where a torchlight procession escorted his casket to a Lake Erie steamboat and transport to Cleveland, Ohio. A train took him to Columbus and Cincinnati, where a boat took him to Louisville and the funeral coach to Lexington.

On July 10, 1852, some 30,000 Americans joined local, state, and federal dignitaries and a huge military escort for Clay's burial in the plot he had acquired in Lexington Cemetery a year earlier. Lucretia and three of her four surviving sons—Thomas, James, and John attended.

Across the nation public officials eulogized the fallen Kentuckian, but few mourned as deeply as Abraham Lincoln.

"I worshiped him as a teacher and leader . . . ideal statesman . . . and the man for whom I fought all my humble life," Lincoln declared.

"I recognize his voice, speaking as it ever spoke, for the Union, the Constitution, and the freedom of mankind."[3]

Lincoln would echo Clay's words the rest of his life, often quoting long passages—forty-one times in his legendary debates with Senator Stephen A. Douglas when the two were vying for the Senate seat from Illinois in 1858. Although Lincoln embellished his first presidential Inaugural Address in March 1861 with Clay's words, many Americans forgot them.

In 1854 Congress repealed Clay's Missouri Compromise with the passage of the Kansas-Nebraska Act, which allowed settlers to decide whether or not they wanted slavery. Widespread fighting ensued between slaveholders and abolitionists that spread across state lines.

On April 12, 1861, South Carolina seceded from the Union, firing at the federal installation at Fort Sumter. Six months later ten other southern states joined South Carolina in a civil war that slaughtered some 750,000 Americans, with brothers often battling brothers, fathers fighting sons.

On June 5, 1862, Henry Clay III died serving in the Union Army; on October 12, 1863, his brother, Thomas J. Clay, died serving in the Confederate Army.

Although Kentucky was a slave state, the patriotic attachment to the Union instilled by Henry Clay and the state's ties to Ohio, Indiana, and nearby northern states kept Kentucky neutral at the outset of the Civil War. An invasion by Tennessee troops, however, infuriated the majority of Kentuckians, and they turned against the South in favor of Clay's beloved Union. Kentucky's military contribution to Union victory was less striking than the symbolism of its participation. Kentucky symbolized the West, and, as President Lincoln put it, "To lose Kentucky [was] nearly the same as to lose the whole game."[4]

Ten years to the day after Clay's death President Lincoln wrote a fateful letter to *New York Tribune* editor Horace Greeley, translating Clay's call for Union into his own presidential policy. Clay had put it, "If anyone desires to know the leading and paramount object of my public life, the preservation of the Union will furnish him the key."[5]

As he did throughout his life, Lincoln relied on Clay's words to guide him:

> My paramount object in this struggle is to save the Union, and is not either to save or destroy slavery. If I could save the Union without freeing any slave, I would do it, and if I could save it by freeing all the slaves, I would do it, and if I could save it by freeing some and leaving others alone, I would also do that. What I do about Slavery and the colored race, I do because I believe it helps to save this Union, and what I forbear, I forbear because I do not believe it would help to save the Union. I have here stated my purpose . . . and I intend no modification of my oft-expressed personal wish that all men, everywhere, could be free.[6]

A month later, on September 22, 1862, President Lincoln issued the Emancipation Proclamation declaring all slaves free in rebel states, effective at the beginning of the new year, on January 1, 1863.

On April 9, 1865, four years after the Civil War had started, Robert E. Lee, commander-in-chief of the Confederate Army, ended the conflict by surrendering to General Ulysses S. Grant, commander-in-chief of the Union Army. A week later, on April 15, 1865, an assassin shot and killed President Abraham Lincoln.

Only Clay's Union survived the carnage.

Appendix

HENRY CLAY'S "AMERICAN SYSTEM"

1. Establishment of a protective tariff of 20 to 25 percent on imported goods that compete with domestic goods.
2. Establishment of a government-operated national bank to receive, hold, and disburse federal funds, float government loans and bonds, and print and distribute a national currency to replace state and private currencies.
3. Federal government investment in a national transportation system of roads, bridges, and canals to link the entire nation and its people and make commercial, military, and individual transportation faster and easier.

   (As an adjunct to the American System, Clay proposed federal government improvements of harbors to increase seaboard commerce and distribution of proceeds from the sale of federal lands to state governments for internal improvements. He called for restricting presidential veto powers and a single-term limit for the President.)[1]

HENRY CLAY'S GREAT COMPROMISES

Missouri Compromise

1. Retained the balanced ratio of slave-state senators to free-state senators in Congress by admitting Missouri as a slave state and Maine as a free state.
2. Slavery was forbidden in territory lying above latitude 36°30'—a line determined by the southern boundary of Missouri and extending westward to the Pacific Ocean.

The Tariff and Nullification Crisis of 1833

Rather than free trade, on one extreme, or prohibitively high tariffs on the other extreme, Clay's compromise called for gradual annual reductions over ten years of all tariffs to no more than 20 percent of the value of the imported goods (*ad valorem*).

The Texas Annexation Crisis of 1836

Rather than annexing Texas and giving slave states a congressional majority, Clay's compromise called for US recognition of Texan independence but indefinite postponement of annexation, ensuring the even division between slave and free states in the United States.

Compromise of 1850

1. California admitted as a free state.
2. Utah and Nevada admitted as territories, with squatter or popular sovereignty, allowing settlers to determine whether or not to prohibit slavery.
3. Concession to the North: abolition of the slave trade (though not slavery) in District of Columbia.
4. Concession to the South: enactment of new, stricter Fugitive Slave Law; US marshals ordered to aid recovery of runaway slaves; fugitive negroes denied right to trial by jury or appeal of magistrate decisions; fine for aiding a runaway slave raised to $1,000, with six months mandatory imprisonment.
5. Texas awarded $10 million in exchange for abandoning territorial claims in New Mexico.

HENRY CLAY'S ESTATE

Henry Clay left Ashland and all his household possessions to Lucretia, whom he made an executor of his estate. She died twelve years after her husband, on April 6, 1864, and lies beside him. Standing above the gravesite is a 130-foot-tall memorial column, dedicated on July 4, 1861, and topped with a twelve-and-a-half-foot-tall statue of Clay.

40. Dedicated on July 4, 1861, a memorial column with a statue of Clay stands above Henry Clay's gravesite in Lexington, Kentucky. Lucretia Hart Clay, Henry Clay's wife of more than 50 years lies beside him. (Library of Congress)

Although Henry Clay willed four slaves to his son James, he freed his other slaves. Adhering to the principles he helped establish at the American Colonization Society, his will directed that children of his slaves born after January 1, 1850, be freed when they turned twenty-five if female, and twenty-eight if male. They were all to be taught to read, write, and calculate, and during the three years before they reached "the age of freedom" they were to be paid wages to cover costs of transportation to Africa and establishing themselves there.

None of Clay's six daughters and only four of his five sons survived him. He set aside a bequest to ensure proper care for Theodore Wythe, his oldest son, who died in 1870 at sixty-eight, after spending much of his life in the Kentucky Lunatic Asylum. Thomas and John were each living on farms Clay had bought near Ashland and willed to them—a 125-acre farm for Thomas and a 200-acre farm for his youngest son, John. Lucretia sold Ashland to her son James and went to live with John, who would live to be sixty-six. Knowing how much Lincoln admired Henry Clay, John sent the President "a snuff box . . . which belonged to my late father, whose avowed sentiment that he owed 'a higher allegiance to the Constitution and government of the United States than to the constitution and government of any state' is mine and whose other noblest sentiment, that he would 'rather be right than be President' I hope may ever be yours." He signed the letter, "With great respect, Your friend, John M. Clay."

Lincoln sent John his "thanks for this memento of your great and patriotic father. Thanks also for the assurances that in these days of dereliction you remain true to his principles."

James bought Ashland from his mother for just under $50,000, but the mansion had deteriorated so badly that he pulled it down and replaced it with a near-replica, which stands today as a museum. A Confederate sympathizer when the Civil War began, he fled Kentucky for the South, then to Cuba, and, finally, to Montreal, where he found refuge with other Confederate ex-patriots. He died there of tuberculosis. His wife sold Ashland to Kentucky University (later University of Kentucky), which sold it back to the Clay family sixteen years later. It remained in the Clay family until 1948, when the Henry Clay Memorial Foundation purchased the mansion, outbuildings, and about 325 acres. Founded by Clay's great-granddaughter, the foundation restored and continues to preserve Clay's Ashland home as a museum for the public.

Thomas Hart Clay, who had been at the bedside when his father died, won election to his father's old seat in the Kentucky legislature before

President Abraham Lincoln appointed him ambassador to Nicaragua. He died at his farm, next to Ashland, in 1871 at the age of sixty-eight.

Henry Clay had thirty-one grandchildren, of whom twenty-two survived infancy. He left a bequest of $7,500 to each survivor at the time of his death.

In 1929 a statue of Henry Clay was installed in Statuary Hall in the Capitol in Washington (see Frontispiece). In 1857 the number of representatives outgrew the House Chamber where Clay had served as Speaker. The House then moved to a new, larger space, where it now sits, and the original chamber was redesigned and converted to Statuary Hall, with space for two statues from each state.

ASHLAND TODAY

The Henry Clay Estate is a National Historic Landmark, Museum and Educational Center that includes a restoration of Henry Clay's magnificent 18-room mansion in the heart of Lexington's most beautiful residential district. The mansion houses a museum with a collection of original Clay family items and stands on 17 acres of wooded parklands that include a formal garden and a group of historic outbuildings.

Notes

INTRODUCTION

1. Abraham Lincoln, First debate with Stephen A. Douglas, at Ottawa, Illinois, August 21, 1858, *Collected Works of Abraham Lincoln*, 3:1–37, esp. 29. (Henceforth, *Works . . . Lincoln*.)

2. Henry Clay [henceforth, HC] to Sen. William C. Preston, South Carolina, before delivering a speech on abolition to the Senate on February 7, 1839, reported in *Congressional Globe*, 25th Congress, 3rd Session, 177; *National Intelligencer*, March 30, 1839; *Niles' Weekly Register*, March 23, 1839.

3. Abraham Lincoln, "Eulogy of Henry Clay," Springfield, Illinois, July 6, 1852, *Works . . . Lincoln*, 2:121–132; Abraham Lincoln, speech in Carlinville, Illinois, August 31, 1858, ibid., 3:77–85, esp. 79.

4. *National Intelligencer*, August 8, 1844, in Van Deusen, *Life of Henry Clay*, 374.

5. Abraham Lincoln, "Eulogy of Henry Clay," *Works . . . Lincoln*, 2:121–132; Abraham Lincoln to Daniel Ullmann, February 1, 1861, ibid., 4:183–184.

CHAPTER 1: SPITTING IN THE FACE OF CONGRESS

1. Ibid.

2. *Congressional Globe*, 27th Congress, 376–377; *Annals of Congress*, 18th Congress, 1st Session, 1311–1317.

3. *Niles' Weekly Register*, October 29, 1842, quoting speech given by Clay in Indianapolis, Indiana, October 5, 1842.

4. Thomas Hart Clay, *Henry Clay*, 19.

5. Lincoln, *Works . . . Lincoln*, 2:121–132.

6. HC Speech "On Retiring to Private Life," Lexington, Kentucky, June 9, 1842, *Works of Henry Clay*, 9:359–384, esp. 362–363. (Henceforth, *Works*.)

7. HC, *Works*, 1:69.

8. Van Deusen, *Life of Henry Clay*, citing M. Taul, "Memoirs," *Kentucky State Historical Society Register*, vol. 27 (January 1929), 357–359.

9. License to Practice Law, Henry Clay, *Papers of Henry Clay*, 1:2–3. (Henceforth, *Papers*.)

10. HC speech "On Retiring to Private Life," Lexington, Kentucky, June 9, 1842, *Works*, 9:359–384.

11. Ibid.

12. HC to the Electors of Fayette County, April 16, 1798, in *Kentucky Gazette*, April 25, 1798, *Papers*, 1:3–8.

13. Ibid.

14. [Resolution] In the House of Representatives, November 10, 1798.

15. Prentice, *Biography of Henry Clay*, 22–25.

16. Ibid.

CHAPTER 2: NO FIGHTING HERE

1. Thomas Hart to William Blount, in Peter Brackney, "The House at Second and Mill Called 'Home' by Several Notable Kentuckians," in *Kaintuckeean*, July 17, 2013.

2. Ibid.

3. HC, *Private Correspondence of Henry Clay*, 24, 615. (Henceforth, *Private Correspondence*.)

4. Ibid. See also Schurz, *Life of Henry Clay*, 1:22.

5. Ibid.

6. HC to Rodney Dennis, April 15, 1849, *Works*, 5:587.

7. *American Citizen*, March 1, 1804.

8. Aaron Burr to Joseph Alston, March 22, 1805, Davis, *Memoirs of Aaron Burr*, 589–590.

9. Thomas Jefferson, October 22, 1806, *Anas*, Jefferson, *Writings of Thomas Jefferson*, Ford, ed., 1:318–319.

10. Thomas Jefferson to Monsieur DuPont de Nemours, July 14, 1807, *Life and Selected Writings of Thomas Jefferson*, 536.

11. Aaron Burr to HC, November 27, 1806, *Papers*, 1:256–257.

12. HC to Dr. Richard Pindell, October 15, 1828, Thomas Hart Clay, *Henry Clay*, 42–44.

13. Ibid.

14. HC, quoted in Frankfort *Western World*, December 18, 1806, *Papers*, 1:258–259.

15. HC to James Pindell, October 15, 1828, Clay, *Private Correspondence*, 207.

16. HC to Aaron Burr, undated, ibid., 257n.

17. de Beaujour, *Sketch of the United States*, 78.

18. Cresson, *James Monroe*, 201.

19. The Marqués de Casa Yrujo to Don Pedro Antonio de Cevallos, January 28, 1807, Henry Adams, *History of the United States*, 3:342–343.

20. HC to Dr. Richard Pindell, October 15, 1828, Thomas Hart Clay, *Henry Clay*, 42–44.

21. Plumer, *William Plumer's Memorandum*, 608.

22. HC to Thomas Hart, *Papers*, 1:273–275.

23. Henry Adams, *History of the United States*, 2:185.

24. *Annals of Congress*, 10th Congress, 1st Session, 44.

25. Kaminski, *James Madison*, 100.

26. Governor Jonathan Trumbull to the opening of a special session of the Connecticut state legislature, February 23, 1809.

27. HC Speech on Domestic Manufactures, *Papers*, 1:458–463.

28. Ibid.

29. Ibid.

30. George Bancroft, "A Few Words About Henry Clay," *Century Magazine* (July 1885), 8:480.

31. Burr, *Reports of the Trials of Colonel Aaron Burr*, 2:446.

32. Burr, *Examination of Col. Aaron Burr*, 34–35.

33. Ibid.

34. HC, Amendment of Resolution on Foreign Relations, December 15, 1808, *Papers*, 1:388–389.

35. HC, Resolution to Encourage Use of American Manufactures, January 3, 1809, ibid., 1:396–397.

36. Van Deusen, *Life of Henry Clay*, citing letter by eye witness H. Blanton, June 3, 1879, in Mrs. J. T. Cannon Collection, Frankfort, Kentucky.

37. *Journal of the House of Representatives of the Commonwealth of Kentucky* (Frankfort: William Gerard, Printer to the State, 1809), 93.

38. HC to Humphrey Marshall, January 4, 1809, *Papers*, 1:397.

CHAPTER 3: AN IMPERIOUS DESPOT

1. HC to Dr. James Clark, January 19, 1809, ibid., 1:400.

2. James Johnson to HC, January 28, 1809, ibid., 1:401.

3. HC Speech on proposed repeal of Non-Intercourse Act, February 22, 1810, *Papers*, 1:448–452.

4. HC Speech on the Occupation of West Florida, December 28, 1810, *Papers*, 1:507–517, esp. 516.

5. Bouldin, *Home Reminiscences of John Randolph*, 94.

6. *Federalist Papers, No. 57.*

7. HC to James Monroe, November 13, 1810, *Papers*, 1:497–498.

8. Abraham Lincoln, "Eulogy of Henry Clay," Springfield, Illinois, July 6, 1852, *Works . . . Lincoln*, 2:121–132.

9. Margaret Bayard Smith, *First Forty Years of Washington Society*, 86.

10. Wharton, *Social Life in the Early Republic*, 212.

11. Margaret Bayard Smith, *First Forty Years of Washington Society*, 86–87.

12. Winthrop, *Memoir of Henry Clay*, 6.

13. HC, Personal Anecdotes, Incidents, Etc., *Harper's New Monthly Magazine*, vol. 5, no. 27, August 1852.

14. [Speaker] Winthrop, *Memoir of Henry Clay*, 27.

15. Risjord, *Old Republicans*, 42.

16. S. T. Mason, quoted in Duane, *Mississippi Question*, 152.

17. Bruce, *John Randolph of Roanoke*, 2:197.

18. South Carolina Representative Langdon Cheves to HC, July 30, 1812, quoting John Randolph's address to Congress, Grossman, *Speakers of the House of Representatives*, 41.

19. Quincy, *Life of Josiah Quincy*, 255.

20. Heidler and Heidler, *Henry Clay*, 88.

21. Poore, *Perley's Reminiscences*, 14.

22. HC editorial, *National Intelligencer*, April 14, 1812.

23. James Monroe to Committee on Foreign Relations, June 3, 1812, Morgan, *Life of James Monroe*, 315–316.

24. Quincy, *Life of Josiah Quincy*, 259.

25. Ibid., 255.

26. Dispatch from Oliver Hazard Perry aboard US Brig *Niagara* to General William Henry Harrison, September 10, 1813, Lossing, *Pictorial Field-Book*, 530.

27. HC to _____, January 27, 1814, *Papers*, 1:856.

28. HC toast, January 28, 1814, cited in Ketcham, *James Madison*, 568.

29. Lucretia Clay to HC, March 10, 1814, *Papers*, 1:870–871.

30. John Quincy Adams to Louisa Adams, July 22, 1814, reel 418; August 19, 1814, reel 419, Adams Family Papers, Massachusetts Historical Society online.

31. John Quincy Adams, *Memoirs of John Quincy Adams*, 3:2.

32. HC, *Works*, 1:119–120.

CHAPTER 4: "THEY WILL FOMENT WAR NO MORE"

1. Wharton, *Salons Colonial and Republican*, 206–207.

2. HC Speech on the Bank of the United States, June 3, 1816, *Papers*, 2:199–205.

3. HC to William Jones, December 12, 1817, *Papers*, 2:410–411.

4. George Washington Ranck, *History of Lexington, Kentucky*, 163.

5. A. T. Mason to J. T. Mason, July 15, 1816, Van Deusen, *Life of Henry Clay*, 114.

6. *Works*, 1:121.

7. James Monroe to General Andrew Jackson, March 1, 1817, Monroe, *Writings of James Monroe*, 6:4–6.

8. William Crawford to Albert Gallatin, March 12, 1817, Gallatin, *Writings of Albert Gallatin*, 1:25.

9. James Monroe, Inaugural Address, March 4, 1817, Monroe, *Writings of James Monroe*, 6:6–14.

10. Margaret Bayard Smith, *First Forty Years of Washington Society*, 301–302.

11. Ibid., 302.

12. Ibid.

13. Ibid., 302–303.

14. HC Speech at Organization of American Colonization Society, December 21, 1816, *Papers*, 2:263–264.

15. HC Speech on Internal Improvements, March 7, 1818, ibid., 2:446–464.

16. HC Remarks on Appropriations for Commissioners to South America, March 24, 1818, ibid., 2:508–541; HC Speech on Independence of Latin America, ibid., 2:541–562.

17. Ibid.

18. Ibid.

19. John C. Calhoun to Edmund P. Gaines, December 16, 1817, Remini, *Henry Clay*, 118.

20. James Monroe to Andrew Jackson, July 19, 1818, Monroe, *Writings of James Monroe*, 6:54–61.

21. James Monroe to Andrew Jackson, December 28, 1817, ibid., 118–119.

22. Andrew Jackson to James Monroe, January 6, 1818, Remini, *Life of Andrew Jackson*, 118.

23. Ibid., 120.

24. Jackson to James Monroe, June 18, 1818, ibid., 123–124.

25. Ibid.

26. HC Speech on the Seminole War, January 20, 1819, *Papers*, 2:636–662.

27. Remini, *Life of Andrew Jackson*, 127.

28. Ibid.

29. Andrew Jackson to Major William B. Lewis, January 25, 30, 1819, Remini, *Henry Clay*, citing Jackson-Lewis Papers, New York Public Library.

30. *Annals of Congress*, 15th Congress, 2nd Session, 1204.

31. Jefferson, *Writings of Thomas Jefferson*, Ford, ed., 10:159.

32. HC to Adam Beatty, January 22, 1820, HC, *Private Correspondence of Henry Clay*, 61.

33. HC, speech at Organization of American Colonization Society, December 21, 1816, *Papers*, 2:263–264.

CHAPTER 5: THE GREAT PACIFICATOR

1. Frost, *Life of Henry Clay*, 171.

2. HC Speech on Internal Improvements, February 4, 1817, *Papers*, 2:308–311.

3. Cresson, *James Monroe*, 328.

4. Remini, *Henry Clay*, 205.

5. HC to James Brown, April 17, 1830, *Papers*, 8:192–193.

6. James Monroe, Seventh Annual Message to Congress, December 2, 1823, *Writings of James Monroe*, 6:325–342.

7. Ibid.

8. HC Speech on the Independence of Latin America, March 28, 1818, *Papers*, 2:541–562.

9. HC Speech on Internal Improvements, January 14, 1824, *Papers*, 3:572–593.

10. *Annals of Congress*, 18th Congress, 1st Session, 1296–1313.

11. James Monroe to James Madison, May 10, 1822, *Writings of James Monroe*, 284–291.

12. John Quincy Adams, *Memoirs*, 5:325.

13. Levasseur, *Lafayette in America*, 282.

14. Ibid., 413.

15. HC Address to Lafayette, December 10, 1824, *Papers*, 3:893–894.

16. Poore, *Perley's Reminiscences*, 31.

17. Levasseur, *Lafayette in America*, 443.

18. HC to Francis Preston Blair, January 8, 1825, *Papers*, 4:9–11.

19. HC to Francis T. Brooke, January 28, 1825, ibid., 4:45–46.

20. HC to Francis Preston Blair, January 29, 1825, ibid., 4:46–48.

21. *Niles' Weekly Register*, March 12, 1825, 21.

22. Louis McLane to his wife, January 13, 1825, McLane Papers, Library of Congress, cited in Remini, *Henry Clay*, 257.

23. Ibid.

24. Diary of John Quincy Adams, January 9, 1825, Massachusetts Historic Society (online).

25. Roberts, *Ladies of Liberty*, citing Sara Gales Seaton, February 24, 1825, 393.

26. John Quincy Adams to John Adams, February 9, 1825, reel 467, Adams Papers, Massachusetts Historical Society (online).

27. John Adams to John Quincy Adams, February 18, 1825, ibid.

28. Remini, *Life of Andrew Jackson*, 153.

29. Andrew Jackson to John Overton, February 14, 1825, ibid., 155.

30. *Columbian Observer*, January 25, 1825, HC, *Works*, 1:317–318.

31. *National Intelligencer*, January 31, 1825.

32. Parker, *Golden Age of American Oratory*, 36, cited in Jones, *Influence of Henry Clay upon Abraham Lincoln*, 13.

33. Remini, *Life of Andrew Jackson*, 153.

34. McLane to Mrs. McLane, February 6, 1825, McLane Papers, Library of Congress, cited by Remini, *Henry Clay*, 261–262.

35. HC to Francis Preston Blair, January 29, 1825, *Papers*, 4:46–48.

36. HC Speech in Lexington, June 9, 1842, ibid., 9:708–716.

37. Andrew Jackson Donelson to John Coffee, February 19, 1825, Donelson Papers, Library of Congress, cited in Remini, *Henry Clay*, 266.

38. Margaret Bayard Smith, *First Forty Years of Washington Society*, 183.

39. Ibid.

40. Ibid.

41. Ibid.

CHAPTER 6: CORRUPT BARGAIN

1. Ibid., 212–213.

2. Andrew Jackson to William B. Lewis, February 20, 1825, Remini, *Henry Clay*, 269.

3. Ibid.
4. HC to Amos Kendall, October 18, 1825, *Papers*, 4:746–748.
5. HC to Lucretia Hart Clay, August 24, 1825, ibid., 589–590.
6. HC to Henry B. Bascom, August 30, 1825, ibid., 600.
7. HC to Charlotte Mentelle, October 24, 1825, ibid., 755–756.
8. Webster, *Papers of Daniel Webster*, 1:3, 6–17.
9. Daniel Webster to HC, September 28, 1825, ibid., 698–699.
10. John Quincy Adams, *Diary*, June 13, 1825, Massachusetts Historical Society (online).
11. Ibid.
12. John Quincy Adams, First Annual Address, December 6, 1825, Koch and Peden, *Selected Writings of John and John Quincy Adams*, 360–367.
13. Ibid.
14. Nathaniel Macon to B. Yancey, December 8, 1825, Wilson, *Congressional Career of Nathaniel Macon*, 76.
15. Remini, *Life of Andrew Jackson*, 160, citing Edward P. Gaines to Andrew Jackson (1826), Jackson Papers, Library of Congress.
16. Ibid., citing Andrew Jackson to John Branch, March 3, 1828, Branch Family Papers, Southern Historical Collection, Chapel Hill, North Carolina.
17. George Washington Farewell Address to Congress, September 19, 1796, *Writings of George Washington*, Fitzpatrick, ed., 35:214–238, esp. 214–215.
18. Poore, *Perley's Reminiscences*, 27.
19. *Register of Debates*, 19th Congress, 1st Session, II, 393, 395–399, 401; Bruce, *John Randolph of Roanoke*, 511–512.
20. Ibid.
21. Ibid.
22. Merrill D. Peterson, *Great Triumvirate*, 140. See also Henry Fielding, *The History of Tom Jones, a Foundling* (London: A. Millar, 1749).
23. HC to John Randolph, March 31, 1826, *Papers*, 5:208–209.
24. HC to Charles Hammond, April 19, 1826, ibid., 253–254.
25. HC to Francis T. Brooke, April 18, 1826, ibid., 253.
26. Prentice, *Biography of Henry Clay*, 298.
27. Ibid., 297.

CHAPTER 7: A MASK OF SMILES

1. *National Intelligencer*, April 10, 1826; General Jessup to James B. Clay, January 19, 1853, Colton, *Private Correspondence of Henry Clay*, 146–147.
2. Christopher Hughs to HC, August 18, 1826, *Papers*, 5:626–629.
3. Thomas Hulme to HC, August 24, 1826, ibid., 5:645–646.

4. John Quincy Adams, *Diary*, May 31, 1828, Massachusetts Historical Society (online).

5. To Miss Susan D. Smith, February [?], 1828, Margaret Bayard Smith, *First Forty Years of Washington Society*, 212.

6. HC, Speech "On Retiring to Private Life," Lexington, Kentucky, June 9, 1842, *Works*, 9:359–384, esp. 365.

7. John Quincy Adams, March 3, 1829, in *Niles' Weekly Register*, vol. 36, April 11, 1829, 107.

8. John Quincy Adams, in Colton, *Works of Henry Clay*, 1:413.

9. HC Address to the Public, December 29, 1827, *Papers*, 4:1394–1396.

10. Lincoln, "Eulogy to Henry Clay," *Works . . . Lincoln*, 2:121–132.

11. To Mrs. Boyd, December 21, 1827, Margaret Bayard Smith, *First Forty Years of Washington Society*, 211.

12. To Miss Susan H. Smith, ibid., 212–213.

13. Andrew Jackson to Sam Houston, December 15, 1826, Remini, *Henry Clay*, 326, citing Jackson Papers, Library of Congress.

14. Ibid.

15. To J. Bayard H. Smith, January [?], 1829, Margaret Bayard Smith, *First Forty Years of Washington Society*, 255–258, 276.

16. To Mrs. Boyd, February 16, 1829, ibid., 276–281.

17. HC to Henry Clay Jr., April 2, 1827, *Papers*, 6:385–386.

18. To Mrs. Boyd, February 16, 1829, Margaret Bayard Smith, *First Forty Years of Washington Society*, 276–282.

19. John Quincy Adams, *Diary*, February 28, 1829, Massachusetts Historical Society (online).

20. To Mrs. Kirkpatrick, January 12, 1829, Margaret Bayard Smith, *First Forty Years of Washington Society*, 258–262.

21. Ibid.

22. To Mrs. Boyd, Spring of 1829, ibid., 285–290.

23. HC Speech at Farewell Dinner, Washington, March 7, 1829, *Papers*, 8:4–6.

24. Henry Clay Jr. to HC, March 29, 1829, ibid., 8:17–18.

25. HC to Henry Clay Jr., May 24, 1830, ibid., 8:213–214.

26. Theodore W. Clay to HC, January 8, 1832, ibid., 8:442–443.

27. HC to Henry Clay Jr., May 24, 1830, ibid., 8:215–216.

28. Henry Clay Jr. to HC, July 4, 1830, ibid., 8:231–232.

29. HC to Henry Clay Jr., August 24, 1830, ibid., 8:256–257.

30. HC to Henry Clay Jr., March 31, 1831, ibid., 8:329–330.

31. James Brown Clay to HC, January 11, 1831, ibid., 8:319–320.

32. John Morrison Clay to HC, January 14, 1831, ibid., 8:321.

33. Daniel Webster to HC, April 4, 1831, ibid., 8:330–332.

34. Wood, "One Woman So Dangerous to Public Morals," 17:237–275.

35. To Mrs. Boyd, Spring of 1829, Margaret Bayard Smith, *First Forty Years of Washington Society*, 285–290.

36. To Mrs. Kirkpatrick, (undated), ibid., 305–306.

37. John C. Calhoun to Andrew Jackson, May 29, 1830, Bartlett, *John C. Calhoun*, 171, citing Calhoun *Papers of John C. Calhoun*.

38. Andrew Jackson to John C. Calhoun, May 30, 1830, Bartlett, *John C. Calhoun*.

39. HC to Francis T. Brooke, April 24, 1831, *Papers*, 8:337–339.

40. HC Speech in Senate, February 4, 1835, ibid., 8:759–760.

41. HC to John Gunter, ibid., 8:358–359.

42. Ibid.

43. See Joseph Pérez, *The Spanish Inquisition* (New Haven, CT: Yale University Press, 2005) and Donald Greer, *The Incidence of the Terror During the French Revolution: A Statistical Interpretation* (Cambridge, MA: Harvard University Press, 1935). See also Jean Tulard, Jean-François Fayard, Alfred Fierro, *Histoire et Dictionnaire de la Révolution Française* (Paris: Éditions Robert Laffont, 1987).

44. John Quincy Adams, *Memoirs*, 8:262–263.

45. *United States Reports* [*Reports of Cases . . . in the Supreme Court of the United States, 1828–1843*], 6:534–63.

46. William Lumpkin's "Annual Message to the Legislature," November 6, 1832, Letter Books of the Governors, 1832, Georgia Department of Archives and History.

47. *Debates and Proceedings*, 21st Congress, 1st Session, 78–80.

48. Ibid.

49. Greeley, *American Conflict*, 1:106.

50. HC to Adam Beatty, May 4, 1830, *Papers*, 8:201.

51. To Mrs. Kirkpatrick, December, 15, 1831, Margaret Bayard Smith, *First Forty Years of Washington Society*, 332.

52. HC to Thomas Speed, June 25, 1830, *Papers*, 8:230–231; HC to Henry Clay Jr., October 31, 1830, ibid., 8:284–286.

CHAPTER 8: AMBITION!

1. To Mrs. Kirkpatrick, December 15, 1831, Margaret Bayard Smith, *First Forty Years of Washington Society*, 332.

2. Poore, *Perley's Reminiscences*, 58.

3. John Quincy Adams, *Memoirs*, 8:449.

4. George Dallas to Henry Gilpin, July 13, 1832, Remini, *Henry Clay*, 36, citing Dallas Papers, Historical Society of Pennsylvania.

5. Remini, *Henry Clay*, 398.

6. HC Speech in Senate, July 12, 1832, *Papers*, 8:552–553.

7. Abridgement of the Debates of Congress from Gales and Seaton's *Annals of Congress* (New York: D. Appleton and Company, 1859, 16 vols.), 11:519.

8. *Register of Debates in Congress of the First Session of the 22nd Congress*, 8:1293–1294.

9. Ibid.

10. Ibid.

11. Ibid.

12. Henry Clay Jr. to HC, June 7, 1832, *Papers*, 8:529–531.

13. President Jackson's Proclamation Regarding Nullification, December 10, 1832, Library of Congress.

14. HC to Charles Hammond, November 17, 1832, *Papers*, 8:599–600.

15. HC to James Brown, October 23, 1832, ibid.

16. Remini, *Henry Clay*, 421.

17. Ibid., 422.

18. JC in Senate, February 12, 1833, *Works*, 7:536–550, esp. 550.

19. HC Speech in the U.S. Senate on the Compromise Tariff, February 13, 1833, *Papers*, 7:536–567, esp. 538–540, 566–567.

20. Remini, *Henry Clay*, 427.

21. HC Speech in the U.S. Senate on the Compromise Tariff, February 13, 1833, ibid., 7:536–567, esp. 567.

22. HC to James A Meriwether, October 1843, ibid., 9:863.

23. HC to Henry Clay Jr., July 23, 1833, ibid., 8:659.

24. William Sullivan to HC, Boston, January 24, 1834, ibid., 8:692.

25. HC to Henry Clay Jr., January 23, 1834, ibid., 8:692.

26. HC to Francis T. Brooke, December 16, 1833, ibid., 8:678–679.

27. Ibid.

28. HC Speech in Senate, December 26, 1833, *Works,* 575–620.

29. Ibid.

30. Power, *Impressions of America*, 1:197–198, cited in Van Deusen, *Life of Henry Clay*, 281.

31. HC Speech to Senate: "The General Distress Caused by the Removal of the Deposits," March 7, 1834, *Works*, 7:621–623.

32. Ibid.

33. HC Speech on the Expunging Resolution, September 25, 1837, ibid., 8:45–60, esp. 59.

34. HC Senate Speech on the State of the Country After the Removal of Deposits, April 14, 1834, ibid., 7:624–631.

35. HC to Henry Clay Jr., February 19, 1839, *Papers*, 8:763.

36. HC to Enoch Cobb Wines, February 16, 1835, ibid., 8:761–762.

37. HC to Lucretia Hart Clay, November 19, 1835, ibid., 8:803.

CHAPTER 9: BLACKGUARDS, BANKRUPTS, AND SCOUNDRELS

1. James Erwin to HC, December 15, 1835, ibid., 8:807–808.

2. To Mrs. Boyd, Christmas Day, 1835, Margaret Bayard Smith, *First Forty Years of Washington Society*, 375.

3. HC to Lucretia Hart Clay, December 19, 1835, *Papers*, 8:308–309.

4. HC to Francis T. Brooke, January 1, 1836, ibid., 8:813–814.

5. HC to Thomas Speed, January 2, 1836, ibid., 8:814–815.

6. HC to Lucretia Hart Clay, January 23, 1836, ibid., 8:820–821.

7. HC Speech to Senate, December 29, 1835, ibid., 8:812–813.

8. *Register of Debates*, 12, Pt. 3, 3758–3778, May 18–19, 1836.

9. John Quincy Adams, *Memoirs*, 10:199–200.

10. HC to Peter B. Porter, December 24, 1837, *Papers*, 9:113–114.

11. Remini, *Henry Clay*, 508.

12. David G. Burnet to HC, March 30, 1836, *Papers*, 8:838–839.

13. HC Speech to Senate, January 9, 1838, ibid., 9:123–126.

14. HC to Thomas Hart Clay, May 19, 1836, ibid., 8:850–851.

15. HC to Margaret Bayard Smith, May 14, 1836, ibid., 8:850.

16. Van Deusen, *Life of Henry Clay*, 136.

17. Thomas Hart Clay, *Henry Clay*, 106.

18. HC Speech to Colonization Society of Kentucky, December 17, 1829, *Papers*, 8:138–158.

19. Ibid.

20. HC Speech to Senate, January 9, 1838, ibid., 9:123–126.

21. Ibid.

22. Ibid.

23. HC to John G. Whittier, July 22, 1837, ibid., 9:64–65.

24. HC Speech to Senate, January 9, 1838, ibid., 9:123–126.

25. Ibid.

26. Morris, *Encyclopedia of American History*, 178.

27. HC to Francis T. Brooke, June 27, 1835, *Papers*, 8:775–776.

28. HC to Ralph Randolph Gurley, December 22, 1836, ibid., 8:874.

29. HC to the General Assembly of the State of Kentucky, January 16, 1837, ibid., 9:7–8.

30. HC Speech to the Senate on the Plan of the Sub-treasury, February 19, 1838, *Works*, 8:94–133, esp. 123–124.

31. Ibid.

32. Ibid.

33. *Congressional Globe*, 25th Congress, 2nd Session, 632.

34. Calhoun to Armistead Burt, December 24, 1838, Calhoun, *Papers of John C. Calhoun*, 14:498.

35. HC to Harrison G. Otis, June 26, 1838, *Papers*, 9:208–210.

36. Poore, *Perley's Reminiscences*, 56.

37. HC to Henry A. Wise, February 28, 1842, *Papers*, 9:662–665.

38. HC to Henry Clay Jr., March 2, 1838, ibid., 9:152.

CHAPTER 10: DOUBLE DEALING

1. November 1, 1830, Coit, *John C. Calhoun*, 230–231.

2. Timothy Pickering to Richard Peters, Henry Adams, *Documents Relating to New-England Federalism*, 338.

3. HC in Senate, February 12, 1833, *Works*, 7:536–550, esp., 550.

4. William Jones Jr., to HC, December 8, 1837, *Papers*, 9:98.

5. HC "On the Subject of Abolition Petitions," a Speech to the Senate, February 7, 1839, *Works*, 8:139–159.

6. Ibid.

7. Ibid.

8. Ibid.

9. Ibid.

10. John C. Calhoun to Armistead Burt, February 18, 1839, Remini, *Henry Clay*, 526, citing Calhoun, *Papers of John C. Calhoun*, 15:555.

11. Edward Everett to Daniel Webster, February 14, 1839, Remini, *Henry Clay*, citing Webster, *Papers of Daniel Webster*, 4:343.

12. *Niles' Weekly Register*, March 23, 1839; *Daily National Intelligencer*, March 30, 1839.

13. *Morning Courier and Enquirer*, August 16, 1839, HC, *Papers*, 9:333.

14. HC to Peter B. Porter, July 23, 1839, ibid., 9:332.

15. Isaac Fletcher to James J. Polk, September 4, 1839, Polk, *Correspondence of James K. Polk*, 5:330.

16. Clarke, *Narrative of the Sufferings of Lewis Clark*.

17. Lewis Garrard Clarke, "Henry Clay: Personal Anecdotes, Incidents, etc.," in *Harper's New Monthly Magazine* 5 (June to November 1852) (New York: Harper & Brothers), 393–399.

18. Seward to Thurlow Weed, July 31, 1843, Thurlow Weed Papers, cited in Van Deusen, *Life of Henry Clay*, 363.

19. *Burlington Free Press*, August 23, 1839.
20. Remini, *Henry Clay*, 541.
21. *Niles' Weekly Register*, August 31, 1839.
22. HC to Lucretia Hart Clay, March 6, 1840, *Papers*, 9:393–395.
23. Ibid.
24. HC to Oliver H. Smith, September 14, 1839, ibid., 9:340–341.
25. William Henry Harrison to HC, September 20, 1839, ibid., 9:342–343.
26. John Tyler to HC, September 18, 1839, ibid., 9:341–342.
27. Sargent, *Public Men and Events*, 2:93–94.
28. Ibid., 92.
29. HC to Henry Clay Jr., December 14, 1839, *Papers*, 9:36.
30. HC Speech in Washington, DC, December 11, 1839, ibid., 9:363–364.
31. Van Deusen, *Life of Henry Clay*, 327, citing *National Intelligencer*, July 26, 1839.
32. HC to Henry Clay Jr., February 20, 1840, *Papers*, 9:391–392.
33. HC to Lucretia Hart Clay, February 21, 1840, ibid., 9:392.
34. Ibid.
35. William Henry Harrison to HC, January 15, 1840, ibid., 9:374–375.
36. *Baltimore Republican*, December 11, 1839.

CHAPTER 11: GET OUT DA WAY!

1. Tyler, *Letters and Times of the Tylers*, 2:33–34.
2. Ibid., 121–122.
3. HC to Francis T. Brooke, October 28, 1841, *Papers*, 9:617.
4. John Tyler to Robert McCandlish, July 10, 1842, *Letters and Times of the Tylers*, 2:173.
5. HC to Henry Clay Jr., *Papers*, 9:625.
6. HC to Peter B. Porter, January 16, 1842, ibid., 9:631–632.
7. HC Speech to Senate, January 24, 1842, ibid., 9:636–640; HC to Peter B. Porter, February 7, 1842, ibid., 647.
8. HC to John H. Clayton, November 1, 1841, ibid., 9:619–620.
9. HC, *Works*, 9:356.
10. Ibid.
11. HC Speech in Senate, March 31, 1842, ibid., 691–696.
12. Ibid.
13. Remini, *Henry Clay*, 609, citing Crittenden, *Life of Crittenden*, 1:177.
14. Helm, *True Story of Mary*, 1–2.
15. Abraham Lincoln et al. to Henry Clay, August 29, 1842, *Works . . . Lincoln*, 1:297.

16. From Hiram Mendenhall et al., October 1, 1842, *Papers*, 9:777.

17. HC Speech in Richmond, Indiana, October 1, 1842, ibid., 9:777–782.

18. Ibid.

19. Ibid.

20. Ibid.

21. Abraham Lincoln, Seventh and Last Debate with Stephen Douglas, in Alton, Illinois, October 15, 1858, *Works . . . Lincoln*, 3:283–325, esp. 304–305.

22. HC Speech in Indianapolis, October 5, 1842, *Papers*, 9:782–785.

23. HC to Lucretia Hart Clay, December 9, 1842, ibid., 9:790–791; January 18, 1843, 797–798.

24. HC to John J. Crittenden, January 14, 1843, ibid., 9:796–797.

25. Ibid.

26. HC to John J. Crittenden, December 5, 1843, ibid., 9:897–900.

27. Resolution Adopted by the Whig Convention at Peoria, Illinois, June 19, 1844, *Works . . . Lincoln*, 1:338–340.

28. Abraham Lincoln to Andrew Johnston, April 18, 1846, *Works . . . Lincoln*, 1:377–378.

29. "Get Out Da Way," sung to the tune of *Old Dan Tucker*, Littell, *Clay Minstrel*, 175–176.

30. *National Intelligencer*, August 8, 1844, in Van Deusen, *Life of Henry Clay*, 374.

31. U.S. National Archives and Records Administration, Washington, DC.

32. Abraham Lincoln to Williamson Durley, October 3, 1845, *Works . . . Lincoln*, 1:347–348.

33. Mrs. Robert S. Todd to Mary Todd Lincoln, Van Deusen, *Life of Henry Clay*, 376, citing "A letter in possession of the Helm family," Lexington, Kentucky, and quoted by Townsend, *Lincoln and His Wife's Home Town*, 109–110.

34. Van Deusen, *Life of Henry Clay*, 377.

35. John Quincy Adams, *Memoirs*, 12:103.

36. Remini, *Henry Clay*, 660–661, citing Andrew Jackson to Amos Kendall, November 23, 1844, Jackson Papers, Library of Congress.

37. HC to Henry Clay Jr., March 17, 1845, *Papers*, 10:207–208.

38. Remini, *Henry Clay*, 686.

39. HC to John M. Clayton, April 16, 1847, *Papers*, 10:322–323.

40. HC to Charles S. Morehead, December 14, 1848, ibid., 10:362–363.

41. Henry Clay to Henry Clay III, June 26, 1850, ibid., 10:756; September 24, 1850, 10:818.

42. Henry Clay to Henry Clay III, November 22, 1850, ibid., 10:832–833.

43. Henry Clay to Henry Clay III, August 15, 1851, ibid., 10:910.

44. HC to Charles S. Morehead, December 14, 1848, ibid., 10:362–363.

45. Citation of HC in *Daily National Intelligencer*, March 1, 1848, ibid., 10:410.

46. Thomas B. Stevenson to HC, May 22, 1848, ibid., 10:469–470.

47. HC to a Committee of Louisville, June 28, 1848, Colton, *Private Correspondence of Henry Clay*, 566–568.

48. Ibid.

49. HC to Richard Pindell, February 17, 1849, *Papers*, 10:574–581, esp. 575.

50. Ibid.

51. Ibid., esp. 576–577.

52. Ibid., esp. 580.

53. HC to James Brown Clay, March 3, 1849, ibid., 10:582.

54. HC to Lucretia Hart Clay, September 5, 1849, ibid., 10:615–616.

55. Colton, *Private Correspondence of Henry Clay*, 593.

CHAPTER 12: ON BOARD OUR OMNIBUS

1. HC to Lucretia Hart Clay, December 28, 1849, *Papers*, 10:638.

2. Ibid., 642.

3. HC to the Senate, January 24, 1850, ibid., 10:652–653.

4. Ibid.

5. Horace Mann to Mary (Peabody) Mann, March 8, 1850, Mann, *Life of Horace Mann*, 293.

6. HC Speech in Senate, July 22, 1850, *Papers*, 10:772–783.

7. Ibid.

8. A symbolic montage of those responsible for the Missouri Compromise and the Compromise of 1850, which saved the Union. Lewis Cass, holding document "Protest [illegible] Treaty," was a brigadier general in the War of 1812 and an unsuccessful candidate for President in 1848. Scott is in his uniform as commanding general in the War of 1812 and the Mexican War and grasps a portfolio with papers and maps from his Mexican War victories. In the left background are (left to right): Speaker of the House Howell Cobb of Georgia, Virginia Representative James McDowell, Thomas Hart Benton of Missouri, and former Secretary of State John M. Clayton of Delaware. In the second row at right: Ohio Senator Thomas Corwin, James Buchanan of Pennsylvania, Stephen A. Douglas of Illinois, Attorney General John J. Crittenden of Kentucky, and Senators Sam Houston of Texas and Henry Foote of Mississippi. Behind, beneath a genius

carrying a laurel branch and liberty staff, are Senators Willie P. Mangum of North Carolina and W. R. King of Alabama. At far right below an eagle are Daniel S. Dickinson of New York, Supreme Court Justice John Mc-Lean of Ohio, and Senators John Bell of Tennessee and John C. Fremont of California.

9. *Kentucky Statesman*, October 5, 1850, cited in Remini, *Henry Clay*, 763.

10. HC at the Free Barbecue, Lexington, Kentucky, October 16, 1850, *Papers*, 10:820–821.

11. HC to James Brown Clay, May 9, 1851, ibid., 10:889–890.

12. Lewis Garrard Clarke, "Personal Anecdotes," *Harper's New Monthly Magazine* (New York: Harper & Brothers, 1852), 393–399.

EPILOGUE

1. Abraham Lincoln to the Illinois Hall of Representatives, Springfield, Illinois, July 6, 1852, *Works . . . Lincoln*, 2:121–132.

2. *National Intelligencer*, July 1, 1852.

3. Abraham Lincoln, "Eulogy of Henry Clay," July 6, 1852, *Works . . . Lincoln*, 2:121–132, esp. 123; Abraham Lincoln to John M. Clay, August 9, 1862, ibid., 5:363–364.

4. Abraham Lincoln to O. H. Browning, September 22, 1861, ibid., 4:531–533.

5. *National Intelligencer*, August 8, 1844, in Van Deusen, *Life of Henry Clay*, 374.

6. Letter from President Abraham Lincoln to Horace Greeley, *New York Tribune*, August 24, 1862.

APPENDIX

1. HC Speech in Indianapolis, October 5, 1842, *Papers*, 9:782–785.

Selected Bibliography

ARCHIVES

Annals of Congress. New York: D. Appleton and Company, 1859, 16 vols.

Henry Clay Papers. Library of Congress.

Congressional Globe 1837–1873.

The Debates in the Congress of the United States, 1789–1824.

Andrew Jackson Papers. Library of Congress.

Letter Books of the Governors, 1832. Georgia Department of Archives and History.

The Register of Debates in Congress 1824–1837. Washington, DC: Gales and Seaton, 1834–1856, 42 vols.

Zachary Taylor Papers. Library of Congress.

John Tyler Papers. Library of Congress.

Martin Van Buren Papers. Library of Congress.

Thurlow Weed Papers. University of Rochester Library.

United States Reports [*Reports of Cases . . . in the Supreme Court of the United States, 1828–1843*]. Philadelphia: 17 vols.

BIBLIOGRAPHY

Adams, Henry. *Documents Relating to New-England Federalism, 1800–1815*. Boston: Little, Brown, 1877.

———. *History of the United States, 1801–1817.* 9 vols. New York: Charles Scribner's Sons, 1889.

Adams, John. *Works of John Adams.* Charles Francis Adams, ed. 10 vols. Boston: Little, Brown and Company, 1856.

Adams, John Quincy. *Diary of John Quincy Adams.* Adams Family Papers. Massachusetts Historical Society (online).

———. *Memoirs of John Quincy Adams.* Charles Francis Adams, ed. 12 vols. Philadelphia: J. B. Lippincott and Company, 1874–1877.

American State Papers, Foreign Relations, 1789–1828. 6 vols. Washington, DC: Gales and Seaton, 1833–1858.

American State Papers, Military Affairs, 1789–1832. 7 vols. Washington, DC: Gales and Seaton, 1832–1861.

Ames, Fisher. *Works of Fisher Ames.* Seth Ames, ed. 2 vols. Boston: T. B. Wait, 1854.

Ammon, Harry. *James Monroe: The Quest for National Identity.* Newtown, CT: American Political Biography Press, 1971.

Bartlett, Irving H. *Daniel Webster.* New York: W. W. Norton & Co., 1978.

———. *John C. Calhoun: A Biography.* New York: W. W. Norton & Co., 1993.

Beeman, Richard. *The Penguin Guide to the United States Constitution.* New York: Penguin Books, 2010.

Bergeron, Paul. *The Presidency of James K. Polk.* Lawrence: University Press of Kansas, 1987.

Bickford, Charlotte Bangs, and Kenneth R. Bowling. *Birth of the Nation: The First Federal Congress, 1789–1791.* Lanham, MD: Madison House Publishers, 1989.

Bordewich, Fergus M. *America's Great Debate: Henry Clay, Stephen A. Douglas, and the Compromise That Preserved the Union.* New York: Simon & Schuster, 2012.

Bouldin, Pohatan. *Home Reminiscences of John Randolph.* Richmond, VA: Clemmin & Jones, 1878.

Bruce, William Cabell. *John Randolph of Roanoke, 1773–1833.* 2 vols. Boston: Houghton Mifflin, 1922.

Burr, Aaron Jr. *The Examination of Col. Aaron Burr Before the Chief Justice of the United States, upon the Charges of a High Misdemeanor and of Treason Against the United States.* Richmond: S. Grantland, 1807.

———. *Reports of the Trials of Colonel Aaron Burr for Treason and for a Misdemeanor Taken in Shorthand by David Robertson, Counselor at Law.* 2 vols. Philadelphia: Hopkins and Earle, 1808.

Calhoun, John C. *A Discourse on the Constitution and Government of the United States.* Columbia, SC: A. S. Johnson, 1851.

———. *A Disquisition on Government.* South Bend, IN: St. Augustine's Press, 2007.

———. *The Papers of John C. Calhoun.* 28 vols. Columbia: University of South Carolina Press, 1959–2003.

———. *Union and Liberty: The Political Philosophy of John C. Calhoun.* Ross M. Lence, ed. Indianapolis, IN: Liberty Fund, 1992.

Carroll, E. Malcolm. *Origins of the Whig Party.* Durham, NC: Duke University Press, 1925.

Clarke, Lewis Garrard. *Narrative of the Sufferings of Lewis Clarke, During a Captivity of More than Twenty-Five Years, Among the Algerines of Kentucky, One of the So-Called Christian States of North America.* Boston: David H. Ela, 1845.

Clay, Henry. *The Life and Speeches of Henry Clay.* Daniel Mallory, ed. 2 vols. New York: Van Amringe and Bixby, 1844.

———. *The Papers of Henry Clay.* James F. Hopkins, ed. 10 vols. Lexington: University of Kentucky Press, 1959.

———. *The Private Correspondence of Henry Clay.* Calvin Colton, ed. New York: A. S. Barnes & Co., 1855.

———. *The Works of Henry Clay.* Calvin Colton, ed. 10 vols. New York: G. P. Putnam's Sons, 1904.

Clay, Thomas Hart. *Henry Clay.* Philadelphia: George W. Jacobs & Company, 1910.

Coit, Margaret L. *John C. Calhoun: American Portrait.* Boston: Houghton Mifflin, 1950.

Colton, Calvin, ed. *The Private Correspondence of Henry Clay.* New York: A. S. Barnes & Co., 1855.

———. *The Works of Henry Clay.* 10 vols. New York: G. P. Putnam's Sons, 1904.

Cresson, W. P. *James Monroe.* Chapel Hill: University of North Carolina Press, 1946.

Crittenden, John J. *The Life of Crittenden.* Mrs. Chapman Coleman (Ann Murray Butler Crittenden), ed. 2 vols. Philadelphia: J. B. Lippincott & Co., 1873.

Cullop, Floyd G. *The Constitution of the United States: An Introduction.* New York: New American Library, 1984.

Cunningham, Noble E. Jr. *The Presidency of James Monroe.* Lawrence: University Press of Kansas, 1996.

Davis, Matthew L. *Memoirs of Aaron Burr.* 2 vols. New York: Harper and Brothers, 1836.

The Debates and Proceedings in the Congress of the United States 1789–1824 [usually called *Annals of Congress*]. 42 vols. Washington, DC: Gales and Seaton, 1834–1856.

de Beaujour, Henri Felix. *Sketch of the United States of North America at the Commencement of the Nineteenth Century, 1800–1810.* London: Hay, Turner and Co., 1814.

DeConde, Alexander. *This Affair of Louisiana.* New York: Charles Scribner's Sons, 1976.

Duane, William. *Mississippi Question: Report of a Debate in the Senate of the United States, on the 23d, 24th, & 25th February, 1803, on Certain Resolutions Concerning the Violation of the Right of Deposit in the Island of New Orleans.* Philadelphia: W. Duane, 1803.

The Federalist Papers. New York: The New American Library of World Literature, 1961.

Follett, Mary Parker. *The Speaker of the House of Representatives.* New York: Longmans, Green and Company, 1896.

Fox, Early Lee. *The American Colonization Society, 1817–1840.* Baltimore: Johns Hopkins University Press, 1919.

Frost, John. *Life of Henry Clay, The Statesman and the Patriot, Containing Numerous Anecdotes.* Boston: Lee and Shepard, 1869.

Gallatin, Albert. *The Writings of Albert Gallatin.* Henry Adams, ed. 3 vols. Philadelphia: J. B. Lippincott, 1879.

Gordon, John Steele. *An Empire of Wealth: The Epic History of American Economic Power.* New York: HarperCollins Publishers, 2004.

Greeley, Horace. *The American Conflict.* 2 vols. Hartford, CT: O. D. Case and Company, 1864, 1867.

Grossman, Mark. *Speakers of the House of Representatives.* Amenia, NY: Grey House Publishing, 2009.

Heidler, David S., and Jeanne T. Heidler. *Henry Clay: The Essential American.* New York: Random House, 2010.

Helm, Katherine. *The True Story of Mary, Wife of Lincoln, by Her Niece Katherine Helm.* New York: Harper & Brothers, 1928.

Henry, William Wirt. *Patrick Henry: Life, Correspondence, and Speeches.* 3 vols. New York: Charles Scribner's Sons, 1891.

Jefferson, Thomas. *The Life and Selected Writings of Thomas Jefferson.* Adrienne Koch and William Peden, eds. New York: The Modern Library, 1944.

————. *The Papers of Thomas Jefferson*. Julian P. Boyd, ed. [in progress, multiple volumes]. Princeton, NJ: Princeton University Press, 1950.

————. *Thomas Jefferson Writings*. New York: The Library of America, 1984.

————. *The Works of Thomas Jefferson*. Paul Leicester Ford, ed. 12 vols. New York: G. P. Putnam's Sons, 1904–1905.

————. *Writings of Thomas Jefferson*. Paul Leicester Ford, ed. 10 vols. New York: G. P. Putnam's Sons, 1892–1899.

————. *The Writings of Thomas Jefferson*. Andrew A. Lipscombe, ed. 20 vols. Washington, DC: The Thomas Jefferson Memorial Association, 1903–1904.

Jensen, Merrill, John P. Kaminski, Gaspare Saladino, Richard Leffler, and Charles H. Schoenleber, eds. *The Documentary History of the Ratification of the Constitution* [in progress, multiple volumes]. Madison: State Historical Society of Wisconsin, 1976.

Johnson, David. *John Randolph of Roanoke*. Baton Rouge: Louisiana State University Press, 2012.

Jones, Edgar DeWitt. *Influence of Henry Clay upon Abraham Lincoln*. Lexington, KY: The Henry Clay Memorial Foundation, 1952.

Journal of the House of Representatives of the Commonwealth of Kentucky. Frankfort: William Gerard, Printer to the State, 1809.

Kaminski, John P. *James Madison, Champion of Liberty and Justice*. Madison, WI: Parallel Press, 2006.

Ketcham, Ralph. *James Madison: A Biography*. Charlottesville: University of Virginia Press, 1990.

Koch, Adrienne, and William Peden, eds. *The Selected Writings of John and John Quincy Adams*. New York: Alfred A. Knopf, 1946.

Levasseur, Auguste. *Lafayette in America in 1824 and 1825: Journal of a Voyage to the United States*. Alan R. Hoffmann, trans., from the 1829 French edition, *Voyage en Amérique*. Manchester, NH: Lafayette Press, 2006.

Lincoln, Abraham. *The Collected Works of Abraham Lincoln*. Roy P. Basler, ed. 9 vols. New Brunswick, NJ: Rutgers University Press, 1953–1955.

Lipsey, Robert E. *U.S. Foreign Trade and the Balance of Payments, 1800–1913*. Cambridge, MA: National Bureau of Economic Research, 1994.

Littell, John S. *The Clay Minstrel; or, National Songster*. New York: Greeley & M'Elrath; Philadelphia: Thomas, Cowperthwaite and Co., 1844.

Lossing, Benson J. *The Pictorial Field-Book of the War of 1812*. New York: Harper & Brothers, Publishers, 1868.

MacNeil, Neil. *Forge of Democracy: The House of Representatives*. New York: David McKay Company, 1963.

Madison, James. *Writings of James Madison*. Gaillard Hunt, ed. 9 vols. New York: G. P. Putnam's Sons, 1900.

Malone, Dumas. *Jefferson and His Time*. 6 vols. Boston: Little, Brown and Company, 1948–1977.

Mann, Mary Tyler Peabody. *Life of Horace Mann, by His Wife*. Boston: Walker, Fuller and Company, 1865.

Mayo, Bernard. *Henry Clay: Spokesman of the New West*. Boston: Houghton Mifflin Company, 1937.

McDonald, Forrest. *The Presidency of George Washington*. Lawrence: University Press of Kansas, 1974.

Messerli, Jonathan. *Horace Mann: A Biography*. New York: Alfred A. Knopf, 1972.

Monroe, James. *The Papers of James Monroe*. Daniel Preston, ed. 2 vols. Westport, CT: Greenwood Press, 2003–2006.

———. *The Writings of James Monroe*. Stanislaus Murray Hamilton, ed. 7 vols. New York, 1898–1903; reprint edition, New York, AMS Press, 1969.

Moore, Glover. *The Missouri Controversy, 1819–1821*. Lexington: University of Kentucky Press, 1953.

Morgan, George. *Life of James Monroe*. Boston: Small, Maynard and Company, 1921.

Morris, Richard B. *Encyclopedia of American History*. New York: Harper & Brothers, 1953.

Niven, John. *John C. Calhoun and the Price of Union*. Baton Rouge: Louisiana State University Press, 1988.

Parker, Edward G. *The Golden Age of American Oratory*. Boston: Whittemore, Niles and Hall, 1857.

Peterson, Merrill D. *The Great Triumvirate: Webster, Clay and Calhoun*. New York: Oxford University Press, 1987.

———. *The Olive Branch and Sword: The Compromise of 1833*. Baton Rouge: Louisiana State University Press, 1982.

Peterson, Norma Lois. *The Presidencies of William Henry Harrison & John Tyler*. Lawrence: University Press of Kansas, 1989.

Plumer, William. *William Plumer's Memorandum of Proceedings in the United States Senate, 1803–1807*. Everett Somerville Brown, ed. New York: Macmillan, 1923.

Polk, James K. *Correspondence of James K. Polk*. Herbert Weaver, ed. 12 vols. Nashville, TN: Vanderbilt University Press, 1969–2013.

Poore, Benjamin Perley. *Perley's Reminiscences of Sixty Years in the National Metropolis.* Philadelphia, Hubbard Brothers, 1886.

Power, Tyrone. *Impressions of America During the Years 1833, 1834, and 1835.* 2 vols. Philadelphia: Lea and Blanchard, 1836.

Prentice, George D. *Biography of Henry Clay.* Hartford, CT: Samuel Hanmer Jr. and John Jay Phelps, Publishers, 1831.

Quincy, Edmund. *Life of Josiah Quincy.* Boston: Fields, Osgood & Co., 1869.

Ranck, George Washington. *History of Lexington, Kentucky.* Cincinnati: Robert Clarke & Co., 1872.

Rayback, Robert J. *Millard Fillmore: Biography of a President.* Buffalo, NY: Buffalo Historical Society, 1959.

Remini, Robert V. *At the Edge of the Precipice: Henry Clay and the Compromise That Saved the Union.* New York: Basic Books, 2010.

———. *Daniel Webster: The Man and His Times.* New York: W. W. Norton, 1997.

———. *Henry Clay: Statesman for the Union.* New York: W. W. Norton, 1991.

———. *The House: The History of the House of Representatives.* New York: HarperCollins Publishers, 2006.

———. *The Life of Andrew Jackson.* New York: Penguin Books, 1988.

Risjord, Norman K. *The Old Republicans: Southern Conservatism in the Age of Jefferson.* New York: Columbia University Press, 1965.

Roberts, Cokie. *Ladies of Liberty: The Women Who Shaped Our Nation.* New York: William Morrow, 2008.

Rothbard, Murray N. *The Panic of 1819: Reactions and Policies.* New York: Columbia University Press, 1962.

Sargent, Nathan. *Public Men and Events in the United States from . . . 1817 to . . . 1853.* 2 vols. New York: Da Capo Press, 1970.

Schurz, Carl. *Life of Henry Clay.* 2 vols. Boston: Houghton, Mifflin Company, 1892.

Siegenthaler, John. *James K. Polk.* New York: Henry Holt and Company, 2004.

Silbey, Joel H., ed. *The Congress of the United States, 1789–1989.* Brooklyn, NY: Carlson Publishing, 1991.

Smith, Elbert B. *The Presidencies of Zachary Taylor and Millard Fillmore.* Lawrence: University Press of Kansas, 1989.

Smith, Margaret Bayard. *The First Forty Years of Washington Society Portrayed by the Family Letters of Mrs. Samuel Harrison Smith.* Gaillard Hunt, ed. New York, Charles Scribner's Sons, 1906.

Stampp, Kenneth M. *The Peculiar Institution in the Ante-Bellum South*. New York: Random House, 1989.

Taussig, Frank William. *The Tariff History of the United States*. New York: G. Putnam's Sons, 1888.

Townsend, William H. *Lincoln and His Wife's Home Town*. Indianapolis, IN: Bobbs-Merrill, 1929.

Tyler, Lyon G. *The Letters and Times of the Tylers*. 2 vols. Richmond, VA: Whittet and Shepperson, 1884.

Unger, Harlow Giles. *John Marshall: The Chief Justice Who Saved the Nation*. Boston: Da Capo Press, 2014.

———. *John Quincy Adams*. Boston: Da Capo Press, 2012.

———. *The Last Founding Father: James Monroe and a Nation's Call to Greatness*. Boston: Da Capo Press, 2009.

Van Deusen, Glyndon G. *The Life of Henry Clay*. Boston: Little, Brown and Company, 1937.

Washington, George. *The Papers of George Washington, Confederation Series, January 1784–September 1788*. W. W. Abbot, ed. 6 vols. Charlottesville: University Press of Virginia, 1992–1997.

———. *The Papers of George Washington, Presidential Series*. W. W. Abbot, ed. [in progress, multiple volumes]. Charlottesville: University of Virginia Press, 1985.

———. *The Papers of George Washington, Revolutionary War Series*. W. W. Abbott, ed. [in progress, multiple volumes]. Charlottesville: University of Virginia Press, 1985.

———. *The Writings of George Washington*. John C. Fitzpatrick, ed. 39 vols. Washington, DC: US Government Printing Office, 1931–1944.

———. *The Writings of George Washington*. Worthington Chauncey Ford, ed. 14 vols. New York: G. P. Putnam's Sons, 1891.

Watson, Harry L. *Andrew Jackson vs. Henry Clay: Democracy and Development in Antebellum America*. Boston: Bedford/St. Martins, 1998.

Webster, Daniel. *The Papers of Daniel Webster, Speeches and Formal Writings*. Charles M. Wiltse et al., eds. [in progress, multiple volumes]. Hanover, NH: University Press of New England, 1986.

Wharton, Anne Hollingsworth. *Salons Colonial and Republican*. Philadelphia: J. B. Lippincott Company, 1900.

———. *Social Life in the Early Republic*. Philadelphia: J. B. Lippincott Company, 1902.

Wilson, Edwin M. *The Congressional Career of Nathaniel Macon*. Chapel Hill: University of North Carolina Press, 1900.

Winthrop, Robert C. *Memoir of Henry Clay*. Cambridge, MA: John Wilson and Son, 1880.
Wood, Kristen E. "One Woman So Dangerous to Public Morals." *Journal of the Early Republic*. Philadelphia: University of Pennsylvania Press, March 1997.

REFERENCE WORKS

Encyclopedia of American History. Richard B. Morris, ed. New York: Harper & Brothers, 1953.
Encyclopedia of Kentucky. New York: Somerset Publishers, 1987.

PERIODICALS

American Citizen
[Boston] *Atlas*
Baltimore Republican
Burlington Free Press
Century Magazine
Columbian Observer [Philadelphia]
Harper's New Monthly Magazine
[Frankfort, Kentucky] *Western World*
Journal of the Early Republic
Lexington Observer & Kentucky Reporter
Kaintuckeean
[Lexington] *Kentucky Statesman*
[New York] *Morning Courier and Enquirer*
New York Tribune
Niles' Weekly Register
Rochester [New York] *Telegraph*
United States Telegraph
[Washington, DC] *Daily National Intelligencer*
[Washington, DC] *National Intelligencer*

Index